T0261245

Splash 2
FPGAs in a Custom Computing Machine

Splash 2
FPGAs in a Custom Computing Machine

Duncan A. Buell
Jeffrey M. Arnold
Walter J. Kleinfelder

Editors
Center for Computing Sciences
Bowie, Maryland

IEEE
COMPUTER
SOCIETY
http://computer.org

WILEY-
INTERSCIENCE
A JOHN WILEY & SONS, INC., PUBLICATION

Library of Congress Cataloging-in-Publication Data

Buell, Duncan A.
  Splash 2: FPGAs in a custom computing machine / Duncan A. Buell,
Jeffrey M. Arnold, Walter J. Kleinfelder.
      p.   cm.
  Includes bibliographical references and index.
  ISBN 0-8186-7413-X
  1. Spash 2 (Computer)   2. Electronic digital computers—Design
and construction.   I. Arnold, Jeffrey M.   II. Kleinfelder, Walter J.
III. Title.
QA76.8.S65B84   1996
004.2 ' 2—dc20

                                                        95-47397
                                                        CIP

IEEE Computer Society Press
10662 Los Vaqueros Circle
P.O. Box 3014
Los Alamitos, CA 90720-1264

IEEE Computer Society Press
Customer Service Center
10662 Los Vaqueros Circle
P.O. Box 3014
Los Alamitos, CA 90720-1264
Tel: +1-714-821-8380
Fax: +1-714-821-4641
Email: cs.books@computer.org

IEEE Service Center
445 Hoes Lane
P.O. Box 1331
Piscataway, NJ 08855-1331
Tel: +1-908-981-1393
Fax: +1-908-981-9667
mis.custserv@computer.org

IEEE Computer Society
13, Avenue de l'Aquilon
B-1200 Brussels
BELGIUM
Tel: +32-2-770-2198
Fax: +32-2-770-8505
euro.ofc@computer.org

IEEE Computer Society
Ooshima Building
2-19-1 Minami-Aoyama
Minato-ku, Tokyo 107
JAPAN
Tel: +81-3-3408-3118
Fax: +81-3-3408-3553
tokyo.ofc@computer.org

Assistant Publisher: Matt Loeb
Technical Editor: Dharma P. Agrawal
Acquisitions Assistant: Cheryl Smith
Advertising/Promotions: Tom Fink
Production Editor: Lisa O'Conner
Cover Image: Dan Kopetzky, Center for Computing Sciences

 The Institute of Electrical and Electronics Engineers, Inc

Contents

v

Preface

The Splash 2 project began at the Supercomputing Research Center[1] in September of 1991 and ended, with success, in the spring of 1994. Splash 2 is an attached processor system using Xilinx XC4010 FPGAs as its processing elements. As such, it is a *custom computing machine*. That is to say that much of what would be the instruction set architecture of the processing elements is not specified except in the details of the program developed by the application programmer. Although a higher-level block diagram of processing elements, memories, interconnect, and dataflow exists in the hardware structure of Splash 2, the details of the instruction set architecture level of the machine will vary from one application to the next.

The Splash 2 project is significant for two reasons. First, Splash 2 is part of a complete computer system that has achieved supercomputer-like performance on a number of different applications. By "complete computer system" we mean that SRC created or caused to be created an extant hardware system (replicated a dozen times), a complete programming and runtime environment, and a collection of application programs that exercised the unique hardware.

The second significant aspect of Splash 2 is that we were fortunate enough to be able to build a large system, capable of performing real computations on real problems. One common complaint about performance results on novel computing machines or environments is that results on small problems cannot be accurately extrapolated to large problems. The Splash 2 system that was designed and built is a full-sized machine and does not suffer from this defect.

To get to the point: why a book?

---

[1]Renamed the Center for Computing Sciences in May 1995, but referred to throughout this book as SRC.

This is a novel computing machine. In order to understand what happens when the application programmer is permitted, indeed required, to design the processor architecture of the machine that will execute his program, it is necessary to see the system as a whole. Programmability and problems to be run on this machine both had major influences on its architecture, just as its architecture and its unique nature influence the kinds of problems one would expect to program for this machine and the nature of that programming. And standing between the user and the machine, as the old joke goes, is a new kind of programming environment and an evolving understanding of how this environment must allow the use of the hardware, without forcing every programmer to be a hardware-design engineer.

At the first IEEE Workshop on FPGAs for Custom Computing Machines, one of the industrial attendees remarked that, although nearly everyone would agree, as part of a coffee-room discussion or the like, that it would be *interesting* to think about building a "computer" using FPGAs, no one in management (except perhaps at SRC and DEC PRL) had put up the commitment necessary in time and money to do a real test of the idea. It was then remarked that, given the nature of the marketplace and of engineering management, these first attempts had to be successful in order to open the door for future work. We feel we have been successful, and we offer in this book an in-depth look at one of the handful of data points in the design space of this new kind of machine.

We would hope that this book has a broad appeal and is readable with understanding by nearly all computer scientists and computer engineers. To the hardware designer, perhaps we can offer a new look at programming applications on a moderately general FPGA-based computing machine instead of designing circuits for a specific board incorporating FPGAs. The engineering world has viewed FPGAs, to a great extent, as the next logical step in a continuum of electronic devices; we offer, we feel, the option of viewing them much more broadly than that. To the computer architect we offer a variant hardware platform and an indication of how that general platform can be used. Much of computer architecture is a compromise between the functionality desired and the limits of what can be built given existing technology; we offer the use of a new technology that can offer, to a limited extent now, and could offer much more generally later, greatly increased functionality. For some of those who have hard problems in computation, we offer much of the power of special-purpose hardware without the inflexibility and uncertain delivery times of hardware. The long-term task is not to map a high-level language to a particular architecture or range of architectures, but in some sense to create for each application program a suitable architecture to which the high-level language will be mapped. And to the language designers and compiler writers we offer a world to conquer. We have presented one imperfect but usable approach to programming such a computing machine, and we trust that others interested in the critical problem of making these machines programmable can learn both from what we did right and what we did wrong.

Chapter 1 discusses the general concept of Custom Computing Machines, of which Splash 2 is one example. Chapters 2 and 3 describe at a high level and then in some detail the hardware architecture of Splash 2. Chapter 4 covers the design considerations and decisions in arriving at the second-generation Splash 2 architecture. We present this chapter at the end of the section on hardware, on the basis that it is easier to understand variations in a design when those variations are compared against something concrete.

Chapters 5 and 6 describe, also first at a higher and then at a lower level, the software architecture of Splash 2. All the application programs in the latter chapters were done using VHDL as an applications programming language and these tools in support. The main goal of the Splash 2 project was to show that software, as described in Chapters 5 and 6, could make a computer using FPGAs as its processing elements into something that reasonable people would call "programmable," and, in that sense, the heart of the Splash 2 project is in Chapters 5 and 6. Throughout the life of Splash 2, however, there has been an alternative view of programming. This view is reflected in Chapter 7 on the Splash 2 version of the programming language dbC. The approach taken in dbC is to permit the programmer to use a version of C as the programming language. It is the compiler which then becomes responsible for, in essence, recognizing the instruction set architecture necessary to execute the program and then creating in the FPGA the requisite registers, logic units, and control.

Chapters 8 through 11 then describe four different applications programmed to conclusion on Splash 2. The first of these—the sequence comparison problem—was the driving application, in the sense that funding for Splash 2 was based on its perceived ability to perform this computation. This and the text processing application were done at SRC.

The Splash 2 project team was fortunate in that SRC's parent company, the Institute for Defense Analyses, issued two contracts, to Virginia Polytechnic Institute and to Michigan State University, for applications work on Splash 2 in image processing and fingerprint identification. Both applications seemed good matches with the Splash 2 architecture but lay outside the normal realm of SRC's research program. The faculty members involved have each prepared a chapter on these applications.

We close in Chapter 12 with some opinions and speculations about the future. In an appendix, the project manager presents a chronology of the entire Splash 2 project.

It is incumbent on us, and a genuine pleasure, to thank the Center for Computing Sciences of the Institute for Defense Analyses and the CCS Director, Francis Sullivan, for supporting us in our writing and editing of this book. All royalties will be donated to the Center for Excellence in Education, formerly known as the Rickover Foundation, in McLean, Virginia. The Center for Excellence in Education supports science and engineering education through its sponsorship of the Research Science Institute each summer for high school seniors, its Role Models and Leaders Project in Washington, D.C., Los Angeles, and Chicago for promising women and minority high school students intending to study science and engineering, and its support and preparation of the United States Informatics Olympiad team each year.

The Splash 2 project was a success in large part due to the ability of those who were involved nearly full-time, but it might not have taken the course it did had the hard-core Splash 2 players not had the chance to get advice and occasional help from a much larger group of experts both at SRC and elsewhere.

We acknowledge, therefore, the help and advice of Nate Bronson, Dan Burns, Bill Carlson, Neil Coletti, Maripat Corr, Steve Cuccaro, Hillory Dean, Chuck Fiduccia, Brad Fross, Charles Goedeke, Maya Gokhale, Frank Hady, Dzung Hoang, Bill Holmes, Amy Johnston, Elaine (Davis) Keith, Dan Kopetzky, Andy Kopser, Steve Kratzer, Jim Kuehn, Sara Lucas, Michael Mascagni, Marge McGarry, John McHenry,

Ron Minnich, Lindy Moran, Fred More, Mark Norder, Lou Podrazik, Dan Pryor, Craig Reese, Paul Schneck, Brian Schott, Nabeel Shirazi, Doug Sweely, Dennis Sysko, Mark Thistle, Bob Thompson, Ken Wallgren, Alice Yuen, Neal Ziring, and Jennifer Zito.

Duncan A. Buell
Jeffrey M. Arnold
Walter J. Kleinfelder
Bowie, Maryland
March 1996

CHAPTER 1

Custom Computing Machines: An Introduction

Duncan A. Buell[1]

1.1 INTRODUCTION

It is a basic observation about computing that generality and efficiency are in some sense inversely related to one another; the more general-purpose an object is and thus the greater the number of tasks it can perform, the less efficient it will be in performing any of those specific tasks. Design decisions are therefore almost always compromises; designers identify key features or applications for which competitive efficiency is a must and then expand the range as far as is practicable without unduly damaging performance on the main targets.

This thesis has certainly been true in processor architecture of computers aimed at computationally intense problems. Vector processors and vector supercomputers have targeted computationally intense, array-oriented floating point problems, usually in the hard sciences and engineering, but have not sacrificed the necessary speed on their core applications in order to be all things to all people. Thus, on computationally intense problems that do not fit well on traditional supercomputers, perhaps due to such things as integer arithmetic or scalar code, fast workstations can often outperform supercomputers.

To counter the problem of computationally intense problems for which general-purpose machines cannot achieve the necessary performance, special-purpose processors, attached processors, and coprocessors have been built for many years, especially

[1]A version of this chapter appeared as Buell and Pocek [11] and is used with permission.

in such areas as image or signal processing (for which many of the computational tasks can be very well defined). The problem with such machines is that they are special-purpose; as problems change or new ideas and techniques develop, their lack of flexibility makes them problematic as long-term solutions.

Enter the FPGA. Field Programmable Gate Arrays, first introduced in 1986 by Xilinx [34], were seen rather immediately by a few people to offer a totally new avenue to explore in the world of processor engineering. The great strength of the computer as a tool is in its ability to be adapted, via programming, to a multitude of computational tasks. The possibility now existed for an FPGA-based computing device not only to be configured to act like special-purpose hardware for a particular problem, but to be reconfigured for different problems and for this reconfiguration to be a programming process. By being more than single-purpose, such a machine would have the advantage of being flexible with at least a limited range of different applications. By being programmable, such a machine would open up "design of high-performance hardware" to individuals who can "design hardware" in an abstract sense but not a concrete sense. Finally, by being designed to operate as if they were hardware, the applications for these machines can achieve the hardware-like performance one gets from having explicitly parallel computations, from not having instructions and data fetched and decoded, and from having the ability to design processing units that reflect precisely the processing being done.

It is no exaggeration to say that machines using FPGAs as their processing elements have demonstrated that very high performance on an absolute scale, and extraordinary performance when measured against price, is possible with this technology. The PeRLe machines built at DEC's Paris Research Laboratory have been programmed on a number of applications with impressive results [7, 8, 9, 31]: An implemented multiplier can compute a 50-coefficient, 16-bit polynomial convolution FIR filter at 16 times audio real time. An implementation of RSA decryption executes at 10 times the bit rate of an AT&T ASIC. A Hough Transform implementation for an application in high-energy physics achieves a compute rate that a standard 64-bit computer could not equal without a 1.2 GHz clock rate.

As can be seen from the later chapters of this book, some of the applications programmed on Splash 2 have achieved similarly promising results. It was a general observation made by those involved in the Splash 2 project that, on applications that fit the machine, one Splash 2 Array Board could deliver approximately the compute power of one Cray YMP processor. One of the commercial licensees of the Splash 2 technology sells its system for about $40,000. Of course, not all applications fit well, and most that do not fit well actually fit very badly indeed, but this is nonetheless a performance-to-price ratio substantial enough to warrant continued investigation and experimentation.

The idea of reconfiguring a computer is certainly not new. The Burroughs B1700 had multiple instruction sets with different targets (Fortran, COBOL, and such) implemented with different microcode. In another way, the Paris functions of the Thinking Machines Corp. CM-2 differed from one version to the next. In the former case, standard views of hardware instructions were implemented. In the latter case, with a novel machine and a new architecture, we presume that an effort was made to implement function calls that users were seen to need and to delete unneeded functions when the instruction store ran out.

A certain amount of disagreement exists over what label to give to these machines and how to refer to them. The group at DEC's Paris research lab refers to their machine as a Programmable Active Memory (PAM) [7, 9, 29, 31]. Another commercial entity uses the term "virtual computer" [12]. From Brown University we have Processor Reconfiguration through Instruction Set Metamorphosis (PRISM) [4, 5, 6, 32]. We have already used the term "FPGA-based computing device" here. That none of these are truly satisfactory was evidenced in the spring of 1994 when the comp.arch.fpga newsgroup was discussed and established; the most contentious point was over the name. Both the new newsgroup and the IEEE workshops we have organized use the term FPGA, thus being in some sense bound in terminology to a particular technology (unless, of course, one can convince the developers of the next technology that its name should allow FPGA as its acronym). We have chosen to use the term Custom Computing Machine (CCM). None of these terms is perfect, but we believe that this one is no worse than any of the others.

The work on CCMs also differs from what is considered reconfigurable computer architecture, in that the term "reconfigurable" usually refers to a much higher level of the system. In the case of CCMs, that which is reconfigurable and significant by virtue of its reconfigurability is the "processor architecture" itself. A reconfigurable computer, by contrast, is likely to be either a multiprocessor in which the interconnections among the processors can change, or a heterogeneous machine with processors of different kinds that a user can choose to include or exclude in the view he/she has of "the computer."

It is to be emphasized that this is not a mature computing technology and that CCMs are not a panacea for all problems in high-performance computing. Among the many issues and problems are the following:

1. Are FPGAs large enough, or will they become large enough, so that a significant unit of computation can be put on a single chip so as to avoid both the loss of efficiency in going off-chip and the problems in partitioning a computation across multiple chips?

2. With current technology, even in the best of circumstances, the user must be exposed to the hardware itself. What is the level of understanding about chip architecture, signal routing delays, and so forth, that a "programmer" must know in order to use a CCM? How much more must be known in order to obtain the performance that would warrant using a CCM instead of a general-purpose computer?

3. If these machines are to be viewed as "computers," then they must be capable of being programmed. How will this be done? What sort of programming language is appropriate? How do we "compile" when we have eliminated the underlying machine model?

4. Granting the point that these are limited-purpose, but not special-purpose, machines, what is the range of architectures needed to cover the spectrum of applications for which these machines make sense?

5. What are the cost/performance figures necessary to make this a viable approach for getting a computing task done? General-purpose machines are cheaper and easier to use but can be slow. ASICs and special-purpose devices are faster but more expensive in small quantities, take longer to develop, and are hard to modify. Where might CCMs fit between these two?

One problem faced by those involved in Splash 1 and Splash 2 at the Super-computing Research Center[2] has been a stubborn refusal from some quarters to believe that achieving high performance on a CCM is possible without a design or programming agony so great as to be offputting to all but the most dedicated of "application designers/programmers." Even in the face of our evidence to the contrary, the case has been difficult to make to some critics.

The case is especially hard because what is needed is to build a complete hardware system, to create or cause to be created a programming environment worthy of being called a programming environment, and then to develop a variety of different applications so that the proof of concept is complete. Further, since the goal is to demonstrate a competitive performance with more expensive and sophisticated machines, the CCM must be big enough to do real work and to be part of complete computational processing environments; it cannot be just a toy machine suitable only for doing kernels of problems. To our knowledge, only two such machines have been built that meet these criteria—Splash 2 and the larger of the DEC PAM systems.

The goal in this book is to present the Splash 2 experience as a whole. Splash 2 was designed and developed in an iterative process from top to bottom to top and back again.

1.2 THE CONTEXT FOR SPLASH 2

1.2.1 FPGAs

FPGAs in general have a wide spectrum of characteristics, but the FPGAs used for CCMs have been of two distinct types. The Xilinx XC4010, a typical example of one type, is a chip containing a 20×20 square array of Configurable Logic Blocks (CLBs) [34]. Each CLB can serve one of three functions, either as two flipflops, or as Boolean functions of nine inputs, or as 32 bits of RAM. The function use has two 4-input functions, each producing an output; these two bits combine with a ninth input in a 3-input Boolean function. The RAM usage simply takes advantage of the fact that the 4-input functions are done with lookup tables to allow the input bits to be viewed as addresses.

Connecting the CLBs to one another and to special Input Output Blocks (IOBs) on the periphery of the chip are routing resources running from CLB to CLB, skipping one CLB, or running the full length of the chip. Configuration of the FPGA is done by loading a bit file onto on-chip RAM.

In contrast to the relatively coarse granularity of the Xilinx chips, the second type of FPGA, by Algotronix, Ltd., and by Concurrent Logic, Inc. [1, 13], is fine-grained. The Algotronix chip is a 32×32 array of 2-input, 1-output Boolean function logic cells, with the signal lines running only point to point from one cell to its neighbors in each rectangular direction.[3]

---

[2]The Supercomputing Research Center was renamed the Center for Computing Sciences in May 1995, but will be referred to throughout this book as SRC.

[3]Algotronix is now a part of Xilinx.

To a first-order approximation, the chips first marketed by Concurrent Logic and now by Atmel[4] resemble the Algotronix chip. Interestingly enough, the unscientific best-guess estimates at the SRC in the fall of 1991, when Splash 2 was being designed, suggested that the then-high-end XC4010 and Concurrent Logic CLi6000 chips had roughly the same "compute power" in spite of the radically different architectures.

1.2.2 Architecture

There have been several architectures proposed and built for CCMs. Although any taxonomy runs the risk of pigeonholing some particular machine into a category distasteful to its designer, the following is a reasonable categorization.

Special-Purpose Devices.   The first and most obvious use of FPGAs for CCMs is in special-purpose machines built to perform a particular computation or kind of computation and not intended to be very flexible, except perhaps from one instance of the problem to the next. There have been several machines built for neural network computations (Ganglion, for example [15]). Here, the computation is clearly parallel, the individual compute nodes are neither standard nor very large, and one feature of neural nets is that a moderately high degree of connectivity is desired among the compute nodes; but the precise connectivity and multiplier constants at each compute node vary from application to application. Other applications for which special-purpose devices have been built include statistical physics, embedded control, and network control [14, 19, 25, 33].

Somewhat more general than a special-purpose device, but still very much in a narrow band of applications, is the use of an FPGA-based computer for rapid prototyping, not just of ASICs or of single circuit boards, but of an entire system. A CCM can be a complete system—processors, memory, data path, and so on—at the block diagram level, and the characteristics and details needed can be programmed into functioning hardware. Similarly, in an appropriate niche market, a CCM could be used in low-volume applications, cheaper in development cost than special-purpose hardware but faster than what one could obtain from a programmed microprocessor.

Coprocessors.   One of the most tantalizing possible uses for FPGAs as compute resources is as coprocessors tightly coupled to the main processor of a computer. The development of RISC processors has meant that some instructions that used to be part of a processor's repertoire are no longer present; these functions must now be performed in software routines that are inherently slower. Some computations have natural kernels that have never been part of the instruction set architecture of any processor. Much of the PRISM [4, 5, 6, 32] work has focused on two points: 1) the language, compiler, and system issues involved in determining that a particular core computation occurs frequently enough that it warrants being put onto the coprocessor, and 2) arranging the computation so that "hardware" exists in the FPGA coprocessor when it is needed and that data can be transferred to and from the coprocessor at speeds great enough to make use of the coprocessor worthwhile. Several such machines are described in [17, 18, 21, 22, 23, 24, 30]. In a similar vein, the SRC worked with Thinking Machines Corp. on the production of the "CM-2X,"

---

[4]National Semiconductor also had rights to and sold a version of this chip.

described by Cuccaro and Reese [16], a 512-node CM-2 in which Xilinx XC3090 chips replaced the floating-point chips as coprocessors.

Attached Processors.   As we have said, there have been two notable examples of FPGA-based attached processors—the PeRLe-0 and PeRLe-1 machines built by DEC's Paris research lab [8, 9, 29, 31], and the Splash 1 and Splash 2 machines built at SRC [2, 3, 20, 26]. The PeRLe-1 board featured 23 Xilinx XC3090 chips, with the core computational unit being a 4×4 grid, connected by a TURBOchannel to a DEC workstation. Splash 2, in contrast, is used primarily either as a linear array of 16 XC4010 chips per board or with data being broadcast to the 16 chips simultaneously. Both have achieved supercomputer performance on a range of applications including image processing, computational science benchmarks, data compression and encryption benchmarks, and molecular biology.

Some machines, which have for one reason or another been built with a particular purpose in mind, are general enough that they would find wider application. The CHAMP machine, described by Box [10], designed for image processing, is certainly among these. Other examples are described in Quenot et al. [27] and Raimbault et al. [28].

1.2.3 Programming

Notwithstanding the tremendous effort necessary to engineer the hardware of a CCM, the fundamental test of these machines is, and no doubt will continue to be, a software problem. Regardless of the architecture or the potential peak performance of the machine, if the effort to achieve that peak requires either an extraordinarily important problem or a fanatically dedicated user, the machine cannot be termed truly successful.

By this criterion we believe that CCMs have not yet silenced all their critics, but that we have turned important corners and have achieved a genuine understanding of the needed directions for research and development.

One problem in developing software for a CCM is that the programming process is far more vertically complex than for a standard computer. At the highest level are all the usual problems encountered when looking for performance from a computer—the user must be generally aware of the architecture of the CCM and program accordingly. But even from this top level working down, issues from deep within the FPGA must be dealt with. Must one partition the computation onto distinct chips in advance, or will an automatic partitioner be able to obtain sufficient utilization and speed? Even after partitioning, will a given chip be so densely packed with logic that routing delays will reduce the speed below a minimally acceptable level?

Apart from issues such as these, there are other factors to be considered. Logic synthesis and placement and routing on Xilinx chips presently takes several minutes to an hour for a chip with any substantial fraction of the logic used in a given application. How long will users be willing to wait, in this era of interactive computing, between iterations of this process? To what extent will they be willing to program in a language that is not Fortran or C? At what level can they or should they get involved in the performance-improving details of logic synthesis and/or placement and routing in order to gain the necessary speed improvements of a given application?

These problems actually differ from one kind of CCM to another. In an attached processor, the entire computation (or a definable portion of it) is taking place on the CCM. In a coprocessor system, the CCM portion must be extracted from the existing code (possibly with the help of compiler directives or annotations). The CCM code is similarly different from one sort of machine to another. On a coprocessor, one can assume that some effort might be expended by a user to optimize a particular "instruction," and the key issues would lie in recognizing its applicability and arranging for data to be delivered to and retrieved from the coprocessor. In an attached processor system, the CCM code could normally be much larger, allowing for more optimization (and thus more of the structure of the source to be obscured).

A final issue in programming is worthy of mention. The Algotronix chips have a feature that the Xilinx chips do not; part of the logic of the chip could be reconfigured without having the rest of the chip affected by the change. The reason for this lies in the different routing resources. On the Xilinx chip, no block of the chip can be assumed to be free of signals routed to or from some other block of the chip. On the Algotronix chip, however, the possibility of swapping hardware designs in and out like programs in and out of virtual memory was incorporated in the design from the beginning. The potential of such a feature for a CCM coprocessor is obvious.

REFERENCES

[1] Algotronix Ltd., *The Configurable Logic Data Book*, Algotronix Ltd., Edinburgh, Scotland, UK, 1990.

[2] J.M. Arnold, D.A. Buell, and E.G. Davis, "Splash 2," *ACM Symp. Parallel Algorithms and Architectures*, ACM Press, New York, 1992, pp. 316–322.

[3] J.M. Arnold et al., "The Splash 2 Processor and Applications," *Proc. Int'l Conf. Computer Design*, CS Press, Los Alamitos, Calif., 1993, pp. 482–485.

[4] P.M. Athanas, "Functional Reconfigurable Architecture and Compiler for Adaptive Computing," *Proc. 1993 Int'l Phoenix Computer and Comm. Conf.*, CS Press, Los Alamitos, Calif., 1993, pp. 49–55.

[5] P.M. Athanas and H.F. Silverman, "An Adaptive Hardware Machine Architecture for Dynamic Processor Reconfiguration," *Proc. Int'l Conf. Computer Design*, CS Press, Los Alamitos, Calif., 1991, pp. 397–400.

[6] P.M. Athanas and H.F. Silverman, "Processor Reconfiguration through Instruction Set Metamorphosis: Architecture and Compiler," *Computer*, Vol. 26, No. 3, Mar. 1993, pp. 11–18.

[7] P. Bertin, *Mémoires Actives Programmables: Conception, Réalisation et Programmation*, PhD thesis, Université Paris 7, 1993.

[8] P. Bertin, D. Roncin, and J. Vuillemin, "Programmable Active Memories: A Performance Assessment," in G. Borriello and C. Ebeling, eds., *Research on Integrated Systems*, MIT Press, Cambridge, Mass., 1993, pp. 88–102.

[9] P. Bertin and H. Touati, "PAM Programming Environments: Practice and Experience," *Proc. IEEE Workshop FPGAs for Custom Computing Machines*, CS Press, Los Alamitos, Calif., 1994, pp. 133–139.

[10] B. Box, "Field Programmable Gate Array Based Reconfigurable Preprocessor," *Proc. IEEE Workshop FPGAs for Custom Computing Machines*, CS Press, Los Alamitos, Calif., 1994, pp. 40–49.

[11] D.A. Buell and K.L. Pocek, "Custom Computing Machines: An Introduction," *J. of Supercomputing*, Vol. 9, 1995, pp. 219–230.

[12] S. Casselman, "Virtual Computing and the Virtual Computer," *Proc. IEEE Workshop FPGAs for Custom Computing Machines*, CS Press, Los Alamitos, Calif., 1993, pp. 43–49.

[13] Concurrent Logic Inc., *Cli6000 Series Field-Programmable Gate Arrays*, Concurrent Logic Inc., Sunnyvale, Calif., 1992.

[14] C.P. Cowen and S. Monaghan, "A Reconfigurable Monte-Carlo Clustering Processor (MCCP)," *Proc. IEEE Workshop FPGAs for Custom Computing Machines*, CS Press, Los Alamitos, Calif., 1994, pp. 59–66.

[15] C.E. Cox and W. Ekkehard Blanz, "Ganglion—a Fast Hardware Implementation of a Connectionist Classifier," IBM Research Report RJ8290, *Proc. 1991 IEEE Custom Integrated Circuits Conf.*, IEEE Press, Piscataway, N.J., 1991, pp. 6.5.1–6.5.4.

[16] S.A. Cuccaro and C.F. Reese, "The CM-2X: A Hybrid CM-2/Xilinx Prototype," *Proc. IEEE Workshop FPGAs for Custom Computing Machines*, CS Press, Los Alamitos, Calif., 1993, pp. 121–131.

[17] B.U. Heeb, *Debora: A System for the Development of Field-Programmable Hardware, and Its Application to a Reconfigurable Computer*, PhD thesis, VDF, Informatik Dissertationen 45, ETH Zürich, Zürich, Switzerland, 1993.

[18] B.U. Heeb and C. Pfister, "Chameleon, a Workstation of a Different Color," in H. Grünbacher and R.W. Hartenstein, eds., *Field Programmable Gate Arrays: Architectures and Tools for Rapid Prototyping*, Springer-Verlag, Berlin, 1993, pp. 152–161.

[19] H.-J. Herpel et al., "A Reconfigurable Computer for Embedded Control Applications," *Proc. IEEE Workshop FPGAs for Custom Computing Machines*, CS Press, Los Alamitos, Calif., 1993, pp. 111–121.

[20] D.T. Hoang, "Searching Genetic Databases on Splash 2," *Proc. IEEE Workshop FPGAs for Custom Computing Machines*, CS Press, Los Alamitos, Calif., 1993, pp. 185–192.

[21] C. Iseli and E. Sanchez, "Spyder: A Reconfigurable VLIW Processor Using FPGAs," *Proc. IEEE Workshop FPGAs for Custom Computing Machines*, CS Press, Los Alamitos, Calif., 1993, pp. 17–25.

[22] C. Iseli and E. Sanchez, "A C++ Compiler for FPGA Custom Execution Units Synthesis," *Proc. IEEE Symp. FPGAs for Custom Computing Machines*, CS Press, Los Alamitos, Calif., 1995, pp. 173–179.

[23] C. Iseli and E. Sanchez, "Spyder: A SURE, SUperscalar and REconfigurable, Processor," *J. of Supercomputing*, Vol. 9, 1995, pp. 231–252.

[24] P. Marchal and E. Sanchez, "CAFCA (Compact Accelerator for Cellular Automata): The Metamorphosable Machine," *Proc. IEEE Workshop FPGAs for Custom Computing Machines*, CS Press, Los Alamitos, Calif., 1994, pp. 66–72.

[25] S. Monaghan and C.P. Cowen, "Reconfigurable Multi-Bit Processor for DSP Applications in Statistical Physics," *Proc. IEEE Workshop FPGAs for Custom Computing Machines*, CS Press, Los Alamitos, Calif., 1993, pp. 103–111.

[26] D.V. Pryor, M.R. Thistle, and N. Shirazi, "Text Searching on Splash 2," *Proc. IEEE Workshop FPGAs for Custom Computing Machines*, CS Press, Los Alamitos, Calif., 1993, pp. 172–178.

[27] G.M. Quénot et al., "A Reconfigurable Compute Engine for Real-Time Vision Automata Prototyping," *Proc. IEEE Workshop FPGAs for Custom Computing Machines*, CS Press, Los Alamitos, Calif., 1994, pp. 91–101.

[28]   F. Raimbault et al., "Fine Grain Parallelism on a MIMD Machine Using FPGAs," *Proc. IEEE Workshop FPGAs for Custom Computing Machines*, CS Press, Los Alamitos, Calif., 1993, pp. 2–9.

[29]   M. Shand, P. Bertin, and J. Vuillemin, "Hardware Speedups for Long Integer Multiplication," *Proc. ACM Symp. Parallel Algorithms and Architectures*, ACM Press, New York, 1990, pp. 138–145.

[30]   S. Singh and P. Bellec, "Virtual Hardware for Graphics Applications Using FPGAs," *Proc. IEEE Workshop FPGAs for Custom Computing Machines*, CS Press, Los Alamitos, Calif., 1994, pp. 49–59.

[31]   J. Vuillemin et al., "Programmable Active Memories: Reconfigurable Systems Come of Age," *IEEE Trans. VLSI Systems*, to be published in Mar. 1996.

[32]   M. Wazlowski et al., "PRISM II: Compiler and Architecture," *Proc. IEEE Workshop FPGAs for Custom Computing Machines*, CS Press, Los Alamitos, Calif., 1993, pp. 9–17.

[33]   L.F. Wood, "High Performance Analysis and Control of Complex Systems Using Dynamically Reconfigurable Silicon and Optical Fiber Memory," *Proc. IEEE Workshop FPGAs for Custom Computing Machines*, CS Press, Los Alamitos, Calif., 1993, pp. 132–142.

[34]   Xilinx, Inc., *The Programmable Gate Array Data Book*, Xilinx, Inc., San Jose, Calif., 1993.

CHAPTER 2

The Architecture of Splash 2

Duncan A. Buell and Jeffrey M. Arnold[1]

2.1 INTRODUCTION

In this chapter we present the higher-level architecture of the Splash 2 system. This architecture is what an application programmer would normally be expected to see. Although the current admirable trend in general-purpose computing is to allow the programmer to perform computations without being required to understand or even be aware of hardware structures, it has always been the case in high-performance computing that knowledge of architectural features is necessary. Programmers on vector machines learn how to vectorize their algorithms and how to write code from which compilers can extract vector computations. Programmers on massively parallel machines must study I/O and data layout patterns. Similarly, programmers of Splash 2 must understand the architecture of the machine in order to make effective use of it. More correctly, they must understand the architecture in order to make *any* use of it. Unlike more common machines with a longer history, we have not yet reached the point at which custom computing machines can be used without paying reasonably close attention to the hardware.

Splash 2, as can be seen in the following discussion, has a substantial generality in its structure. Although generality in an architecture can be a very desirable feature, such generality can be anathema to effective use of the machine if all possible details must be considered for routine use. Consequently, every effort was made

---

[1] A version of this chapter appeared as Arnold et al. [1] and is used with permission.

to provide standard avenues for a programmer to use features of the architecture in standard ways. The system was designed with the strong intent that most applications would have data streaming linearly past the FPGA processing elements or have data broadcast to them in SIMD fashion. These capabilities were thus supported both in hardware and software and in example computations and programs, and a reading of the architectural description should be done with a focus on how the architecture supports these two models of computation.

2.2 THE BUILDING BLOCKS

The basic building block from which Splash 2 is made is the Xilinx XC4010 FPGA [3, 4]. As mentioned in Chapter 1, the XC4010 contains a 20 × 20 array of Configurable Logic Blocks (CLBs). The XC4010 CLB (shown in Figure 2.1) contains three lookup tables and two flip-flops. Two tables, labelled F and G, can each implement any Boolean function of up to four inputs. The outputs of the F and G functions can also be combined with a ninth input, H1, to form a single Boolean function of nine inputs. The YF output of the CLB can be taken from the output of either the F table or the H table. Similarly, the YG output can come from either the G or the H table. The F and G tables can also be configured to appear as individual 16 × 1-bit RAMs or a single 32 × 1 RAM. Not shown in Figure 2.1 is additional fast carry logic, which allows a single CLB to implement a two-bit full adder. An additional wire allows the carry-out of one CLB to be connected directly to the carry-in of an adjacent CLB.

Figure 2.2 illustrates the routing structure of the XC4000 series FPGA. Connecting the CLBs are three types of signal routing resources including a single-length interconnect between adjacent switch boxes ("S" in Figure 2.2), a double-length interconnect between alternate switch boxes, and a set of long lines that span the width and height of the chip. The switch boxes contain programmable switches that allow each segment to connect to three others. Configuration of the FPGA is done by loading a bit file into on-chip RAM; the hardware to do this in Splash 2 is implicit in our description in this chapter of the general architecture and is discussed in greater length in Chapter 6.

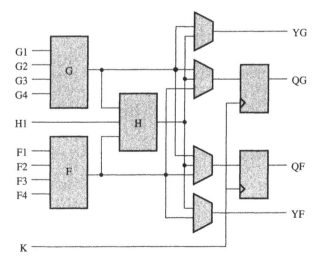

FIGURE 2.1   Xilinx XC4000 CLB Architecture

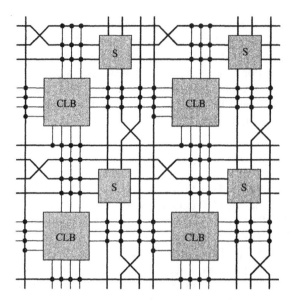

FIGURE 2.2 Xilinx XC4000 Routing Structure

The 400 CLBs can be viewed as 800 flip-flops, which can in turn be thought of as a maximum of twenty-five 32-bit "registers," where by "register" we mean to include registers, adders, comparators, multiplexors, and similar basic structures. For example, a 16-bit object requires eight CLBs. Adders, subtracters, and comparators are implemented by "rippling" the fast carry output from one CLB to the next. In order to reduce the signal propagation time for the carries, one would normally want to have the CLBs physically adjacent to one another in the final design. The Xilinx-supplied tools attempt to do this, and the "Hard Macros" supplied by Xilinx can be used to guarantee that a logic object is placed into contiguous CLBs.

In addition to their use as registers, the Boolean function use of the CLBs is necessary to implement the rather more random control logic that will exist in any program, so the available number of "registers" is certainly always less than the maximum.

2.3 THE SYSTEM ARCHITECTURE

Splash 2 is an attached processor system. Although it was not designed for the purpose of being an attachment specifically for Sun workstations, the system as designed uses a SPARCstation 2 as a host and attaches to the host through the SBus.

The overall system architecture is pictured in Figure 2.3. An SBus adapter card is placed in the host and connects via a cable to the Interface Board of Splash 2. The Interface Board and the Splash 2 Array Boards reside in a separate cabinet on a Futurebus+ backplane.

Splash 2 is designed to execute either synchronously with the host or asynchronously as an attached processor. Programs for Splash 2 are loaded on the system by the host through the SBus connection. In some applications, the processing on Splash 2 is then driven by a clock on the Interface Board, and data is delivered to and taken from Splash 2 by DMA channels on the Interface Board. The Interface Board

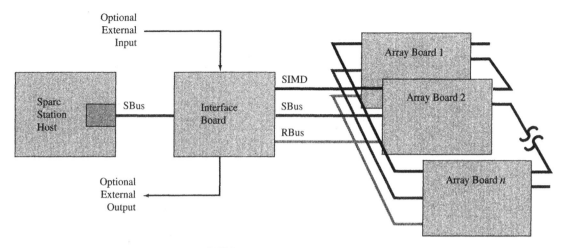

FIGURE 2.3   Splash 2 System Architecture

can also be configured to accept clock and data from an external source; in these applications, the role of the host is only to load programs and provide high-level control. Also supported are synchronous execution of Splash 2 via software clocking and slave data transfers.

The system architecture is designed to accommodate up to 16 Array Boards. A system containing eight Array Boards was built and functioned correctly, but most systems were built with two or four Array Boards in a 5-slot chassis that is 15″ wide, 28″ deep, and 24″ high. The largest possible system was never built because it would have required an expensive special version of the cabinet. There seemed to be no reason based on the eight-board system's operating characteristics to expect any problems with the larger system, and assembling a larger number of smaller systems from the same number of Array Boards allowed a greater breadth of applications to be tested.

2.4 DATA PATHS

Each Splash 2 Array Board contains 17 Xilinx XC4010 FPGA chips [4] as its processing elements (see Figure 2.4). Sixteen of these are connected in a linear array to create a linear data path and the seventeenth provides a broadcast capability to the other 16 chips. To each of these 17 chips is attached 512 Kbytes of memory. Reflecting this basic design, there are three different paths by which data can be delivered to or taken from the Array Boards.

The primary models of computation that were intended to be supported by the Splash 2 architecture were a SIMD or broadcast-of-data model and a linear (but not restricted to "systolic") model. The programmer viewing Splash 2 as a SIMD machine sees, among other things, a 36-bit-wide data path from the Interface Board down the SIMD Bus to each Array Board simultaneously. Xilinx chip X0 on each Array Board can then broadcast the SIMD Bus data to the other FPGAs on its Array

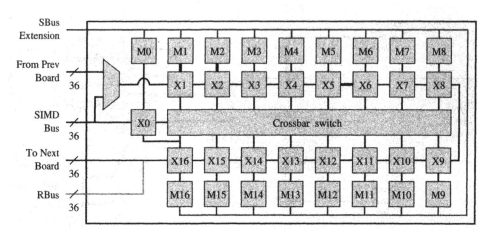

FIGURE 2.4   Array Board Architecture

Board. This mode of transferring data to the Splash 2 system was used, for example, in the text matching computation described later in this book.

Viewed as a machine with a linear data path, the SIMD Bus can be used to transmit data from the Interface Board to the first FPGA on the first Array Board. The data can then be moved through the linear data path on that board, then to the first FPGA on the second Array Board, and so on. Data from the last FPGA on the last Array Board returns to the Interface Board via the RBus. The linear path is also 36 bits wide, and is bidirectional (except for the initial segment along the SIMD Bus), so that data can be streamed in both directions for correlation computations; this was done for some versions of the DNA sequence comparison program detailed in Chapter 8. The definition of "last Array Board" is based upon the contents of a register on the Interface Board. This register can be changed during a program's execution, so the length of the processor array can be changed dynamically.

Data coming from the SPARCstation 2 host is 32 bits wide. The 36-bit-wide data path in Splash 2 arises naturally from this and from the need and desire to have tag bits on the data. Although data coming from an external signal could genuinely be 36 bits wide, in most applications the tag bits are set and read by Xilinx FPGAs on the Interface Board. Since the Splash 2 system executes asynchronously with the host, it is routine for Splash 2 to be able to begin executing before data can be delivered from the host. One use for the tag bits, therefore, is to serve as a "valid data" signal. In linear mode, the Xilinx chips on the Array Boards would pass "data" down the linear data path immediately upon startup, but would not actually begin processing that data until a valid data tag appeared. Similarly, the Xilinx FPGA on the Interface Board that was handling output would discard any "result" it received until a valid data tag appeared on the output path.

Another use for the tag bits arises when the machine is used as if it were a SIMD machine. It is possible to broadcast a 32-bit word to the broadcasting X0 chip as well as a 4-bit instruction opcode. (Actually, of course, there is no structure to the 36 bits being broadcast, so any bits not needed for data could be used for an opcode.) This opcode could be used by X0 to process the data or control the broadcast just as with any other hierarchical SIMD machine.

These paths are not necessarily mutually exclusive, and these configurations are not hardware-controlled by something like a mode bit. For example, it is possible to use the SIMD Bus for broadcast of data to all FPGAs simultaneously, but then to use the linear data path as a sort of "back door" for the return of results or for necessary neighbor-to-neighbor communications. The only restriction on these data paths is that the SIMD Bus can be used only for delivering data and not for returning results to the Interface Board.

In either of the above modes, data from the Interface Board can come either from the host or from an external signal (see Figure 2.5). Each Xilinx XC4010 FPGA on the Interface Board is programmable by the user (some standard programs for common applications also exist). Xilinx chip XL (for "Xilinx Left") handles incoming data for delivery to the SIMD Bus; in addition to setting the tag bits, if necessary, it handles the DMA transfers from the host, possible serial-to-parallel or parallel-to-serial data conversions, or similar massaging of the input data stream. Xilinx chip XR similarly handles data on the RBus, which would normally be the output path from the Splash 2 system. In some applications, especially in circumstances when postprocessing of the results was necessary, XR actually performed that part of the computation. This was true, for example, in the DNA sequence comparison computation.

The third means by which data can be provided to or retrieved from Splash 2 is directly through the 8.5 Mbytes of memory on each Array Board. This memory can be read by or written from the host as part of its normal address space via an

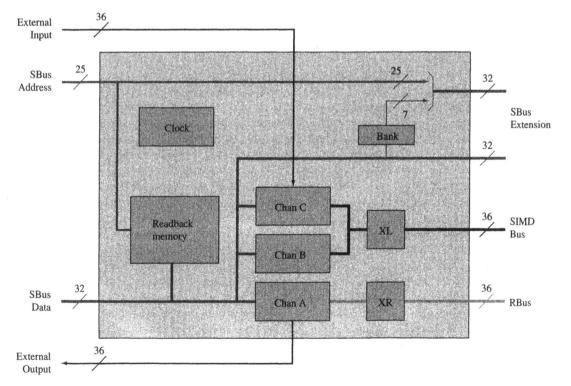

FIGURE 2.5   Interface Board Architecture

SBus extension independent of the FPGAs and their linear data path. The memory, however, is not dual-ported; during such memory read/write operations, the FPGAs are prevented from executing (and thus possibly accessing memory themselves). Thus, this mode of data transfer is not intended to be suitable for highly interleaved accesses of memory by Splash 2 and its host, but rather for bulk transfers before or after large phases of a given computation.

2.5 THE SPLASH 2 ARRAY BOARD

2.5.1 The Linear Array

The Splash 2 Array Board is detailed in Figure 2.4. Each Array Board contains 17 Xilinx XC4010 FPGA chips as processing elements. Sixteen of these, X1 through X16, form the processing array and are connected with a 36-bit-wide data path linearly and via a crossbar. To each FPGA is connected 512 Kbytes of memory. Throughout the Splash 2 system, the normal data object has been assumed to be 32 bits, augmented where possible and sensible with four tag bits. Here, in the connection from FPGA to memory, we find the one instance in which this design has been compromised. Three 36-bit-wide data paths, 18 bits for a memory address, and 32 bits for memory data would have left far too few of the 160 total pins for controlling each FPGA. The compromise was to reduce the memory data width to 16 bits.

2.5.2 The Splash 2 Crossbar

The crossbar for Splash 2 is a truly unique feature. The 36-bit-wide path is made by aggregating nine 4-bit Texas Instruments SN74ACT8841 crossbar chips [2]. Each such chip can be loaded at startup with as many as eight different configurations, with the particular configuration in effect being chosen under program control during execution of a computation. Furthermore, this choice can be made almost on a tick-by-tick basis.[2] The potential thus existed at the beginning of the design of this machine for each of the nine nibbles to have up to eight sources and destinations independent of the other nibbles and varying among the eight possibilities during the computation. This rather formidable choice of possibilities was only slightly reduced when pin constraints on the FPGAs X1 through X16 forced the low-eight nibbles to be paired so that only five independent sources and destinations actually exist on the machine as built. The crossbar, however, permits most "reasonable" configurations to be realized relatively simply.

For example, in an edge-detection program written essentially just for practice by Jeff Arnold, the first three chips on an Array Board are used to circularly buffer incoming lines of pixels so that the image can be streamed continuously into the board; the crossbar changes configuration at the end of every line of pixels to produce the effect of a circular buffer of three input lines on which a 3×3 filter can be applied.

---

[2]This is "almost" tick-by-tick only because one cannot reverse source and destination in one clock period.

In other applications, the presence of the crossbar permitted the programmer to get beyond the rigid structure of a linear data path by "jumping ahead" in time/space in order to maintain a tightly pipelined, systolic-like computation. Although the specific chips chosen for the crossbar were the source of a later problem (more is said about this in Appendix A), we have been unable to find other examples of machines in which processor-to-processor communication can be changed as rapidly or with as much variety as in Splash 2.

2.5.3 Xilinx Chip X0 and Broadcast Mode

The seventeenth Xilinx chip, labelled X0, performs several functions that provide much of the flexibility of the Splash 2 architecture. Three bits from X0, controlled by a program that must be loaded into X0, select which of the eight configurations of the crossbar are in effect at any given point in time. For static configurations lasting throughout a given phase of a computation, this "program" controlling the crossbar is invisible to the programmer; if a varying crossbar is desired, however, the program to control the crossbar must be written by the programmer as part of the complete application.

The other major function of X0 is to broadcast data received on the SIMD Bus to the other 16 Xilinx FPGAs. This is possible because X0 and X16 share wires into the crossbar. Clearly, of course, both FPGAs must not be permitted to drive signals simultaneously on these wires, but this does not normally limit the range of usage; in situations in which X0 needs to serve as a broadcast chip, X16 normally does not need access into the crossbar. When X0 is broadcasting, X16 is receiving just like any other of the FPGAs. Since the crossbar is bidirectional, X0 can in fact receive data from the crossbar as well, adding to its ability to control execution on its Array Board.

Chip X0, like the other FPGAs, has a 256K × 16-bit memory attached to it with a 16-bit data path. In most instances where custom computing machines such as Splash 2 have been built, the use of memory for lookup tables has been important in achieving high performance. The rather limited compute resources on an FPGA requires the use of such memory to reduce the need for processing logic. This is especially true of chip X0.

Most massively parallel SIMD machines have had a front-end processor; chip X0 can, to the limit of its own capability, serve that function in Splash 2. As is described in Chapter 9 on the text processing application, X0 can perform some general computations and data preparation. It is also possible to use the four tag bits (or, for that matter, any other of the 36 bits of the data path) as instruction opcodes to chip X0. In such a situation, the memory would be used to store a "microcode subroutine," which would be executed by a small finite-state or other machine implemented on X0.

2.6 THE INTERFACE BOARD AND CONTROL FEATURES

A detailed description of the Interface Board is presented in Chapter 3 on hardware and implementation details, but now we discuss several aspects of the Interface Board that have to be considered as part of the higher-level architecture of the Splash 2 system. To permit control of parallel programs running searches until some particular event occurs, global `or` and global `valid` bits run to FPGA X0 from each of the 16 FPGAs X1 through X16 on an Array Board. Global `or` and global `valid` bits from X0 of each Array Board are then wire-ORed on the backplane to a register on the Interface Board and appear as inputs to FPGAs XL and XR on the Interface Board. On each Array Board, the `or` and `valid` bits are bidirectional, allowing further control by X0 of computations on the Array Board.

The clock that drives Splash 2 as an asynchronous attached processor resides on the Interface Board. Because various programs could be expected to run (and in fact do run) at widely differing speeds, a clock module was chosen whose frequency could be tuned to the speed at which the synthesized Xilinx chip program could run. Chip XL has control of the clock-regulated computation on the Array Boards; the Array Boards can be single-stepped, n-stepped, or allowed to run freely. To reduce the programming overhead for routine computations, several default programs for XL were written at an early stage in the development of the system and can be selected by a programmer from the library. This is also true of programs for the FPGAs on the Array Boards.

The alert reader will already have noted that the address bits available from the host on the SBus are insufficient to address all the memory potentially available on a full-sized Splash 2 system. The address extension is done on the Interface Board; the particulars of this process appear in Chapter 3 on hardware implementation details.

A final feature of the Splash 2 system is the ability to load or store a configuration state into the Xilinx chips. Readout of the state is invaluable for debugging, program optimization, and monitoring program behavior.

REFERENCES

[1] J.M. Arnold, D.A. Buell, and E.G. Davis, "Splash 2," *Proc. ACM Symp. Parallel Algorithms and Architectures*, ACM Press, New York, 1992, pp. 316–322.

[2] Texas Instruments Inc., *The SN74ACT8800 Family Data Manual (SCSS006A)*, Texas Instruments Inc., Dallas, 1988.

[3] S.M. Trimberger, ed., *Field Programmable Gate Array Technology*, Kluwer Academic Publishers, Boston, 1994.

[4] Xilinx, Inc., *The Programmable Gate Array Data Book*, Xilinx, Inc., San Jose, Calif., 1993.

CHAPTER 3

Hardware Implementation

Walter J. Kleinfelder and Jeffrey M. Arnold

3.1 INTRODUCTION

Figure 3.1 illustrates the system architecture of Splash 2. The system consists of a Futurebus+ backplane enclosure containing one Interface Board and up to 13 Splash 2 Array Boards,[1] and a SPARCstation 2 host computer with Adapter Board. The Adapter Board plugs into the host computer's internal SBus and extends the address and data bus to permit host-resident programs to directly address the memory and control registers in the Splash 2 system. The Adapter Board also provides the interface logic required to permit Splash 2 to perform direct memory access (DMA) transfers to and from the host memory and to generate SBus interrupts. The Splash 2 enclosure is connected to the host system via a cable between the Adapter Board and the Interface Board. To complete the linear data path, each Array Board is also connected to its two neighboring boards through a separate custom backplane in addition to the Futurebus+ backplane.

During the course of the Splash 2 project, two different interface boards were developed to provide the connection between the host computer and the Splash 2 Array Boards. The Development Board was designed with minimal functionality but with an extensible wire-wrap core to allow prototyping of various features. The final Interface Board was built in printed circuit technology and incorporates a number of higher-level functions. Both interfaces extend the host address and data buses to the

---

[1]This is the largest enclosure fabricated for the Splash 2 system. The architecture supports up to 16 Array Boards.

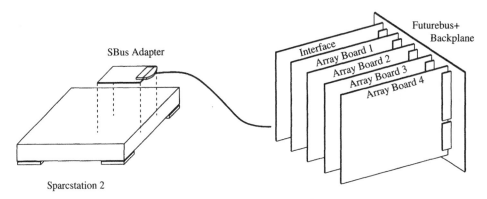

FIGURE 3.1   Splash 2 System Architecture

backplane memory bus, permitting the host to read and write memory and memory-mapped control registers on the Array Boards. All data transfers between the host and the interface are 32 bits wide, the word size of the SBus. Because the 25 bits of physical address space for a single SBus slot is insufficient to address the entire Splash 2 memory space, the address is extended to 32 bits by a 7-bit bank register on the Interface Board.

The Splash 2 system may transfer data to and from the host system memory via DMA. The Interface Board contains up to three independent DMA channels implemented as optional daughter boards that may be plugged onto the Interface Board. In addition to supporting DMA, this daughter board arrangement allows high-speed external input and output devices to be connected directly to Splash 2, bypassing the host SBus. For example, an external video input may be brought directly into Splash 2 by replacing one DMA channel with a specially designed daughter board.

The linear data path extends from the Interface Board along the SIMD Bus, through the set of Array Boards in daisy-chain fashion, and back to the Interface Board along the RBus. The SIMD Bus is a 36-bit unidirectional bus driven by the Interface Board and connected to each Array Board in the system. The Array Board daisy chain and the RBus are 36-bit-wide bidirectional data paths. The linear data path can therefore be used to pass data in either the "left-to-right" direction or the "right-to-left" direction. Left-to-right is defined to be from the SIMD Bus through the Array Boards and back on the RBus. Right-to-left is defined to be from the Interface Board down the RBus to the last, or rightmost, Array Board through the daisy chain and terminating at the first, or leftmost, Array Board. Two data streams can pass simultaneously through the array in opposite directions, with one stream following the left-to-right direction on a subset of the bits of the linear data path and the second stream moving right-to-left on the remaining bits.

Each Splash 2 Array Board contains 16 Processing Elements, X1–X16, with direct 36-bit connections between adjacent elements. Each element can also communicate with all other elements on the same board through a programmable crossbar. A seventeenth Control Element, X0, controls the crossbar and provides support logic. The sixteen Processing Elements and the Control Element each consist of a Xilinx XC4010 FPGA and a 256K × 16 static RAM.

3.2 DEVELOPMENT BOARD DESIGN

The Development Board was designed to serve a variety of purposes during the early development of Splash 2. The original goal of the Development Board was to support the initial debugging of the Array Board design and the system software while the design of the Interface Board proceeded in parallel. The flexibility of the Development Board also made it a convenient vehicle on which to prototype various components of the final Interface Board design. The Development Board eventually became a critical tool for the instrumentation and debugging of the DMA transfer protocol. A modified version of the Development Board was also used as a test fixture for the DMA and Clock daughter boards.

The design philosophy behind the Development Board was to keep the hardware simple by moving as much control as possible to the host software. This was accomplished by placing virtually every signal on the backplane under the direct control of the host computer. Readable and writable registers are connected to the SIMD Bus and RBus data (32 bits each) and tags (4 bits each), and the RBus size and direction controls. Read-only registers provide access to the interrupt request and global OR signals. The system clock mechanism is a register that, when written by the host, generates a single pulse of 100 nsec duration. To generate successive clock pulses the host must write repeatedly to the clock register. Using this mechanism the SPARCstation host is able to achieve a maximum clock rate of 4 MHz. To improve the performance of stream-based applications an additional address is decoded that, when written, loads the SBus data into the SIMD register and then generates a single clock pulse.

The physical design of the Development Board consists of three main components: the SBus interface, the backplane interface, and the wire-wrap core. The data path portion of both the SBus and the backplane interfaces are implemented with surface-mount printed circuit technology along two edges of the board. The center of the board contains a large grid of holes for wire-wrap socket pins. This prototyping area is used to implement the control state machines and to experiment with the DMA and Clock circuits.

3.3 INTERFACE BOARD DESIGN

The Splash 2 system buses are implemented on the P896.2 Futurebus+ profile A backplane with a 128-bit extension. The Splash 2 Interface Board plugs into Slot 1 of the Futurebus+ backplane and accepts the cable from the SBus Adapter Board in the host computer. The Interface Board is responsible for generating all signals required in the backplane and is structured to drive up to 16 Splash 2 Array Boards. The principal functions of the Interface Board include SBus control and data transfer, system clock generation, and pre- and postprocessing of data to and from the Array Boards.

Figure 3.2 illustrates the Splash 2 Interface Board architecture. The host data bus (SD[0:31]) is gated and buffered to drive the backplane memory data bus for memory-mapped reads and writes. The host address bus (SA[2:24]) is buffered and decoded locally for accesses to the Interface Board. The Bank Register is loaded by the host with a 7-bit value. The SBus address and the Bank Register together form

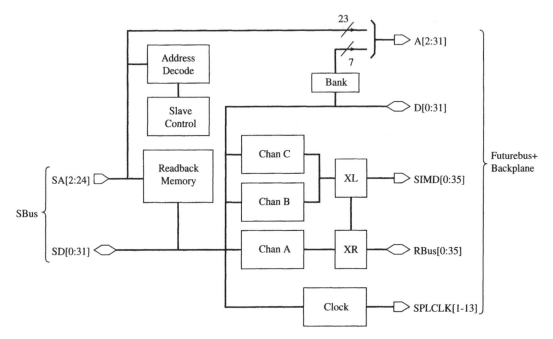

FIGURE 3.2   Interface Board Architecture

the Array Board memory address, A[2:31]. Since only 32-bit accesses are supported, the two least significant bits of the address (A[0:1]) are always zero.

The slave control state machine receives the decoded address and generates internal read and write timing signals in response to SBus slave cycles. The slave machine also controls the timing of the SBus acknowledge signal, ensuring sufficient access time for the various registers and memories. SBus read operations to the Array Board are acknowledged in 9 SBus clock cycles, while write operations are acknowledged in 8 cycles. In accesses to the facilities on the Interface Board, writes are acknowledged in 3 cycles and reads in 4 cycles.

The clock circuit generates the system clock signal for the Splash 2 Array Boards and can be programmed by the host to various frequencies. During execution of Splash 2 programs this signal clocks the user-defined circuitry. To aid debugging of applications, the clock generator can be programmed to stop, single-step, or step a fixed number of times. To prevent DMA data overruns or underruns the clock generator can also be stopped and restarted by user-defined logic in XL or XR. To minimize the clock skew across the system, separate clock signals (SPLCLK) are driven to each Array Board.

XL and XR are user-programmable XC4010 FPGAs that provide the interface between the DMA channels and the backplane bus. XL controls Channels B and C and drives the 36-bit SIMD bus. XR controls Channel A and can receive data from or drive data to the 36-bit RBus. The direction of the RBus is determined by the RDIR output of XR. Data may also be passed between XL and XR through a separate 36-bit bidirectional path.

3.3.1 DMA Channel

The DMA channels perform SBus-compatible burst transfers between the host memory and a 256-word FIFO. Each DMA channel contains an address register, a transfer count register, and a control register. The address register contains the address of the host memory buffer. The transfer count register contains the number of burst transfers to perform. The control register contains an enable bit and a direction bit. All DMA transfers are performed in 16-word bursts, the largest supported by the SBus. The FIFOs contain programmable high- and low-watermark registers, which permit the DMA channel to determine when to request a transfer. When the channel is enabled and the direction bit is set to read from the host memory, if the FIFO has space for at least 16 words, then an SBus READ operation is requested. Similarly, when the direction bit is set to write to the host, memory, and if at least 16 words of data are available in the FIFO, then an SBus WRITE operation is requested.

After each burst transfer completes the address and transfer count registers are updated. The address register is incremented by 64 to point to the next block of 16 words (64 bytes), while the transfer count is decremented by 1. When the transfer count reaches zero an SBus interrupt is requested.

The SBus side of the DMA channel is 32 bits wide, but the FIFO and the Splash 2 data paths are 36 bits wide. When transferring data from the host, the word is extended to 36 bits by concatenating the contents of a 4-bit tag register to the data. When transferring data to the host, the 4 tag bits are saved in a register.

The DMA channel allows direct loading and unloading of the FIFO data from the host by mapping the input and output data registers of the FIFO into the host's address space. This feature allows the host operating system software to handle the boundary conditions of transfers that are not aligned on 64-byte boundaries. See Chapter 6 for more details on DMA data alignment.

3.3.2 XL and XR

The primary function of the two user-programmable FPGAs, XL and XR, is to perform pre- and postprocessing on the input and output data streams. DMA Channel A is controlled by XR, while Channels B and C are controlled by XL. Both XL and XR receive the Splash 2 system clock and a free-running clock that is synchronous with the system clock. Either XL or XR may stop and restart the system clock when the FIFOs, in their respective DMA channels, are empty or full. When XL or XR are used to stop the system clock the free-running clock may be used to drive the controlling state machine, allowing it to restart the system clock when the condition has cleared.

DMA Channels B and C share a common 36-bit-wide data bus with XL, which may select the channel from which to receive data. XL is also responsible for driving the SIMD bus, typically with the input data from one or both of Channels B and C. XR sits between DMA Channel A and the RBus and is typically used to postprocess result data from the RBus before sending it back to the host through Channel A. A separate 36-bit bidirectional bus connects XL and XR. This bus may be used to coordinate clock control, to close the loop through the linear array by passing data from the RBus back to XL and the SIMD bus, or to pass input data from XL through XR to the linear data path in the right-to-left direction. For example, an application can receive input data from both Channels B and C simultaneously, sending the Channel B data along the left-to-right direction and the Channel C data moving from right to left.

3.3.3 Interrupts

The Interface Board receives up to 16 individual interrupt requests, one from each Splash 2 Array Board. Interrupt requests can also be generated by XL, XR, the DMA channels, and the clock. The interrupt circuit logically ANDs each request with a corresponding bit in a mask register and then ORs these results together to form a single SBus interrupt request which, when enabled by a bit in the control register, is passed to the SBus. When handling an interrupt, the host can read the contents of the interrupt register to determine which of the possible sources made the request. If the request came from one of the Array Boards, the host can then interrogate a similar register on the requesting Array Board to determine which PE initiated the request.

3.3.4 Clock

The system clock can be selected from two possible sources: the programmable clock generator or a software-generated clock pulse. The clock generator, or "hardware clock," is a daughter card that plugs onto the Interface Board. The heart of the hardware clock is an Analytic Instruments FS-30 programmable frequency synthesizer, which has a frequency range of less than 1 Hz to 30 MHz. The frequency of the system clock is set by the host and is asynchronous with respect to the SBus clock. Both XL and XR have the ability to immediately stop the system clock, typically in response to a DMA channel nearing the full or empty mark. The host computer also has the ability to start and stop the clock generator, and may program the generation of a specific number of clock cycles. Special synchronization circuitry ensures that the first and last clock pulses are not truncated. The output signal has a nominal duty cycle of 50% plus or minus 5 nsec.

The "software clock" is a register very similar to the clock register on the Development Board. In the interest of performance, a bit in the control register determines whether writes to the software clock generate one or two pulses of 100 nsec each. Another bit in the control register selects either the hardware clock or the software clock to drive the system clock.

3.3.5 Programming and Readback

The configuration and state readback mechanisms for all of the user-programmable FPGAs are implemented on the Interface Board using a single 256K × 32 memory to store the bitstreams. All of the FPGAs on a single Array Board are programmed simultaneously using the serial configuration mode of the XC4010. Prior to programming, the host merges the 17 individual bitstreams (one each for X0 through X16) into a single 17-bit-wide stream. This operation is known as "corner turning." The corner-turned configuration stream is then loaded into the Interface Board memory, and the programming sequence is begun by an on-board state machine. This state machine reads sequential locations from the memory and performs write operations over the SBus extension to a special address on the selected Array Board. A base address register contains the location of the first word in the bitstream and configuration stops when the address counter reaches the top of the memory. Seventeen of the 32 bits are used to store the data for the 17 user-programmable FPGAs on the Array Board. Two additional bits may optionally contain the configuration streams for XL and XR. The remaining bits of the Interface Board memory are not used.

The same basic mechanism is used to perform state readback. Another state machine on the Interface Board reads the internal state information from all 17 FPGAs on a given Array Board and stores the data into successive locations in the Interface Board memory. Readback terminates when the address counter reaches the top of memory. Once the FPGA state information is stored in the Interface Board memory the SPARCstation host can retrieve the specific state bits of interest to the programmer.

Since the configuration and readback operations employ the SBus extension between the Interface Board and the Array Boards, during both configuration and readback the Splash 2 system will not respond to the SBus; any host attempt to access the Splash 2 system during one of these operations will result in a bus time-out.

3.3.6 Miscellaneous Registers

There are several control and status registers on the Interface Board that are accessible to the host. The configuration and readback mechanism contains an 18-bit base address register and a control register with a direction bit (programming versus readback) and a start bit.

The main control and status register (CSR) contains the "bypass" mode bit which, when set, disables XL and XR and enables the bypass registers. These registers allow the Interface Board to mimic the behavior of the Development Board. A separate bypass register contains the RBus size and direction bits and the broadcast bit for use in bypass mode.

The CSR also provides access to the signals that control the programming and readback of XL and XR, including the PROGRAM, INIT, and DONE pins of the Xilinx chips. Another signal, RBTRIG, is used to initiate the readback operation in XL and XR. The clock source select and the interrupt enable bits are also in the CSR.

There are three levels of reset available on the Interface Board. At the lowest level is the system reset signal, which is connected to the host computer's power-on reset. At the second level is the "panic" bit in the CSR. This signal is used to reset various control state machines on the Array Boards. At the highest level is the "program reset" bit in the CSR, which is connected to the individual Processing Elements' global set/reset (GSR) signal.

The Interface Board also contains a 32-bit read-only identification (ID) register implemented using DIP switches. The ID switches are set to contain board version information and a unique serial number.

3.4 ARRAY BOARD DESIGN

Figure 3.3 shows a block diagram of the Array Board architecture. The Array Board contains 16 Processing Elements (PEs) arranged in a linear array. A seventeenth FPGA-memory pair, referred to both as the Control Element or as the seventeenth

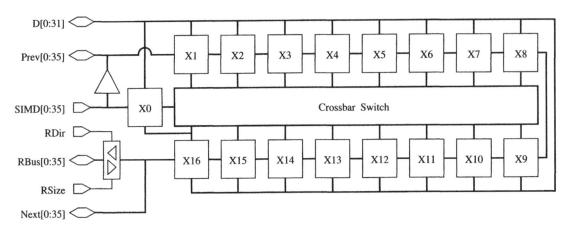

FIGURE 3.3 Array Board Architecture

Processing Element PE0 in some applications, manages the crossbar and can send data to or receive data from the crossbar. The 36-bit linear data path enters the array from the previous board, continues through adjacent PEs, and exits the array to the next board. The first, or leftmost, board in the system detects that it is in slot 2 and receives its input data from the SIMD bus instead of the previous board connection. The last, or rightmost, board is determined by comparing the slot number of each board to the RBus Size value on the backplane. The selected board then either sends data to the RBus or receives data from the RBus, as determined by the state of the RDIR backplane signal. Array Boards that are not at either end of the array simply communicate with adjacent boards via unbussed pins in a custom backplane extension.

Along the front edge of the Array Board are 18 light-emitting diodes (LEDs). One LED (green) is connected directly to power and indicates whether the board is receiving power. A second LED (red) is connected to an output pin of the Control Element (X0). The remaining 16 LEDs (amber) are each connected to an output pin of each PE. These LEDs are available for use by application programs and are used extensively by the diagnostic software.[2]

3.4.1 Processing Element

The organization of the Splash 2 Processing Element is shown in Figure 3.4. The PE consists of a Xilinx XC4010 FPGA and 256K × 16 RAM. The RAM is implemented with four 256K × 4 static RAM chips with 20 nsec access time mounted on a ZIP package. The memory control state machine is implemented in a 22V10 programmable logic device (PLD).

The Processing Element FPGA has four principal data paths, corresponding approximately to the four sides of the chip. There is a 36-bit-wide bidirectional data path to each of the two neighboring PEs (to the left and right), a 41-bit interface to the central crossbar, and a 36-bit interface to the local RAM. The crossbar interface consists of a 36-bit-wide bidirectional data path and five output enable control signals.

---

[2]One programmer wrote a program that scrolled a banner of text across the boards.

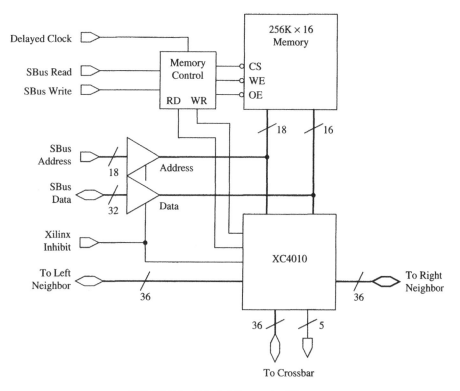

FIGURE 3.4 Splash 2 Processing Element

The 36 bits of data are arranged in four groups of 8 bits and one group of 4 bits, with each group controlled by a separate output enable. The RAM interface consists of a 16-bit data path, an 18-bit address, and separate read and write control signals.

The memory control device is used to present a purely synchronous interface to the programmer. To initiate a memory read operation the FPGA asserts the read control signal and the address at the rising edge of the system clock. Data from the memory is available on the next rising edge of the clock. To initiate a write operation the FPGA asserts the write control signal, the address, and the data on the rising edge. The write enable pulse is generated by the memory control PLD from a delayed version of the system clock. The interface circuitry and the RAM timing guarantee that a write pulse is not applied to the RAM until the address and data have met the setup requirements. The write pulse is released in time to meet the required hold time. To guarantee that these constraints are satisfied, it is necessary to register the memory interface signals in the IOB flip-flops of the FPGA.

There are several other signals available to the Processing Element, including:

- system clock
- broadcast bit from the control element
- program reset signal from the Interface Board
- two handshake register bits

- global OR result and valid bits connected to the control element
- Xilinx Disable bit
- LED control signal

3.4.2 Control Element

The organization of the Control Element (X0) is very similar to that of the Processing Element, consisting of a Xilinx XC4010 and a 256K × 16 RAM. The memory interface of the Control Element is identical to that of the Processing Element. The 36-bit SIMD bus is connected directly to X0. X0 is responsible for selecting the crossbar configuration in use at any given time through a 3-bit "crossbar select" port. X0 may also read or write the 36-bit crossbar through the port it shares with PE X16. An output port allows X0 to override X16's crossbar output enables, effectively taking control of the 36-bit data path.

The bidirectional global OR and Valid bits from each of the 16 PEs are connected to X0. X0 in turn may also drive the open collector systemwide global OR and Valid signals on the backplane. These signals are intended to be used to permit X0 to perform Array Board-level synchronization, and then to participate as the board's representative in systemwide synchronization.

The single-bit broadcast signal from the backplane is an input to X0, which may then drive the board-level broadcast signal to the 16 PEs.

3.4.3 External Memory Access

The SBus extension bus permits the host to directly read and write the PE memories. Since the PE memory is not dual-ported, the address and data bus of each memory is shared between the FPGA and the SBus extension. Therefore it is necessary to ensure that the FPGA does not interfere with SBus accesses to the memory, and vice versa. The host accomplishes this by stopping the system clock and asserting the "Xilinx Disable" signal in the Array Board control register prior to any memory access. The system software must guarantee that the Xilinx Disable pin of each PE is wired to the internal Global Tri-State (GTS) signal within the FPGA. Once the memory access is complete, the host must clear the Xilinx Disable bit and restart the clock.

References from the host to the PE memories are multiplexed such that each 32-bit host access is converted to two 16-bit accesses to sequential memory locations. The RAM multiplexor is clocked with the SBus clock, not the programmable system clock, so the memory can be accessed by the host while the system clock is stopped.

3.4.4 Crossbar

The crossbar network permits the communication between processing elements via a selection of preprogrammed configurations. The Texas Instruments SN74ACT8841 chip, shown in Figure 3.5, is used for this application. The 8841 chip has sixteen 4-bit bidirectional ports, which may be connected in any desired pattern. Each port's output may be selected from any of the other ports. The output port selection is

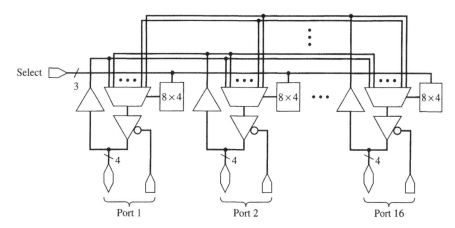

FIGURE 3.5   Architecture of the TI 8841 Crossbar Chip

controlled by an 8×4 register file. The register file entry in use during a given clock cycle is chosen by the external 3-bit Select signal. The output of each port is independently controlled by a separate output enable pin.

On the Splash 2 Array Board, nine 8841 chips are coupled to form the central crossbar. The output enable pins are grouped together in pairs to form five controls for each Processing Element. Each FPGA therefore supplies five signals to control its corresponding crossbar connection, arranged as four 8-bit paths and one 4-bit path.

The crossbar array is preloaded by the host with up to eight connection configurations. During execution, three bits from the Control Element X0 select the desired preloaded configuration, which X0 can change from clock cycle to clock cycle. The crossbar chips are individually loaded, since their configurations will not necessarily be identical.

3.4.5 Programming and Readback

Configuration and readback of the Array Board FPGAs is accomplished by performing write and read operations over the extended SBus. The PROGRAM bit in the Array Board control register causes all 17 FPGAs (X0–X16) to enter program mode. Subsequent writes to the "configuration" register cause each FPGA to extract one bit from the data word and load it into its internal configuration. The INIT and DONE status signals are available as separate registers to be read by the host.

State readback is performed in a similar manner. When written, the RBTRIG bit in the control register puts all 17 FPGAs in readback mode. Subsequent reads from the configuration register return the internal state information to the SBus. An on-board state machine generates the configuration clock (CCLK) timing for both configuration and readback.

3.4.6 Miscellaneous Registers

Most of the registers on the Array Board and the SBus address decoding are actually implemented in an eighteenth Xilinx FPGA. This FPGA is not user-programmable, however, but is configured at power-on from a set of on-board PROMs. The "panic" signal from the Interface Board will also force a reload of the controller's configuration.

All of the programmable features and mode controls are accessible to the host through the SBus address space. All registers are aligned on 32-bit boundaries. The registers are organized into two separate pages of the address space, one to be available in user mode and the other accessible only in supervisor mode. The user mode registers include the control register, the handshake register, the configuration registers, the version and serial number register, and the crossbar configuration registers. The supervisor mode space contains the interrupt status and mask registers.

The control register contains a number of signals effecting the operation of the Array Board, including the PROGRAM and RBTRIG for loading and unloading the FPGAs. The control register also contains the Xilinx Disable signal used to force the FPGA pins to their high impedance state and the Handshake Direction signal used to set the direction of the handshake register. The configuration registers include addresses from which the host may read the INIT and DONE status signals from each FPGA and the location to which the configuration bitstream is written or the readback stream is read.

The handshake register is an asynchronous communication channel between the host and the Processing Elements. One bit of the handshake register is connected to each of the 17 FPGAs. The bits themselves are bidirectional, but the direction of all 17 bits is determined by the Handshake Direction bit of the control register. The version and serial number register contents are hard-coded in the controller's configuration PROM. The version number changes with each revision of the controller PROM program, and the serial number is unique to each Array Board.

The crossbar configuration information is loaded into a set of 4-bit registers within each of the nine TI 8841 crossbar chips. These registers are mapped into the SBus address space of the Array Board, allowing the host to write directly to the TI chips.

The interrupt status register latches the state of the interrupt bits from each of the 17 FPGAs. The controller combines the latched status with the mask information to form the board-level interrupt signal. The interrupt status register is cleared when read by the host.

CHAPTER 4

Splash 2: The Evolution of a New Architecture

Duncan A. Buell

The preceding two chapters have described the hardware designed and built as Splash 2. It is important, however, to trace the design process that led us to the artifact we have today, otherwise there is the danger of seeing only the extant machine and not the potential variations. In this chapter we examine the decisions that led to the final architecture.

4.1 SPLASH 1

The germ of the idea for Splash 1 [2] apparently came from Dick Kunze and Paul Schneck at SRC in late 1986. Discussion took place among Kunze, Schneck, and Dick Lipton from Princeton, in part due to a realization that a Splash-like processor would be a generalization of the special-purpose P-NAC (Princeton Nucleic Acid Comparator) that Lipton was having built. P-NAC was designed to execute the edit-distance (approximate string matching) algorithm used in comparing DNA sequences against each other.

By the spring of 1987, the essential Splash 1 architecture had been laid out; at a meeting among the SRC and Princeton principals held at SRC on February 27, 1987, the linear array of Xilinx chips and memories had already taken shape. As with any such new system, there were several variants that were considered from time to time but never adopted. One early thought was that a 128-board system could be built. This never got beyond the concept stage. Another idea that surfaced again and again and resurfaced briefly in the later design of Splash 2 was the possibility of including floating-point chips in the array path. This idea was studied for Splash 1 but never adopted, the stumbling block being in part that the floating-point chips operated at a fixed speed whereas Splash 1 designs ran at speeds that were dependent on the programming. This implied that the floating point chips could not be substituted one for one with Xilinx chips, leading to rather complicated control paths. Further, while applications that made use of the Xilinx capability—reconfigurable processor architecture—and applications that made use of the floating-point power could be envisioned, there seemed only a limited benefit from mixing the two. Given that numerous floating-point accelerators exist and that the real point of the experiment was to demonstrate the power of FPGAs for computing, there seemed to be no overwhelming reason to add the floating-point capability to Splash 1. In the later design of Splash 2 the subject came up once again. By then the consensus was that Splash 1 was and Splash 2 would be processors with a niche that lies outside the world of floating-point computation. Given more serious consideration for Splash 2, however, was the idea of including a fast microprocessor on each Array Board to provide more general compute capability close to the Xilinx chips themselves.

The final Splash 1 processor was a single multiwire board that plugs into the VMEbus of a Sun workstation (see Figure 4.1).

Each board contained 32 Xilinx XC3090 FPGA chips X0 through X31 as PEs connected in a linear array by a 32-bit-wide path. Chips X0 and X31 could be similarly connected to form a ring, were it necessary to route data around the ring more than once or to send data in both directions through the FPGAs. Data synchronization on and off the board was handled by a pair of FIFOs controlled by X0 and X31, respectively. Between each pair of interior Xilinx chips was a $128K \times 8$ RAM with an 8-bit-wide path to the FPGAs.

The Xilinx XC3090 chips in Splash 1 had a maximum clock rate of 32 MHz. To accommodate Splash 1 designs that could not be run at maximum speed, usually due to placement and routing problems or to the inability of the VMEbus to deliver data at a sufficiently high rate, the clock rate could be set in factors of two from 1 MHz to 32 MHz.

A three-Xilinx-chip (one for input from the host, one for output to the host, and one in the middle) Splash 1 board, nicknamed PUDDLE, was wire-wrapped by hand in order to gain an understanding of the hardware and expose unforeseen problems. This board became operational in March of 1988. When it had been thoroughly debugged, a full 32-chip board was wire-wrapped and become operational at the end of 1988. Finally, schematics for the multiwire "production" version were finished in mid-February of 1989, and the final boards were fully tested just in time for SRC's 1989 summer workshop on Splash 1 applications.

Programming of Splash 1 was originally done with the Xilinx-supplied XACT editor; later tools included the Viewlogic schematic capture package. From the outset, however, there were difficulties in developing application codes; especially for individuals unused to hardware design, programming with XACT was not easy. To make the machine more accessible, the Logic Description Generator (LDG), a higher-level language whose output could be mapped to the Xilinx chips, was designed and implemented at SRC through the fall of 1988 and the winter of 1988–89 by Maya Gokhale [3]. In addition to the software for direct execution, a debugger called `Trigger` was used extensively.

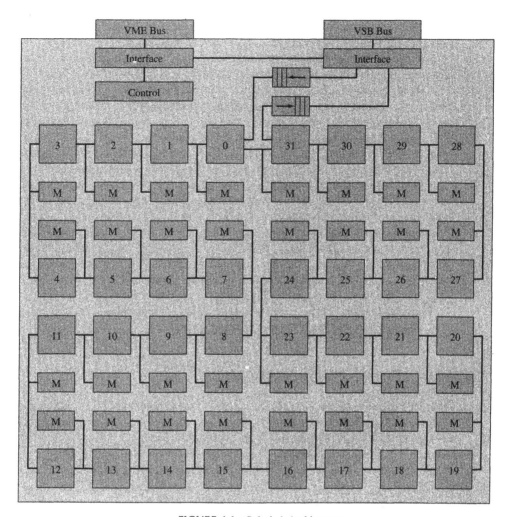

FIGURE 4.1   Splash 1 Architecture

These new tools permitted some escape from the low-level details of hardware design, but programming the Xilinx chips was still a nontrivial task. Problems existed at several levels. Splash 1 programming was still hardware design. Counters and sequencers had to be explicitly constructed and connected to the logical units that they controlled. Timing information about a design was difficult to obtain, and the inability to perform complete state readback and restore hindered the debugging process. One of the hardest problems centered on the `apr` (Automatic Place and Route) software from Xilinx. This program ran slowly and often failed to completely route a chip's design. It was often, if not usually, necessary to provide `apr` with hand-placed designs in order to get fully routed designs with acceptable execution speeds as a result of `apr`'s work. One major focus—which has been successful—in moving from Splash 1 to Splash 2 has been to eliminate the need for such low-level effort in order to get a working design. Programmers have for years been accustomed to the fact that, if speed is the object, the working program (usually in a high-level language) is only a first step; detailed study of execution characteristics and possibly rewriting kernels in assembly language may be necessary. The problem with this "make it right before you make it better" approach for Splash 1 was the level of effort and detailed knowledge necessary to make it right in the first place.

In spite of difficulties, work continued on Splash 1. Several boards were finished and LDG was made robust by the summer of 1989, when Splash 1 applications were the focus of an SRC summer workshop. It was during this workshop and immediately afterward that the DNA sequence comparison program was written and optimized. This became, by the fall of 1989, a submission to the 1989 Gordon Bell prize competition, in which the SRC program received an honorable mention.

It is appropriate in this history to mention one path that was explored for Splash 1 and then abandoned. It was realized early on that getting data to Splash 1 could be a problem. An apparent solution was to install a VSB bus memory board, available commercially from Motorola. It was thought that loading this board with data from the host would allow Splash 1 to access large data streams multiple times without involving the host. Hardware for this was added, but experiments showed that with most applications there was no appreciable improvement in performance, and occasionally some performance degradation occurred. Although some applications did use this "cached" data, most simply accepted a stream for one-time processing from the host, making the VSB board unnecessary.

4.2 SPLASH 2: THOUGHTS ON A REDESIGN

Splash 1 proved to be very successful, as shown in Gokhale et al. [2], although it was not without its limitations. When the design of a follow-on system was contemplated, the first item of business was to address those limitations.

1. **Programmability:** Splash 1 was programmed for the most part in Gokhale's LDG [3]. Although LDG had the obvious advantage of having been done expressly for programming Splash 1, it had the disadvantages associated with being an internally developed system. In addition, the Xilinx tools were unequal to the task of supporting code development for Splash 1. Users often had to perform placement themselves in order for the apr tool to succeed in routing a design. Further, many of the problems in debugging a design required more detailed knowledge of the Xilinx design than could be obtained from the tools. These problems combined made Splash 1 difficult to program by individuals unused to hardware design. One of the key issues in planning Splash 2, then, was to make it *programmable*, to make it a processing system that would be usable, without (undue) agony, by a wide range of programmers.

2. **I/O Speed:** Many of the original applications for Splash 1 were strongly I/O-bound. The VMEbus can deliver about 4 Mbytes/sec (in slave mode; VME using DMA would be significantly better) from the host to a Splash 1 board, but an application running at 16 MHz needs a bandwidth of 32 Mbytes/sec in order to consume and produce one character per clock tick. Any follow-on system would have to overcome the I/O bottleneck of Splash 1 in order to be truly successful.

3. **Memory:** The primary uses of the memory chips in Splash 1 were for lookup tables and for storing microprograms to be executed by state machines implemented in the Xilinx chips. In some instances the lookup tables were small, but in some applications, such as integer multiplication, a single reference to memory would replace complicated and slow logic and the speedup from using lookup tables would be limited only by the memory size. The memory use was encumbered, however, by problems in sustaining peak rates, by the fact that memory loads had to be done down the linear data path of the Splash board, and by the fact that the memories were connected to two Xilinx chips on the linear data path. This last problem required that programmers exercise great care to separate in time the access to memory and the transmission of data from Xilinx to Xilinx. On the other hand, the ability of one Xilinx chip to store data into a memory that the next Xilinx chip would read provided on Splash 1 a communication capability that was useful but which was not retained in the Splash 2 design.

The Splash 1 memories were also not as large as desirable for many applications, and the requirement that memory reads and writes take place by passing data through the FPGAs caused unnecessary complications, requiring that a special Xilinx program for memory read/write be written and used.

4. **Multiboard Scalability:** Some Splash 1 applications quite naturally used (or would have used) more than one Splash 1 board either for larger, more complex computations or for multiphase computations. In order to use a multiboard system, it was necessary to bring the data back to the Sun host from a Splash 1 board and then to send it from the host to the next Splash 1 board. This aggravated the I/O bottleneck problem.

5. **Data Path:** Splash 1 had only a single data path—a linear route through the 32 Xilinx chips. While the linear (which is sometimes systolic) paradigm is very powerful and its application to Splash has been very successful, there were many applications that either could not be done or whose efficiency suffered because the linear path was the only data path. Given that high performance seemed to require careful control of the data pipeline past the somewhat limited processing resources, the cost of transmitting data to the appropriate processing element needed to be diminished.

In Splash 1, the data from the host passed directly into the Splash board, so that handling of the FIFOs and any preconditioning of the data (merging of two input streams, for example) had to be done by the Xilinx chips on the Splash board. This often complicated the programming. Strong suggestions had surfaced early that performance might be substantially improved if the data preconditioning were moved out of the general processing array.

Finally, on Splash 1 it was often observed that 32-bit data widths were sufficient for the data but that extra tag bits sent along with the data would have been very useful. Not having the extra bits either complicated the design of programs or required extra clocks (a major negative factor in a highly pipelined program) in order to transmit the necessary control information from FPGA to FPGA. An extension of the input/output data path width from 32 to 36 bits would probably remedy this shortcoming.

6. Clock: The Splash 1 clock had only power-of-two speeds. Designs that came close to running at 32 MHz could only be run at 16 MHz, for example.

The above list addressed the known and specific limitations of the Splash 1 boards as built. Once a redesign of a Splash-like system was contemplated, however, all the earlier design decisions were reviewed. The original design of Splash 2 by Andy Kopser was given in [4] in a preliminary architecture description. On September 12, 1991, however, all these decisions came up for review at the first of a series of architectural design meetings. These meetings were intended to start from first principles to design a Splash-like FPGA-based processor; although Kopser's earlier thoughts were taken into account, none of his conclusions was accepted as given—all were subject to further scrutiny. Among these were the following:

1. Choice of FPGA chips
2. Choice of host and connecting bus
3. The linear array and any other interconnection of the FPGAs
4. Multiprogramming of multiple Array Boards

4.3 PROGRAMMING LANGUAGE

The decision to use VHDL [5] as the language in which to program applications for Splash 2 was actually made quite early. The use of VHDL would clearly be a compromise. In its favor were the facts that it is a defined standard, that it is a programming language (at least in simulation mode), and that it is supported by commercial tools for both simulation and synthesis. The commercial tools also provide a programmer with most of the bells and whistles of a debugging environment that are now expected by users. Finally, the goal of Splash 2 was to demonstrate the ability to program logic into an FPGA-based machine; although a high-quality translation of a high-level language to Xilinx bitfiles would be necessary for performance, we did not feel that we wanted to make it a significant part of the Splash 2 project itself.

Working with an off-the-shelf VHDL system would not, however, address all the issues involved in programming Splash 2. Quite apart from the "religious" issue that VHDL is an Ada derivative while most modern programmers are using C, there would be known problems both "above" and "below" the VHDL level. At the time Splash 2 was begun, it was not clear that it would be possible to drive a VHDL simulation from a general C-language interactive front end. The user's view of the programming environment might necessarily be that of the VHDL vendors' tools—which were designed for use by engineers doing circuit or VLSI design and might seem unduly foreign or even hostile to application programmers. More important, due to the need to have some example applications achieve high performance, it was not clear that the output of the logic synthesis would produce a Xilinx bitfile that would use crucial performance features of the FPGAs. Much of the success of Splash 1 had come when the programmers had specifically controlled from LDG the resources on the XC3090 FPGAs. A serious question was whether an outside vendor whose tools were aimed at a very different target consumer would provide the resource utilization that we would need.

It has thus always been assumed that VHDL is not perfect and that some language more like C should be developed. We realized, however, that we didn't know enough *a priori* about programming Splash 2 to permit development of "the right language." VHDL was therefore viewed as an acceptable middle ground, with the hope that in the process of programming Splash 2 in VHDL for a varied list of initial applications, enough would be learned about the programming model appropriate for Splash 2 to permit language development after the fact. Meanwhile, useful work would be accomplished by those brave pioneers who had coded the original applications in VHDL.

4.4 CHOICE OF FPGAS

SRC had gained extensive experience with and understanding of the Xilinx XC3090 chips, much of which would translate to the new XC4000 series chips, but the question was opened as to whether a different vendor's chip might be more desirable. Prominent among the options was the Concurrent Logic, Inc. FPGA. The two chips appear remarkably alike to a "computer designer," despite the extremes of granularity between the two products. The Xilinx XC4010 has 400 Configurable Logic Blocks (CLBs) in a square array. Each CLB takes two sets of four inputs and produces any Boolean function of each set, then any Boolean function of the two bits of result together with a ninth input signal. With this coarse structure, Xilinx advertises the XC4010 as roughly equivalent to a gate array of 10,000 gates [6].

The Concurrent Logic chip, by contrast, is very fine-grain. The high-end chip at the time was the CLi6005, a 56×56 array of cells that in most modes serves to produce one output from three inputs. Concurrent Logic advertised its CLi6005 chip as being roughly equivalent to a gate array of 5,000 gates, the similarity between the Xilinx and the Concurrent Logic figures perhaps saying more about the basic complexity of 1992 silicon technology than about the clear superiority of one vendor over another.

In the final analysis, three factors were decisive:

1. The fact that the Xilinx chips were a known quantity made it necessary to have a very good reason to change.
2. The delivery schedule for the Concurrent Logic chips was some months behind that for the Xilinx chips.
3. Most important, as a technical matter, the Concurrent Logic chips had 108 I/O pins compared to the Xilinx's 160. As it was envisioned at the time the decision was made, even the Xilinx's 160 I/O pins seemed insufficient. This was borne out by later experience.

In the process of deciding on a chip, it was necessary to compare not just the chips but to take into account their features and the processing power per Array Board that could be accommodated. A feature new to the XC4010 chip was a fast carry internal to the CLBs, which makes arithmetic computations faster and requires less programming and fewer CLBs. Further, the number and quality of the interconnection lines had increased, which would help more applications run at higher speeds. Finally, the new chips allow for the use of CLBs as a 32-bit RAM, configured either as 32×1 bit or as 16×2 bits.

The major difference between the XC3090 and the XC4010 chips, however, was in the basic size and structure—the XC4010s have 400 Configurable Logic Blocks (CLBs) instead of the previous 320, each CLB has nine input lines instead of five, and the maximum speed is 40 MHz instead of 32 MHz. The improvements in the FPGAs to be used would permit Splash 2 to have 17 Xilinx chips on an Array Board instead of the previous 32. This was both a conscious decision and a necessity. The newer chips were, in the packaging available at the time, physically somewhat larger, and it was not possible to put 32 of them on a single Array Board along with the memories and the crossbar (to be described in Section 6). The hope was that because the newer chips were each more powerful than the old chips, and because it had been more often the case with previous applications that they were I/O-limited rather than processor-limited, the plan to use half as many chips per Array Board, each perhaps somewhat less than twice as powerful, would provide a reasonable processor-to-I/O balance.

As it has come to pass, the decision to use the Xilinx chips has not been without its problems. The VHDL tools used in programming Splash 2 reduced the VHDL program to the gate level in the synthesis step rather than constructing efficient CLB designs, so a natural inefficiency exists in the use of the VHDL language for the Xilinx FPGAs. (To a great extent these issues were addressed in working with Synopsys on their FPGA Design Compiler.)

4.5 CHOICE OF HOST AND BUS

In the design of Splash 2, there were no tacit assumptions, and even the choice of host and bus were open for discussion. The options were narrowed considerably, however, by various practical considerations. Sun workstations continued to be the norm at SRC, and that, coupled with Sun's dominant position in the overall workstation market, made it hard to really consider abandoning Sun as a host. The constant realization existed, however, that the object of study was "the Splash 2 attached processor" and not "attached processors for Sun workstations." By constantly keeping in mind the fact that the choice of hosts contained a nontrivial degree of arbitrariness, we were able to avoid embedding the machine so deeply in the Sun milieu that it could not be re-engineered at modest cost for a different host.

The choice of the particular host was not so arbitrary. The realistic options were the SPARC 1+ and the SPARCstation 2, using the SBus with either. Experiments on SPARC 1+ workstations at SRC showed, however, that the SBus as implemented did not match the SBus as documented by Sun. Since the SBus was the logical choice (for reasons described below), this forced the decision in favor of the SPARCstation 2.

These decisions, together with the decisions on the Futurebus+ backplane, were not made in a vacuum. Another hardware-build was under way at SRC at the same time, also a workstation enhancement a few months ahead of Splash 2 in development, and the decision was made that Splash 2 would use the same bus, backplane, and so on. The real goal of Splash 2 was to demonstrate the capability of FPGA-based computing, and the use of hardware in common with the other project would permit more effort to be directed to the specifics of meeting that goal.

Having decided to use the SPARCstation 2, the decision to use the SBus was rather easy. By far the most limiting hardware feature of Splash 1 was the 4 Mbytes/sec peak data rate of the VMEbus on the Sun host. While the VME-bus protocol is rated as high as 16 Mbytes/sec peak transfer rate, existing implementations of VME buses do not reach that rate. Above all else, we did not want Splash 2 to be, as was Splash 1, I/O bound, and the SBus appeared to provide at least an order of magnitude higher data rate than the Sun VMEbus. Early estimates were 38 Mbytes/sec; tests now show that a CPU-loaded SPARC 2 can sustain about 40 Mbytes/sec through the SBus via DMA and that an unloaded machine can deliver as much as 54 Mbytes/sec. Unfortunately, these are peak transfer rates from the same 16-word DMA buffer of the host. Without further work on the drivers on the host, perhaps to include double-buffering, the data transfer via DMA takes place during only about 40 percent of the time, so transfer rates actually are limited to 20 to 25 Mbytes per second.

Along with the decisions on host and bus, driven by the need to provide Splash 2 with data, the plan for data connections that did not go through the host was an early feature of the design. As is remarked upon by nearly every experimenter with workstation attachments (including Bertin et al. [1]), workstation discs are too slow to produce volumes of data at high speed, memories are too small, and the Ethernet connections simply cannot sustain the load. The external connection could be to a traditional supercomputer functioning as an I/O device (which a supercomputer does quite admirably) or to an array of discs (as one might find in a text search or database search application).

Several different external data connections seemed desirable and potentially usable. An early plan to include several such connections on the Interface Board was dropped in favor of Wally Kleinfelder's idea to put such connections onto a daughterboard. This would allow the DMA to be built and tested on an early-version Interface Board while the final Interface Board was being designed and would also allow future daughterboard designs such as HiPPI.

Finally, another early decision was that the Sun and Splash 2 would use different clocks. It was a simple matter, then, to leave open the option of having the external data also carry the clock to be used by Splash 2.

4.6 CHIP-TO-CHIP INTERCONNECTIONS

One of the major decisions in designing Splash 2 was the choice of chip-to-chip data paths. In this, the 160 I/O pins on the XC4010 chip turned out to be one of the forcing factors.

With 160 I/O pins, one can implement four 36-bit data paths but have only 16 pins left over for control. Even by dropping the tag bits (bits 35–32 of the data path) one cannot get five 32-bit ports (this is exactly 160, leaving nothing for control). We are, therefore, necessarily designing for a four-port array.

The obvious extension from a one-dimensional array would be a two-dimensional array of Xilinx chips. This consumes four ports, so memory connections would have to be shared with the chip-to-chip connectors, as on Splash 1. Two such arrays are given in Figures 4.2 and 4.3.

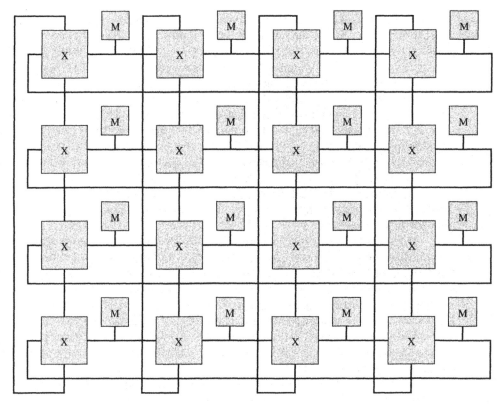

FIGURE 4.2 Two-dimensional Toroidal Mesh

In Figure 4.2 we easily obtain a 2-D mesh, but we cannot easily string the chips together into a 1-D array if the memories are also being used. That problem is fixed in the design of Figure 4.3—at the expense, of course, of the 2-D mesh itself.

The basic problem is simple: If the memories are connected to two processor chips by the same lines that are used for processor-to-processor connection, then a linear array of processors with memories in between uses up two of the four ports per chip. If the memories are active, then with only two ports per processor we can achieve only a linear array.

Similar objections ruled out the use of busses, and a major step was taken in the decision to connect each processor to its own local memory. Some capability was lost with this decision. There were a few Splash 1 programs whose efficiency was due to the ability of the FPGAs to transfer data through the memories; the stored output of one FPGA's work could be accessed in an arbitrary order by the next FPGA. But this would have required a wider data path to accommodate two ports, or the time-multiplexing of access to memory by the FPGAs, and the advantages seemed not worth the hardware investment or the increased complexity of programming the memory use.

With one of the four ports per chip used for memory, three ports become available for chip-to-chip communication. Various three-port configurations were considered, including the chordal ring. A chordal ring (a ring with regularly or irregularly

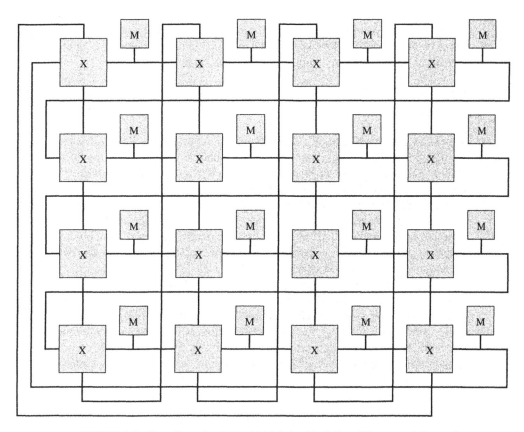

FIGURE 4.3   Two-dimensional Toroidal Mesh with Shift on Wraparound Connections

spaced "chords" as additional connections) can be used as a linear array, or a linear array with shortcuts, and had the advantage of not being tied to "nice" numbers (like 16) of processor chips. A possible drawback, though, is that "normal" programming patterns do not (yet?) include the chordal ring as routine.

For these and similar reasons, the eventual choice was a linear array with two ports per chip and a crossbar connecting the chips with the other port. This choice was made easier when made in conjunction with a choice of the TI reconfigurable crossbar chips (TI SN74ACT8841 were used). Each such chip is a 16-port, 4-bit-wide crossbar and can be programmed with eight different configurations. In this way, data paths in nibble sizes could be programmed (although pin limitations later limited this to byte sizes), and a wide variety of communication patterns could be accommodated.

Although it turned out later to lead to serious problems, the choice of the TI chip seemed an excellent one at the time. In the manner in which we would use the chip, the latency across it was one tick, so the crossbar communications would not differ from communications down the linear array. This would simplify the programming task—slower chips would require the programmer to insert pipeline stages in a program and then to synchronize them carefully. The multiple configurations permitted by the TI chip seemed to provide the logical connectivity needed, and the ability to switch configurations with at most a one-tick delay was a very attractive option. None of the more sophisticated switch chips available at the time, nor the use of FPGAs to implement the switch, offered these features.

4.7 MULTITASKING

Up to now, we have been discussing the architecture of the Splash 2 Array Board or the data paths in and out. The decisions on these were originally made in Kopser's Splash 2 design and then reaffirmed by the architectural committee. One of the design decisions that was changed radically was an original thought that each Splash 2 Array Board would have its own input and output FIFOs and that each Array Board could run a separate Splash 2 process multiprogrammed from the host. This would have required extensive control hardware on the Interface Board as well as complete software protocols for the Sun host's control and context switching of processes running independently and asynchronously on the Splash 2 attached processor.

The possibility of allowing Splash 2 Array Boards to work on separate tasks was hotly discussed for several sessions at the weekly architecture meetings. The goal—which, in the final analysis, seemed impossible to achieve—was that arbitrary subsets of Splash 2 Array Boards could be chained together, each running distinct processes, possibly communicating with each other directly, possibly communicating through the host, and possibly not communicating with each other at all.

It was even envisioned at this time that different users might run different programs on Splash 2 concurrently, in addition to the situation in which a single user might have multiple independent Splash 2 processes.

In the end, all such plans were discarded. The final Splash 2 system is an attached processor in which all the Array Boards in a given system form a linear chain; the only variations in configuration are that broadcast to all Array Boards simultaneously is possible and that the physical chain of Array Boards can be logically shortened. Although use of the entire system can be time-shared, no partitioning of the system for concurrent execution of independent processes in different partitions can occur.

The major factors in this decision were: that the algorithmic complexity of controlling the independent processes would require too much hardware support if it were designed to run at the necessary speeds; that the complexity of the "back-end" network controlling the subsets of Splash 2 Array Boards into chains would be too great; and that insufficient real estate existed even on the large Array Boards planned for Splash 2 to allow for the Xilinx chips, memories, and crossbar, as well as FIFOs, DMA controllers, bus arbitration with the Interface Board, and network communication with the other Splash 2 Array Boards in a chain. A final concern was that each subsystem would have to be able to run at a different clock rate so that maximum efficiency of the Splash 2 processes could be obtained. This would clearly have necessitated complex mechanisms to arbitrate bus and DMA access for data movement on and off Splash 2.

Somewhat reluctantly, then, Splash 2 became a system all of which, at any point in time, would be assigned to a single process. The Array Boards were to form a linear array (although broadcast was still possible). The FIFOs and DMA control for each Array Board were consolidated into one pair of input and one pair of output FIFOs using DMA channels and moved onto the Interface Board. Interrupts and global AND/OR were similarly cascaded from each Xilinx chip to a board-level register and from board level to a system-level register on the Interface Board. The inclusion of Xilinx chips XL and XR on the Interface Board would provide for control of data transfer, clock (even a clock supplied by the external input), and tag bits independent of the Splash 2 Array Boards. In Splash 1, such control had usually been done in the first array chip, leading to asymmetry and crowded designs. With proper programming of XL and XR, the asynchronies of DMA transfer and external input and clock should not be seen by the Splash 2 Array Boards themselves, and the XL and XR programs should function much like a system I/O library.

With the adoption of this more conservative plan, some applications were given up, but the general opinion was summed up by Ron Minnich: "Now, at last, I think we have a real chance that this thing can be built."

4.8 CHIP X0 AND BROADCAST

One of the casualties in moving the I/O off the individual Array Boards onto the Interface Board was that it was no longer as simple to envision broadcast of data from the host or from an external interface to all the processor FPGAs simultaneously; yet this programming model was seen to be equally as important to support as the simpler model in which long streams of data would pass down the linear array. Unfortunately, the basic power-of-two dilemma existed. Earlier Splash 1 programs had occasionally been complicated or suffered decreased efficiency because FPGAs X0 and X31 had handled I/O; this took away somewhat from the power-of-two advantage of the 32-long linear array. When the I/O handling was moved from the beginning and end of the linear array on each Array Board to FPGAs XL and XR on the Interface Board, the power-of-two structure returned to the processing array when viewed as a linear array.

Now, however, something needed to be done for broadcasting data. With some reluctance, FPGA X0 was added to each Array Board. The reluctance came primarily from the realization that 17 is not a very elegant number. Reading and writing the memory on each Array Board would become more complicated (having made a decision to include another FPGA on the Array Board, there was little dispute over making it look as much like the other FPGAs as possible, so it was given the same memory as the other FPGAs), reading and writing the configuration and state of the FPGAs would also be more complicated, and most inelegant of all, X0 would have to share lines into the crossbar with some other FPGA.

Despite the inelegance, the Array Board architecture with the 17 FPGAs has proved to be successful. The complications from not having power-of-two structures have been more than compensated for by the greatly increased ability to move data into the Array Boards and to the PEs.

4.9 OTHER DESIGN DECISIONS

In addition to these "coarse" decisions on the architecture, a number of other changes were made to the Splash 1 design. Data paths were fixed at 36 bits in width. This would accommodate 32-bit words and 4-bit tags carried along with them. An earlier plan for a 40-bit crossbar was scaled back to 36 bits. No good use could be immediately envisioned for the extra four bits, and the I/O pins were needed elsewhere. The only place in which Splash 2 is not a 36-bit machine is in the Xilinx-to-memory path. This path is 16 bits wide, largely because the 160-pin Xilinx XC4010 chip cannot support three 36-bit data paths (two ports for the linear array and one into the crossbar) and a path to memory at least 32 data bits wide ($3 \cdot 36 + 32 = 140$, leaving only 20 pins for Xilinx control and memory address). It was thought to be absolutely necessary that memory be accessible in every clock period, making multiplexing of data and address infeasible.

One change from Splash 1 to Splash 2 was to add a separate memory read/write path that did not require going through the Xilinx chips. The memories could now be directly read/written from the Sun host over the SBus. They are not, however, dual-ported; the FPGAs must be inactive during the read/write operations. This change allows tables to be loaded in bulk and results to be read from the memories without requiring the circuitous path through the Xilinx chips. However, since the memories were 16 bits wide and the "natural" word size of both Splash 2 and its Sun host is 32 bits, an obvious question arose as to where the conversion from 32 to 16 bits would take place. In this case, no answer is perfect. Placing halfword data on word boundaries in the host is easy for the programmer but wasteful of memory space on the host and of I/O bandwidth to Splash 2. Packing halfwords two to one into Sun words is a slight annoyance for the programmer but wastes neither bandwidth nor memory. This latter choice prevailed after it was determined that, in fact, the memories could be double-cycled on the Splash 2 Array Boards fast enough to keep up with accesses from the host; the host would never know that the Splash 2 memories were 16 and not 32 bits wide.

One of the suggestions made and discussed was whether to include on each Splash 2 Array Board a microprocessor to perform tasks not easily or efficiently done by the Xilinx chips. Although this was a suggestion made at a time when independent execution of Splash 2 Array Boards in a multiprogrammed environment was being considered, it was an idea that had a wider context. Many of the uses to which FPGAs for computing have been put have been to augment the instruction set of a microprocessor; one could easily imagine a Splash 2 Array Board being viewed in this way by a user focusing attention on an on-board microprocessor. In the end this idea was not pursued, largely because the control of the Array Boards and programming would be overly complex. The intent, as discussed in the next paragraphs, was to be able to program the machine in a high-level language. It appeared, however, that in order to make effective use of the microprocessor, it would be necessary to control and synchronize processing and data movement on the Array Boards at a very low level. Splash 1 applications had been, and Splash 2 applications were expected to be, highly pipelined, but in order to do this on a Splash 2 Array Board, the output of the microprocessor's compiler would have to mesh closely with the "program" for the Xilinx FPGAs. The software effort for the Xilinx part of the Array Board seemed difficult enough without the complications that the on-board microprocessor would add.

Throughout the design and architecture refinement, the emphasis was on producing a machine that could be programmed at a moderately high level. This fundamental assumption about what it would take to produce a successful computing engine had an effect, as mentioned, on many of the design decisions, especially the decisions involving the degree of independence of one board from another and the control of board-level entities. For example, the inclusion of a microprocessor on each Splash 2 Array Board would have required programmers to code not only asynchronous Sun/Splash 2 execution but also to coordinate the interaction of the on-board microprocessor and the Xilinx chips. It did not seem clear that this could be done in a high-level language in a way that would be tolerated by programmers, and similarly, it did not seem clear that a compiler could readily be written that would deliver the performance that users could have a right to expect.

The discussion about programming continues to this day. VHDL is, on the one hand, sufficiently high-level and sufficiently modern to be recognized and accepted as a "programming language." On the other hand, it does retain many of the quirks of hardware description, and mastering the methods for getting around these quirks does not render much less arcane the art of VHDL. It is not "C-like" and cannot by itself be made to be "C-like."

At the heart of many of the issues surrounding the programming of Splash 2 is the fact that the architecture at present is completely exposed to the user, who sees, in essence, the memory address and data registers, the specific data paths, and so forth.

REFERENCES

[1] P. Bertin, D. Roncin, and J. Vuillemin, "Programmable Active Memories: A Performance Assessment, in G. Borriello and C. Ebeling, eds., *Research on Integrated Systems*, MIT Press, Cambridge, Mass., 1993, pp. 88–102.

[2] M. Gokhale et al., "Building and Using a Highly Parallel Programmable Logic Array," *Computer*, Vol. 24, No. 1, Jan. 1991, pp. 81–89.

[3] M. Gokhale et al., "The Logic Description Generator," Tech. Report SRC–TR–90–011, SRC, Bowie, Md., 1990.

[4] A. Kopser, "Splash 2: Architectural Motivation," tech. report, SRC, Bowie, Md., 1991.

[5] D.L. Perry, *VHDL*, McGraw-Hill, New York, 1991.

[6] Xilinx, Inc., *The Programmable Gate Array Data Book*, Xilinx, Inc., San Jose, Calif., 1993.

CHAPTER 5

Software Architecture

Jeffrey M. Arnold

5.1 INTRODUCTION

As we saw in Chapter 4, the Splash 1 system was programmed at the logic gate level with the macro language LDG [4]. This meant that the process of developing applications for Splash 1 was very labor-intensive, requiring a detailed understanding of the internal structure of the Xilinx devices. For this reason, applications programmers with little or no hardware experience found Splash 1 extremely difficult to program. The result was that there were never more than half a dozen proficient Splash 1 "programmers," and these were people with extensive hardware design backgrounds.

When we set out to design a software environment for Splash 2, our main objective was to improve the ease of programmability of the system, opening it up to a much larger audience of applications developers. The specific design goals of the Splash 2 software environment were to:

- select or develop a procedural language for writing applications
- provide a rich debugging environment that did not require a detailed understanding of the hardware
- provide a smooth and efficient interface between the host computer and Splash 2
- develop a comprehensive set of diagnostic tools for hardware development and maintenance
- leverage commercial off-the-shelf technology wherever possible

With these goals in mind we chose to base the Splash 2 programming environment on the VHSIC[1] Hardware Description Language (VHDL) [6, 10] and modern Computer Aided Design (CAD) tools such as simulation and logic synthesis. Applications for Splash 2 are developed by writing behavioral descriptions of algorithms in VHDL, which are then iteratively refined and debugged within the Splash 2 simulator. During the course of this iteration, the VHDL implementation is manually partitioned by the programmer into a set of individual FPGA programs. Once the partitioned implementation is determined to be functionally correct in simulation, it is compiled and optimized to produce a network of logic gates. This *gate list* is then mapped onto the FPGA architecture by automatic placement and routing tools to form a loadable FPGA object module. Static timing analysis tools are applied to the object module to determine the maximum operating frequency and the set of critical paths. This information is fed back to the user, who may choose to manually optimize the design. The runtime system provides the interface between the host computer and the Splash 2 system and consists of a C language library and an interactive symbolic debugger.

This chapter presents the architecture of the Splash 2 software system. We begin with a background discussion of the underlying CAD technologies that make custom computing possible. We then proceed to justify our choice of VHDL as the programming language of Splash 2. Next is a discussion of the architecture of the programming environment and the system software. Finally, we present the models of the system the programmer sees at each of several levels of abstraction.

5.2 BACKGROUND

The success of Splash 2, and of custom computing in general, has been made possible by the confluence of two important technologies: infinitely reprogrammable logic arrays (static RAM-based FPGAs) and high-level CAD software. Over the past few years the CAD industry has made significant advances in automatic generation of hardware design from high level specification. This process may be divided into two steps: *logic synthesis* and *physical mapping*. Logic synthesis is the process by which procedural descriptions of algorithms are mapped into Boolean logic gates, bypassing traditional structural techniques such as schematic capture. The physical mapping process converts the resulting gate list into a specific hardware technology, such as the static RAM- (SRAM-) based FPGAs used in Splash 2. Together, these technologies move the task of application development for custom computing from the realm of hardware design into the realm of software programming.

Figure 5.1 illustrates the flow through the Splash 2 program development process from design entry through hardware configuration. There are two feedback loops in this flow. The inner loop is used to establish the functional correctness of a program by simulating the design and observing the response to a set of test vectors. The outer loop constructs the physical implementation by synthesizing and optimizing the logic and then mapping the result into the FPGA technology. A static timing analyzer

---

[1]The Very High Speed Integrated Circuits (VHSIC) program was an initiative funded by the U.S. Department of Defense in the late 1970s and early 1980s.

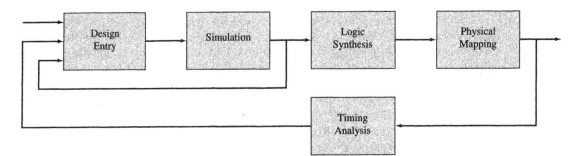

FIGURE 5.1   Splash 2 Program Development Process

is used to predict performance and identify potential bottlenecks. The programmer may use this information to determine overall system performance and possibly guide further optimization.

Logic synthesis [2, 3, 13] is the process of converting a high-level description of an architecture into an optimized logic implementation. The input to the synthesis process is typically in the form of a procedural or mixed procedural and structural description of the intended architecture. The logic synthesis tools extract control and data flow information from this description and produce a set of Boolean equations and module instances that perform the desired function. This internal representation is then optimized to meet user specifications of area and delay. Since the design has not been mapped into the logic blocks of the FPGA technology at this stage in the synthesis process, the optimization must be based upon estimates of logic block packing, logic propagation delays and a fan-out-dependent statistical model of the routing network. Many of the parameters that control the optimization may be set by the user, allowing trade-offs to be made between minimizing area and maximizing performance. The output of the synthesis process is a list of technology-independent logic gates.

The physical mapping [3, 16] process converts the generic gate list produced by logic synthesis into a configuration bitstream for the particular FPGA by *partitioning* the gates into logic blocks, *placing* the logic blocks into the FPGA, and *routing* the signal nets between the blocks. The partitioning phase groups the combinational logic gates into Boolean functions that will fit in the lookup tables of the logic blocks (3 and 4 inputs for the XC4010) and assigns registers to the flip-flops of the logic and I/O blocks. During the partitioning phase it is often possible to trade chip area (gates) for speed by replicating functions that have a high fan-out. Unfortunately, this trade-off requires a close coupling between the synthesis and mapping processes that is not present in today's tools.

The placement step accepts the partitioned design and determines a good placement for the logic blocks in the FPGA array [16]. Most FPGA placement algorithms use a stochastic optimization algorithm such as simulated annealing to minimize a cost function such as total net length. Traditional integrated circuit routing techniques are based on decomposing the area available for wiring into rectangular "channels" that can be routed independently. Unfortunately, this approach does not work well for FPGAs, because the interconnect resources are fixed in place. Therefore, most FPGA routers use a form of maze router that does not decompose the problem into independent routing channels. User-specified timing requirements can be used to guide the router by building a detailed delay model from the physical interconnect parameters of the FPGA. Finally, the router must handle additional constraints imposed by the FPGA such as special clock networks and carry-chain routing.

Once the detailed routing is complete, the static timing analyzer is able to make an accurate prediction of the maximum operating frequency and determine the critical paths of the design based upon the known logic block and routing resource delays. The programmer may use the critical path information to manually optimize the design or restructure the program for resynthesis. The delay information extracted from the design by the static timing analyzer may also be used to construct a structural simulation model of the design, which in turn can be used to perform detailed timing simulation.

A great deal of research and development in the area of FPGA design tools is taking place in academia and industry, with the result that the quality of the available tools is rapidly improving. We therefore felt it was efficacious to leverage "commercial off-the-shelf" technology for Splash 2 as much as possible, allowing ourselves to concentrate on the system integration issues.

5.3 VHDL AS A PROGRAMMING LANGUAGE

One of the most important objectives of the Splash 2 software effort was to move the task of application development from the realm of hardware engineering to the realm of software programming. This desire led to several selection criteria for a "production" programming language for Splash 2. Among these criteria were support for the use of procedural as well as structural specification, and the ability to build higher levels of abstraction through encapsulation of function. To support high-performance applications, we felt that the language should include an escape mechanism to allow the programmer to explicitly specify hardware details. Finally, the language had to be directly executable to allow interactive source-level debugging of application programs.

In the early stages of the Splash 2 effort we explored the option of developing our own language based upon a subset of C. Such a language would have the advantage of familiarity to most users, be directly executable on a wide variety of platforms, and come complete with a rich development environment. However, we felt that the task of compiling a subset of C into hardware would quickly become a major research project in its own right, detracting from the Splash 2 system development effort. Therefore we chose to focus our efforts on system integration, leveraging commercial logic synthesis tools by basing the Splash 2 programming environment on VHDL.

Ultimately, we believe the best programming model for custom computing machines is to develop higher-level programming languages that can be compiled into a form suitable for input to commercial CAD tools. Such a language would synthesize an application-specific architecture, perhaps use VHDL as an intermediate language, and use commercial logic synthesis in the "assembly" process. One such effort, based upon the dbC language [5], is described in Chapter 7.

5.3.1 History and Purpose of VHDL

VHDL evolved from an effort to develop a design specification and interchange language common to all of the participants of the VHSIC program [8]. The language traces its roots back to a planning session in 1981, although the initial development effort was not begun until 1983. The importance of this work became clear to the broader engineering community with the first release of the language and simulator in 1985. A standards committee of the IEEE was established to further refine the language, which was released in 1987 as IEEE STD-1076 [6]. IEEE standards are reviewed and renewed every five years, and as part of the 1992 renewal of VHDL the language was extended to include a number of new features, such as a foreign-language interface, impure functions, and shared variables [7].

5.3.2 VHDL Language Features

Rather than develop an entirely new language, the designers of VHDL chose to base the syntax and semantics of their language upon an existing well-defined standard, Ada [11]. Many of the high-level programming features of Ada are therefore found in VHDL. Like Ada, VHDL is a strongly typed language with user-definable and -extensible data types. Structured objects such as vectors, arrays, and records are fully supported. Operators, functions and procedures may be overloaded on the data types of arguments and return results. VHDL supports data abstraction through the use of packages, which present a clean interface to objects and operations on objects while insulating the programmer from the details of the object implementation. VHDL explicitly represents concurrency and synchronization through the `Process` and `Wait` constructs and supports the automatic inference of registers and latches through signal assignment within sequential processes. VHDL also supports a wide range of abstraction levels by allowing the mixture of behavioral and structural representations, with `Generate` constructs and `Generic` parameters to control the instantiation of structural components.

VHDL also includes a number of features specifically designed to support simulation. File input and output are supported directly by the language, and the `TEXTIO` package is provided to support formatted ASCII I/O. Dynamic storage allocation is supported through the use of *access* types (that is, pointers), the object allocator `new`, and the implicit `Deallocate` procedure. The `assert` statement may be used to check that a specified condition is true. If the condition is not true, an error at one of several different severity levels may be reported. Although these language features have no direct analog in physical hardware (that is, they are not *synthesizable*), together they greatly facilitate the implementation of a system simulator, as is shown in Chapter 6.

The compilation process for VHDL is separated into an *analysis* phase and an *elaboration* phase, which are roughly analogous to compilation and object module loading in a conventional programming language compiler. VHDL provides the programmer with a great deal of control over the compilation process by deferring the binding of generic parameters and architecture instances until elaboration time. The elaboration time binding is controlled by the `Configuration` statement, which allows the user to specify the architecture to use for each component instance in the design and to override any generic parameter values passed to the architecture. This in turn allows the user to select component architectures from a library and to control the instantiation of those components without requiring a detailed understanding of the library implementation.

5.3.3 Problems with VHDL

VHDL is not a panacea. VHDL is a large language with many features, which often takes a long time to learn. The syntax, although very similar to Ada, is unfamiliar to many programmers, who may find it verbose and cumbersome. The stateless nature of VHDL functions and procedures forces the use of structural representations for complex state machines. Finally, although VHDL has explicit constructs for concurrency and synchronization, many programmers find that coordinating many parallel fine-grain tasks can be difficult and time-consuming.

When we began development of Splash 2 in 1991, some features of the VHDL language were not supported by commercial synthesis tools; in particular, the use of Generic parameters, multidimensional arrays, and constant folding for multiply and divide operations were unsupported. The level of compliance of the tools has improved significantly over the last several years, and today there are very few VHDL constructs that synthesis tools cannot handle.

The other leading candidate for the role of Splash 2 programming language was the Verilog [15] hardware description language. Like VHDL, Verilog supports both simulation and synthesis from the same source code, so there was no fundamental impediment to using Verilog for Splash 2. The syntax of Verilog is closer to the C language and thus would be more familiar to many programmers. We felt, however, that Verilog would not be as rich a *programming* language as VHDL, because it did not have many of the language features we were looking for. The built-in data types of Verilog are very closely tied to hardware constructs such as wire-AND logic and high impedance (tristate) drivers, and there is no support for building abstract data types above these. Verilog also does not support the overloading of operators or procedures based upon data type. For these reasons we felt that we would not be able to provide the same level of abstraction with Verilog that we could with VHDL.

5.4 SOFTWARE ENVIRONMENT

The VHDL programming environment for Splash 2 consists of a system simulator, a logic synthesis package, a VHDL library that is common to both tools, and a SunOS-based runtime system. The Splash 2 simulator is a hierarchical model of the Splash 2 system comprising a set of VHDL models for each of the components of the system. The simulator provides a framework for the development and debugging of applications. Within the simulator, an application program is able to interact with the system exactly as it would with the physical hardware. The system models also verify that the application program meets various hardware constraints, such as memory sequencing and setup and hold times. The user may also specify crossbar configurations and initial memory contents with separate ASCII files, which are read by both the simulator and the runtime system.

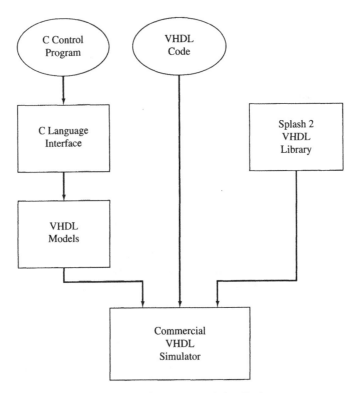

FIGURE 5.2   The Splash 2 Simulation Environment

The components of the simulation environment are shown in Figure 5.2. The ovals represent the two components of the user's application code: the VHDL program(s) for the computing elements and the C control program, which will run on the host computer. The C Language Interface is an optional piece of the environment that allows the simulation to be controlled by the same program that will run on the host. The VHDL Models block is the set of simulation models for the system, including the central crossbar, the external memories, and the Interface Board. The Splash 2 VHDL Library contains a set of data types, constants, procedures, and components designed to facilitate the interface between the application VHDL code and the rest of the system and to provide access to the Xilinx hard macros. Hard macros are predefined components, such as adders and counters, which provide guaranteed performance. Hard macros also provide the only access to special hardware features such as the fast-carry logic. Finally, the Commercial VHDL Simulator provides the simulation engine and the graphical user interface.

The VHDL simulation environment allows Splash 2 applications to be developed in either a top-down or bottom-up fashion. Top-down design is supported by beginning with a single high-level VHDL model for the entire Splash 2 system and iteratively descending through levels of hierarchy corresponding to the structure of the simulator down to the computing element, adding detail at each level. Bottom-up design is supported through the use of a library of default components for all of the pieces of the system except for the element being developed. As each element is completed, the corresponding library component is replaced with the actual design.

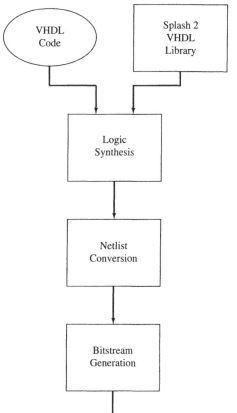

FIGURE 5.3 The Splash 2 Compilation
Environment

A mix of logic synthesis and standard compilation techniques are used to compile the VHDL programs into FPGA configurations, as shown in Figure 5.3. The VHDL Code that was developed in the simulation environment (Figure 5.2) is compiled with the same VHDL Library used to produce the Splash 2 object module. The logic synthesis tools from Synopsys Inc.[13, 14] map the VHDL code into a gate list. During the course of the Splash 2 project we used two different generations of Synopsys logic synthesis tools: the version 2.2 Design Compiler [12] and the version 3.0 FPGA Compiler [14].

At the beginning of the project we chose what was then the state-of-the-art Synopsys Design Compiler as the basis of our compiler. This tool was not tailored specifically to the FPGA technology and therefore required some customization to suit our needs. We developed a technology library that allowed the Design Compiler to produce a generic gate list from a reasonable subset of VHDL, and a net list conversion program called `edif2xnf`. Edif2xnf parsed the hierarchical EDIF net list, flattened the structure, and produced another file in Xilinx Net list Format (XNF) that was suitable for mapping onto the physical hardware by the Xilinx-provided bitstream generation tools [17]. Along the way it also performed some minor optimizations specific to both Splash 2 and the FPGA architecture.

Our experiences with the Synopsys Design Compiler and with our own `edif2xnf` program were fed back to Synopsys to help direct the development of their FPGA Compiler product. By the middle of 1993 Synopsys released their version 3.0 FPGA Compiler [14], which was able to compile logic directly into Xilinx RAM-based lookup tables and produce XNF net lists. The FPGA Compiler removed the need for our custom technology library and `edif2xnf`, but we found that some minor modification of the net list was still necessary. The program `xnfer` was written to fix XNF net list errors and to automatically insert logic common to all Splash 2 designs, such as the control for the internal Global Tri State (GTS) signal.

The major components of the runtime environment are shown in Figure 5.4. There are two host software interfaces to the Splash 2 system, a C library, which can be linked into an application-specific control program, and an interactive symbolic debugger called T2. Both interfaces are built upon the same underlying runtime system, `libsplash.a`, and provide the same functionality. The runtime system implemented by `libsplash.a` allows the user to open the device, map the Splash 2 memory into the host address space, establish input and output data streams, and control the system clock. The clock may be singly stepped, multiply stepped, or allowed to run free. The user can establish software handlers for interrupts generated by individual Processing Elements. The runtime library and the hardware diagnostic suite rely on the services provided by the Unix device driver, including memory

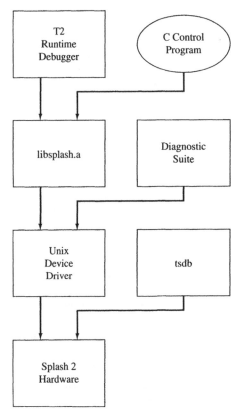

FIGURE 5.4 The Splash 2 Runtime Environment

management and several system calls (see Chapter 6). At the lowest level is a hardware debugger called "tsdb" (for Trivial SBus Debugger) that allows the designer to examine and set locations in the hardware based upon the physical address space of a single SBus slot.

The user interface of T2 is built upon the tool command language Tcl [9]. Tcl is an interpreted language with a C-like syntax which may be embedded into applications to provide an extensible user interface. The Tcl interface to T2 allows users to write simple programs to aid with debugging and experimentation on Splash 2. T2 also supports symbolic debugging by reading back the internal state of all FPGAs at the end of every clock cycle and associating the state of each flip-flop with the corresponding VHDL signal name. From T2 the user can step through the execution of the program, continuously displaying the contents of some or all of the registers in the design.

5.5 PROGRAMMER'S VIEW OF SPLASH 2

Every Splash 2 application may be divided into three main components: the portions that run on the Array Boards, the Interface Board, and the host computer. At the Splash 2 Array Board level, the programmable components consist of the Processing Elements, X1 through X16, the Control Element, X0, and the crossbar. At the Interface Board level, the Control Elements XL and XR are user-programmable, as are many of the control registers. The host interface must provide the input data streams, handle the output data streams, and control the operation of the Splash 2 system. In this section we discuss the process by which applications programs are developed, and then look at the programming model presented at each of the three levels. More details of the implementation may be found in Chapter 6 and in the Splash 2 Programmer's Manual [1].

5.5.1 Programming Process

Developing an application for Splash 2 is not unlike designing a program for a massively parallel computer. The programmer must choose an overall control paradigm, typically either data parallel (SIMD) or pipelined, and then plan the data flow among the Processing Elements, including the use of the crossbar and memories. On massively parallel computers the data layout among the processors is often critical to performance. In pipelined Splash 2 applications, it is the *control* layout that is critical. An algorithm must be partitioned carefully among the Processing Elements to maximize the efficiency of the inter-PE communication. Unfortunately, we know of no good automated tools that will find and exploit the structure of the design, so this partitioning must be performed manually by the programmer.

Once the basic control paradigm is chosen and the algorithm is partitioned, the communication and control protocols among the Processing Elements may be designed. Since Splash 2 is a globally synchronous system, these protocols are implemented as a set of finite state machines (VHDL `processes`) communicating through a set of `signals`. Input data from the Interface Board may be tagged as valid, or the clock may be controlled such that all input data seen by the Array Boards are valid.

A principal design goal in most applications is to maximize the utilization of one or more of the resources of Splash 2. For example, to maximize the memory bandwidth, many applications pipeline the accesses such that a new memory read or write operation occurs in every clock cycle. This is accomplished by registering the address and data within the IOBs of the Processing Elements, as is discussed in Chapter 6.

One major shortcoming of the programming methodology for FPGAs is the inability to determine the "size" (percent utilization) of a design without running through the entire compilation procedure. Splash 2 programmers have developed a crude "rule of thumb" to estimate the size of a design. The number of bits of register storage (including state machines) is summed, and if the number is within about 25 percent of the total number of flip-flops in the XC4010 (800 CLB flip-flops plus input and output flip-flops on the principal data ports), the design may be too large to fit. The 25 percent margin allows for inefficiencies in the placement and routing tools and the crude estimation heuristic. Many Splash 2 applications were in fact able to achieve or exceed a 98 percent CLB utilization rate.

5.5.2 Processing Element View

Programs for the individual Processing Elements of the Splash 2 Array Board are written in VHDL and must conform to the predefined Processing Element `Entity` declaration. The Processing Element `Entity` is essentially "boilerplate" code, common to all Splash 2 applications, and specifies the names and data types of the interface ports. The body of a PE program is a VHDL `Architecture` corresponding to the standard `Entity`. The interface ports include the data paths to the left- and right-hand neighbor PEs, the data path and control signals to the crossbar, the address and data path to the external memory, and a variety of control signals such as the global OR signals, the broadcast, interrupt, and handshake signals.

It is often important for timing considerations and CLB utilization to exploit the flip-flops in the input/output cells (IOBs) of the Processing Elements. To avoid long propagation delays between the logic core of one Processing Element to another, it is standard practice (although not required) to register data both entering and leaving the PE. Since the propagation delay on the major buses is significant, it is strongly recommended that input data from the SIMD Bus and output data to the RBus be registered. The timing of the external memory control requires that the address and control signals be registered in the Processing Element. This final constraint is enforced by the gate list postprocessor, `edif2xnf` or `xnfer`.

The set of configurations for the central crossbar is specified by an ASCII file that is interpreted by both the simulator and the runtime system. The configuration in use at any given time is selected by the Control Element (X0), but the output enable signals of the crossbar must still be set correctly by the individual Processing Elements. Another user-provided ASCII file may be used to specify initial contents of any of the external memories.

The Control Element (X0) is typically used to implement Array Board-level controller functions, such as SIMD instruction decode, and to store and broadcast common data tables. The Control Element has a different I/O interface than the Processing Element, and hence a unique `Entity` declaration. X0 has an input data port from the SIMD Bus and a bidirectional data port to the crossbar that is shared with

X16. Another three-bit output port is used to select the current crossbar configuration. The two global OR signals from each of the Processing Elements may be used to perform reduction and synchronization operations among all 16 PEs and the results combined with other Array Boards in the system via the systemwide global OR signals. Since the internal global OR signals are bidirectional, they may also be used to signal sequencing information from X0 to the individual PEs.

5.5.3 Interface Board View

The Development (or "Quick and Dirty") Board was built to assist in the debugging of the Splash 2 Array Boards while the final Interface Board was still being designed, and to provide an early application development environment. The Development Board maps every signal from the backplane side of the Interface Board to a host-accessible register, allowing the host to emulate in software the behavior of the Final Interface Board. The system clock is generated by host accesses to one of two special registers: the "Software Clock" register, which produces a fixed-width clock pulse, and the "SIMD Clock" register, which places the write data in the SIMD register and then generates a clock pulse. The functionality of the Development Board was retained in the Final Interface Board by incorporating a "bypass" mode that allowed applications and diagnostics written for the Development Board to run on the Final Interface Board by simply recompiling the code.

The Final Interface Board (IB) is responsible for controlling the data streams to and from Splash 2, the system clock, the RBus master and direction, and the FPGA configuration and state readback. The two FPGAs on the IB, XL and XR, are user-programmable, but the Splash 2 VHDL Library includes several standard designs that perform the most common control operations such as tagging input data with a "valid" indicator and only writing output data so tagged. More complicated designs can be implemented by modifying one of these programs. The input data source to the SIMD bus is selected from Channel B or C by XL, which may also perform preprocessing on the data, such as parallel-to-serial conversion. The output data is typically received by XR from the RBus and sent back to the host on Channel A, although XR may also send or receive data from XL. Both XR and XL have the ability to stop and restart the system clock, depending upon the state of the data channels. For example, if an input DMA channel is empty or an output channel is full, the clock may be stopped until the condition is cleared by the host (for instance, when another DMA operation occurs). The state machines in XL and XR that control the system clock may be clocked by a separate free-running clock signal. XR also controls the ownership of the RBus by setting the linear array size (RSize) and the direction (RDir) backplane signals.

5.5.4 Host View

A complete Splash 2 application includes a C program running on the host, which plays a pivotal role in the initialization and control of the hardware. This role includes downloading the configuration data to the FPGAs, establishing the input and output data streams, and controlling the system clock. The host program can also interact with the FPGA programs through a variety of both synchronous and asynchronous means.

The output of the compilation process is a set of configuration bitstream files, typically one for each FPGA. The host is responsible for merging the set of bitstream files for each Array Board into a single configuration stream called a "raw" file, which can then be downloaded directly to the Array Board. The host must also initialize the crossbar by reading and downloading the crossbar configuration file.

Symbolic debugging of running programs is supported by the state readback mechanism. To examine the internal state of a program, the host may stop the system clock and initiate a readback operation, which dumps the internal state of all of the FPGAs into a special buffer. The debugger may then extract the state of individual registers from the buffer, and associate the value with the VHDL symbol name.

The memory associated with the Processing Elements is mapped into the address space of the host program such that each PE memory appears as an array of integers. This allows the host program to read and write the memory using standard C data structures and pointer references. The kernel device driver is responsible for coordinating memory accesses with the FPGAs.

On systems with the Development Board, the SIMD and RBus data registers are mapped directly into the address space of the host program. To create an input stream to Splash 2 the host program simply writes data to the SIMD register. Likewise, an output stream is handled by reading from the RBus register. A set of library routines are available to facilitate these operations. The various asynchronous communications mechanisms such as the handshake registers may be accessed through C macros.

The Final Interface Board supports the use of standard Unix `read` and `write` system calls. An input data stream is created by writing the contents of an internal buffer or file to the device, while an output stream may be read from the device into a buffer or file. Higher-level library routines allow the concurrent handling of input and output streams. Another set of library routines permit the host to set the clock frequency, and start and stop the system clock.

REFERENCES

[1]   J.M. Arnold and M.A. McGarry, "Splash 2 Programmer's Manual," Tech. Report SRC-TR-93-107, SRC, Bowie, Md., 1993.

[2]   R.A. Bergamaschi, "High-Level Synthesis in a Production Environment: Methodology and Algorithms," in J.P. Mermet, ed., *Fundamentals and Standards in Hardware Description Languages*, Kluwer Academic Publishers, Boston, 1993, pp. 195–230.

[3]   S.D. Brown et al., *Field-Programmable Gate Arrays*, Kluwer Academic Publishers, Boston, 1992.

[4]   M. Gokhale et al., "The Logic Description Generator," Tech. Report SRC–TR–90–011, SRC, Bowie, Md., 1990.

[5]   M. Gokhale and R. Minnich, "FPGA Programming in a Data Parallel C," *Proc. IEEE Workshop FPGAs for Custom Computing Machines*, CS Press, Los Alamitos, Calif., 1993, pp. 94–102.

[6]   *IEEE Standard VHDL Language Reference Manual*, Std 1076-1987, IEEE Press, New York, 1988.

[7]   *IEEE Standard VHDL Language Reference Manual*, Std 1076-1992, IEEE Press, New York, 1992.

[8] P.J. Menchini, "An Introduction to VHDL," in J.P. Mermet, ed., *Fundamentals and Standards in Hardware Description Languages*, Kluwer Academic Publishers, Boston, 1993, pp. 359–384.

[9] J.K. Ousterhout, *Tcl and the Tk Toolkit*, Addison-Wesley, Reading, Mass., 1994.

[10] D.L. Perry, *VHDL*, McGraw-Hill, New York, 2nd ed., 1994.

[11] *Reference Manual for the Ada Programming Language*, ANSI/MIL-STD-1815A-1983, U.S. Department of Defense, Washington, D.C., Feb. 1983.

[12] Synopsys, Inc., *Design Compiler Reference Manual*, Synopsys, Inc., Mountain View, Calif., 1991.

[13] Synopsys, Inc., *VHDL Compiler Reference Manual*, Synopsys, Inc., Mountain View, Calif., 1991.

[14] Synopsys, Inc., *FPGA Compiler Reference Manual*, Synopsys, Inc., Mountain View, Calif., 1994.

[15] D.E. Thomas and P.R. Moorby, *The Verilog Hardware Description Language*, Kluwer Academic Publishers, Boston, 1991.

[16] S.M. Trimberger, ed., *Field Programmable Gate Array Technology*, Kluwer Academic Publishers, Boston, 1994.

[17] Xilinx, Inc., *The XC4000 Data Book*, Xilinx, Inc., San Jose, Calif. 1994.

CHAPTER 6

Software Implementation

Jeffrey M. Arnold

6.1 INTRODUCTION

An important goal of the Splash 2 software effort was to provide a working programming environment as quickly as possible without sacrificing the ability to grow and evolve as the project progressed. We therefore chose to base the implementation on software standards and readily available tools as much as possible, allowing us to concentrate on the system integration and the development of applications. The standards we chose included the VHDL and C programming languages and the Unix operating system. This chapter shows how these standards and the tools that support them were assembled to produce a complete programming environment.

6.2 VHDL ENVIRONMENT

The Splash 2 VHDL programming environment consists of a library of useful VHDL constructs and a set of standard entity declarations for the various levels of the Splash 2 hierarchy. This section presents some details of that environment, and then discusses aspects of the VHDL programming style that was evolved by the Splash 2 programmers.

6.2.1 Splash 2 VHDL Library

The `Splash2 Library` contains a set of `Packages` that are used for the development of VHDL application code for Splash 2. The `TYPES` package contains definitions of the data types used for interchip communication and is essentially a superset of the IEEE 1164 Standard Logic data type package. All bidirectional interface ports are built upon a four-state subtype (`'X'`, `'0'`, `'1'`, and `'Z'`) of the `Standard_Logic` type, called `RBit3`.[1] Assignment of a value of `'Z'` to a signal implies the synthesis of a tri-state driver. The `'X'` state is used only in simulation, primarily to identify tri-state bus conflicts. All of the standard logical operators as well as signed and unsigned arithmetic operators are supported over vectors of `RBit3`.

The `SPLASH2` package contains a variety of constants, data types, and functions that are specific to either the Splash 2 architecture or the Splash 2 simulator. For example, constants are defined that specify the width and depth of the memories and the width of the linear data path. Subtypes are also defined to specify the Processing Element data ports.

The `COMPONENTS` package contains a set of components and procedures useful in writing applications. These include the "Pad" procedures, which can be used to interface between the tri-state (`RBit3` type) signals external to the Xilinx chips and the standard logic levels (`Bit` type) internal signals. There are four pad procedures, each overloaded to accept scalar and vector arguments of `Bit` and `RBit3` types. `Pad_Input` is used to receive inputs from off-chip; `Pad_Output` is used to drive off-chip; `Pad_InOut` is used to conditionally receive and drive off-chip signals; and `Pad_XBar` is used to receive and drive the crossbar data path, conditioned by the crossbar output enable signals.

The `HMACROS` package contains component declarations and simulation models for the set of *hard macros* [4] provided by Xilinx. Hard macros are logic modules that have been hand-optimized with fixed relative placement and routing for maximum efficiency. Until the release of the Xilinx XACT 5.0 tools in 1994, hard macros were the only mechanism for accessing special-purpose hardware such as the fast-carry-chain logic. The `HMACROS` package provides the means to structurally instantiate hard macros within an application.

6.2.2 Standard Entity Declarations

All Splash 2 applications programs must conform to the input and output behavior defined by the standard `ENTITY` declarations. There are four unique FPGA entities visible to the programmer: the Processing Element (X1 through X16) and the Control Element (X0) on the Array Board, and XL and XR on the Interface Board. The entity declaration for the Processing Element is shown in Figure 6.1. The generic parameters `BD_ID` and `PE_ID` are constant values, unique to each PE, provided by the software environment; they permit the application to customize each PE program to its physical position in the system. The port declarations represent the connections of the PE to its neighbors and the rest of the system. The ports of type `DataPath` represent the data paths to the left and right neighbors and the crossbar. For example,

---

[1]The original `RBit3` data type was a resolved three-state (0, 1, Z) logic developed before the release of IEEE 1164.

```
ENTITY Processing_Element IS
   GENERIC(BD_ID          : Integer;
           PE_ID          : Integer);
   PORT(XP_Left           : inout DataPath;
        XP_Right          : inout DataPath;
        XP_XBar           : inout DataPath;
        XP_XBar_EN_L      : out   Bit_Vector(4 downto 0);
        XP_Mem_A          : inout MemAddr;
        XP_Mem_D          : inout MemData;
        XP_Mem_RD_L       : inout Bit;
        XP_Mem_WR_L       : inout Bit;
        XP_Int            : out   Bit;
        XP_Broadcast      : in    Bit;
        XP_Reset          : in    Bit;
        XP_HS0, XP_HS1    : inout RBit3;
        XP_GOR_Result     : inout RBit3;
        XP_GOR_Valid      : inout RBit3;
        XP_LED            : out   Bit;
        XP_Clk            : in    Bit);
END Processing_Element;
```

FIGURE 6.1   Standard Processing Element Entity Declaration

XP_Right of one PE is connected to XP_Left of the next PE. The interface to the PE memory consists of an address bus (XP_Mem_A), a data bus (XP_Mem_D), and separate read and write control signals (XP_Mem_RD_L and XP_Mem_WR_L). The "_L" appended to the name indicates the signal is active low. The user must set these signals to a '1' when the memory is not in use. XP_Int is the interrupt output signal. The interrupt signals from each of the FPGAs X0 through X16 are logically ANDed with the contents of the Array Board mask register, and then ORed to form the board-level interrupt. XP_Broadcast is an input signal driven by X0 and is common to all 16 PEs. XP_Reset is the systemwide reset signal, which may be set by the host. By default, XP_Reset is automatically connected to the Global Set/Reset (GSR) signal of the Xilinx XC4010, but it is also available as a user input. The Array Board handshake registers appear to the PE as XP_HS0 and XP_HS1. Each PE is connected to a unique bit of the HS0 register, while HS1 is common to all PEs on the Array Board. XP_GOR_Result and XP_GOR_Valid are bidirectional signals between the Control Element (X0) and each of the Processing Elements. The signal names reflect their intended purposes (global AND/OR reduction and barrier synchronization), but the bidirectionality makes these ports useful for signaling state changes from X0 to individual PEs. The port XP_LED is connected directly to a light-emitting diode (LED) on the front edge of the Array Board and is typically used for diagnostics. Finally, XP_Clk is the global synchronous clock shared by every PE in the system.

The entity corresponding to the Control Element (X0) is similar to the Processing Element entity, although the port names are prefixed by X0_ rather than XP_ (see Figure 6.2). In place of the XP_Left and XP_Right data buses, the Control Element has 36-bit ports to the SIMD bus (X0_SIMD) and to the crossbar (X0_XB_Data). X0_GOR_Result_In and X0_GOR_Valid_In are each 16-bit vectors of bidirectional

```
ENTITY Control_Element IS
  GENERIC(BD_ID          : Integer;
          PE_ID          : Integer);
  PORT (X0_SIMD          : inout DataPath;
        X0_XB_Data       : inout DataPath;
        X0_Mem_A         : inout MemAddr;
        X0_Mem_D         : inout MemData;
        X0_Mem_RD_L      : inout Bit;
        X0_Mem_WR_L      : inout Bit;
        X0_GOR_Result_In: inout RBit3_Vector(1 to 16);
        X0_GOR_Valid_In  : inout RBit3_Vector(1 to 16);
        X0_GOR_Result    : out   Bit;
        X0_GOR_Valid     : out   Bit;
        X0_Clk           : in    Bit;
        X0_XBar_Set      : out   Bit_Vector(2 downto 0);
        X0_X16_Disable   : out   Bit;
        X0_XBar_Send     : out   Bit;
        X0_Broadcast_In  : in    Bit;
        X0_Broadcast_Out: out    Bit;
        X0_LED           : out   Bit);
END Control_Element;
```

FIGURE 6.2 Standard Control Element Entity Declaration

signals to each of the Processing Elements. X0_GOR_Result and X0_GOR_Valid are outputs connected to the wire-OR backplane signals. Access to the crossbar data is achieved by asserting X0_X16_Disable, which effectively isolates X16 from controlling the crossbar output enables, and then setting X0_XBar_Send high to transmit into the crossbar or low to receive.

The entity for the Interface Board part XL is shown in Figure 6.3. The principal data ports correspond to the data path shared by DMA channels B and C, the SIMD bus, and the data path to XR. There are separate input ports for the system clock and the free-running clock. A clock-enable output port is used to start and stop the system clock. Two separate channel control ports of 14 bits each convey the control and status

```
ENTITY XL IS
  PORT(XL_FIFO           : inout DataPath;
       XL_SIMD           : inout DataPath;
       XL_XR             : inout DataPath;
       XL_Free_Clk       : in    Bit;
       XL_Splash_CLK     : in    Bit;
       XL_Enable_Clk     : out   Bit;
       XL_Chan_B         : inout ChanCtrl;
       XL_Chan_C         : inout ChanCtrl;
       XL_Ctrl           : inout Bit_Vector(4 downto 0);
       XL_GOR_Result     : in    Bit;
       XL_GOR_Valid      : in    Bit;
       XL_BCast          : inout Bit);
END XL;
```

FIGURE 6.3 Standard XL Entity Declaration

signals to and from the DMA channels. The global OR result and valid signals from the backplane are inputs to XL, as is a separate 5-bit handshake register, XL_CTRL.

The XR entity is very similar to XL. Its principal data ports correspond to data paths to DMA channel A, the RBus, and the XL-XR bus. It too has two clock inputs, a clock-enable output, and shares the same 5-bit handshake register. The RBus size and direction signals originate from ports on XR.

6.2.3 Programming Style

Over the course of the Splash 2 project a number of idiomatic VHDL constructs have evolved. Some of these constructs arose from requirements of the synthesis tools; others became a matter of programming style. In this section we examine a few of these idioms.

Signed and unsigned arithmetic is supported for Integer-derived types and for vectors of Bit and RBit3 types. The default word size for both signed and unsigned Integers is 32 bits, which can lead to a tremendous waste of logic and routing resources when the data range is known to be small. Therefore, range constraints on integers are used to assist the synthesis tools in optimizing the width of operator logic. For example, the code in Figure 6.4 will synthesize to a 10-bit unsigned incrementer. Likewise, vector lengths may be used to control operator widths for arithmetic over bit vectors. Since the arithmetic operators are overloaded to work with either, the choice of whether to represent a value as an Integer or a Bit_Vector is one of programming style. It is often more convenient to specify ranges than vector lengths, but vectors allow easier expression of shifts, concatenation, and bitfield extraction.

```
SIGNAL i: Integer range (0 to 1023);
i <= i + 1;
```

FIGURE 6.4 Range Constrained Integer Assignment

All of the Processing Elements in Splash 2 receive a global synchronous clock, XP_Clk. Therefore, all Processing_Element architectures have one or more processes synchronized to this signal. As shown in Figure 6.5, a synchronous process has no *sensitivity list* to limit its execution, but rather contains a single WAIT statement conditioned to trigger execution of the process on the rising edge of the clock. Assignments to SIGNAL objects within the body of the synchronous process are used to imply registers, since assignment occurs only following the execution of the process body, effectively registering the result on the clock edge. Unregistered temporary values may be named within a process by assigning to VARIABLE objects.

The "Pad" procedures (Pad_Input, Pad_Output, Pad_InOut, and Pad_XBar) declared in the COMPONENTS package are typically used to connect logic within the

```
PROCESS BEGIN
  WAIT UNTIL XP_Clk'EVENT and XP_Clk = '1';
  -- Body of synchronous process
END PROCESS;
```

FIGURE 6.5 Synchronous Process

```
ARCHITECTURE Test OF Processing_Element IS
  SIGNAL Left : Bit_Vector(DATAPATH_WIDTH-1 downto 0);
  SIGNAL XBar_in : Bit_Vector(DATAPATH_WIDTH-1 downto 0);
  SIGNAL XBar_out : Bit_Vector(DATAPATH_WIDTH-1 downto 0);
  SIGNAL XBar_dir : Bit_Vector(4 downto 0);
BEGIN
  Pad_Input(XP_Left, Left);
  PROCESS BEGIN
    WAIT UNTIL XP_Clk'EVENT and XP_Clk = '1';
    Pad_XBar(XP_XBar, XBar_in, XBar_out, XBar_dir);
    Pad_Output(XP_XBar_EN_L, XBar_dir);
  END PROCESS;
END Test;
```

FIGURE 6.6   Example of Off-Chip Communication

Processing Element to the external Array Board environment. Figure 6.6 shows an example of the use of two of these procedures. The `Pad_Input` procedure receives data from the left-hand neighbor PE and makes it available on the internal `Bit_Vector` signal `Left`. Since this is a *concurrent* statement, there is no implicit registering of the data. In contrast, the call to `Pad_XBar` is a *sequential* statement within a synchronous process. Therefore, both the input to the PE (`XBar_in`) and the output to the crossbar (`XBar_out`) are registered. The 5-bit vector `XBar_dir` is used to control the direction of the five "bytes" of the crossbar and is also driven out to the crossbar to control the corresponding output enable pins.

Finite-state machines are implemented by embedding flow control constructs such as `IF` and `CASE` statements within synchronous processes. An enumerated type may be used to define the set of valid states and a `SIGNAL` object of this type declared to hold the current state. A `CASE` statement within a synchronous process is used to dispatch on the state variable. Within each `WHEN` clause, input conditions are tested, output signals are assigned, and the next state transition is computed.

Occasionally it is necessary to instantiate one or more components within a Splash 2 application program to create replicated structures or to gain access to specific FPGA features. VHDL provides several structural constructs, including component instantiation and conditional and iterative `Generate` statements. For example, access to the CLB RAM within the Xilinx PE may be accomplished by instantiating a special memory component. Generic parameters to this component are used to configure the width and depth of the memory as well as to specify any initial contents (such as for ROMs). When evaluated by the Splash 2 simulator, the model for this component uses these parameters to create an output file that can be read by the Xilinx-provided `MEMGEN` program. `MEMGEN` in turn creates a macro for the memory, which is incorporated into the FPGA load module by the place-and-route tools.

There are two standard modes of synchronizing the input data with the Splash 2 system. In the first mode, the XL chip on the Interface Board controls the system clock such that the Array Boards see a system clock pulse only when there is valid data on the SIMD bus. In the second mode, the system clock is allowed to run continuously while the presence of valid data is indicated by setting to 1 the most significant bit (bit 35) of the SIMD bus. More complex behavior can be achieved by modifying the XL program.

Access to the external memory is synchronous with the global clock. Memory read operations are performed by placing the address on the XP_Mem_A port in one clock cycle and reading the data from XP_Mem_D in the next cycle. The port XP_Mem_Rd is asserted with the address to indicate a read operation. The address may be changed every cycle to perform back-to-back reads. A write operation is performed by placing both the address and the data on the memory ports and simultaneously asserting XP_Mem_WR. The address and data may be changed every cycle to perform back-to-back writes.

6.3 SPLASH 2 SIMULATOR

The Splash 2 simulator itself is written in VHDL and consists of a hierarchical set of models of the various components of the system. An application program uses the Configuration statement to specify which architectures (models) to use at each of the levels of the hierarchy. The architectures specified at the leaves of the hierarchy may be any mix of user-provided VHDL code and predefined default models. The configuration statement also allows the user to customize individual models by setting the values of generic parameters. Among the parameters specified are the names of any files of test data. The configuration statement therefore specifies the construction of a complete model of the system. This model in turn is interpreted by a simulation engine, effectively executing the user's application.

This section begins by describing the structure of the simulator hierarchy. We then present the use of the configuration statement through a series of examples. Finally, we discuss some details of the system models.

6.3.1 Structure

Figure 6.7 illustrates the structure of the Splash 2 simulator. The root of the hierarchy is the System model, which instantiates the Interface and the S2Boards models.

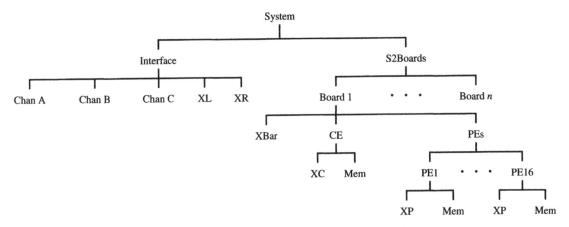

FIGURE 6.7   Structure of the Splash 2 Simulator

The `Interface` model is responsible for instantiating the DMA channels, XL and XR. Instances of the DMA channels are created only if there are values passed in the configuration statement for the corresponding input and/or output filenames. The `Interface` model is also responsible for generating the system clock, at a frequency determined by another generic parameter.

The number of Array Boards generated is controlled by the generic parameter `Number_Of_Boards`. The `S2Boards` model also passes the slot ID number to each Array Board component generated. The Array Board model in turn instantiates the crossbar (XBar) and the Control Element (CE) and contains a `Generate` statement that instantiates the Processing Elements (PEs). Each PE consists of a reference to the Processing Element component (XP) and the Memory component (Mem). The Processing Element reference passes the slot number and the PE number to the user's code through the generic parameters `BD_ID` and `PE_ID`, respectively.

6.3.2 Configuring the Simulator

The Splash 2 simulator assembles an application program according to the directions presented in the VHDL `Configuration` statement. This statement, typically stored in a file called `config.vhd`, identifies the architecture to use for each entity in the design and allows the user to specify values of generic parameters. Figure 6.8 shows the top, or outermost, level of a typical `config.vhd` file. Most of the file is common to all applications and may be copied from the Splash 2 library. In this example, `Top` is just a label to identify the configuration of the `Splash_System` entity. Within the `Structure` architecture there are two component instantiations: one for the `Interface_Board` entity and one for the `Splash2_Boards` entity. Any configuration information needed for the components would normally appear within the `for` clauses.

Figure 6.9 shows an example configuration for the `Interface_Board` component. The `Generic Map` construct is used to pass generic parameter values to the simulator. In this example, input for the application is taken from the file `test.dat` and output is written to the file `output.dat` in hexadecimal format. The clock model runs at a simulated frequency of 20 MHz. The user-programmable FPGAs XL and XR are both loaded with their `Valid` architectures from the `interface` library.

The rest of the Splash 2 simulator is configured in a similar manner. The complete `config.vhd` file contains places for specifying the number of Array Boards,

```
configuration TOP of Splash_System is
  for Structure
    for IFACE: Interface_Board
      -- Interface board configuration
    end for;                        -- IFACE: Interface_Board
    for Splash: Splash2_Boards
      -- Configuration of array boards
    end for;                        -- Splash: Splash2_Boards
  end for;                          -- Structure (of Splash_System)
end TOP;                            -- Configuration TOP
```

FIGURE 6.8   Top Level of Simulator Configuration File

```
for IFACE: Interface_Board
  use entity interface.Interface_Board(Structure)
    Generic Map (input_file1  => "test.dat",
                 output_file1 => "output.dat",
                 File_Type    => Hex,
                 Clock_Freq   => 20);
  for Structure
    for all: XL
      use entity interface.XL(Valid);
    end for;                     -- all: XL
    for all: XR
      use entity interface.XR(Valid);
    end for;                     -- all: XR
  end for;                       -- Structure of IFACE
end for;                         -- IFACE: Interface_Board
```

FIGURE 6.9   Interface Board Model Configuration

the crossbar configuration file, the Control Element and Processing Element architectures, and any initial memory tables.

6.3.3 Input and Output

Input to and output from the Splash 2 system are handled by the Interface Board
model, which contains generic filename parameters for each of the three I/O channels.
If the `config.vhd` file specifies a filename for a channel, the corresponding model
opens the file for reading or writing. Input files are assumed to be ASCII containing
one hexadecimal string per line, each line representing a new data value to be read
from the channel. Output files are written in the same format, one value per line of
the output file.

6.3.4 Crossbar and Memory Models

The crossbar model in the simulator is passed a generic parameter that contains the
name of a file that contains up to eight settings. The first line of each setting consists
of the keyword `configuration` followed by an integer from 0 to 7 (inclusive). The
following lines of the setting are of the form:

output–port–number input–port–specifier

where "output–port–number" ranges from 1 to 16 and corresponds to the Processing
Element number. The "input–port–specifier" is either a single integer (0 to 16) or
five integers (0 to 16). If the input–port–specifier is a single integer in the range
(1 to 16), it specifies a single source port for all 36 bits of the output. A value
of 0 is used to indicate that port "output–port–number" is used as an input to the
crossbar. If "input–port–specifier" consists of five integers, each integer specifies the
source for one byte of the output, from most to least significant. If an output port
number is missing from the configuration, it is assumed to be set to 0 (input to
the crossbar). Note that simply setting "input–port–specifier" to 0 is not sufficient
to disable the crossbar port; the corresponding XP_XBar_EN_L signals must be set
to 1.

```
-- Odd PEs drive, even PEs receive
configuration 0
1 0
2 1
3 0
4 3
5 0
6 5
7 0
8 7
10 9
12 11
14 13
16 15

configuration 1
1 0
2 9 7 5 3 1
```

FIGURE 6.10 Sample Crossbar Configuration File

Figure 6.10 shows an example crossbar configuration file with two settings defined. In the first setting, the odd-numbered PEs are driving into the crossbar while the even-numbered PEs are receiving. The crossbar ports corresponding to PEs X9, X11, X13, and X15 are implicitly set to 0 (disabled). In the second setting, PE X2 is receiving one byte each from X9, X7, X5, X3, and X1. Crossbar ports for X3 through X16 are implicitly disabled.

Users may choose from several predefined memory models available in the Splash 2 simulator, or they may add their own. The predefined memory architectures include the following:

- None: No memory is modeled. Access to the memory generates an error.
- Zero: Read-accesses from any location return a constant zero. Write-accesses are ignored.
- Static: Memory is modeled as a statically allocated, fixed-size array. The size of the array is determined by a generic parameter passed by the configuration file. This model is useful for lookup tables and sequentially accessed data.
- Dynamic: Storage for the memory model is allocated dynamically as needed. The first write to an address allocates a new storage cell, which subsequent reads will fetch. A read from an unwritten address generates an error. This model is useful for programs in which the access pattern is data-dependent (random).

The memory initialization, or "load," file is an optional ASCII file that may be used to specify initial contents of the PE memories. The format of this file is simple. For each set of contiguous blocks of data, the base address of the block is given, followed by one or more data values. The base address is specified by the keyword address followed by an unsigned decimal integer. Subsequent (decimal) integers are interpreted as the 16-bit values to load into consecutive locations. A single load file may contain any number of blocks. Alternatively, the entire memory can be initialized to zero by including the keyword clear in the load file.

6.3.5 Hardware Constraints

One important role of the simulator is to verify that application programs satisfy certain hardware constraints that are difficult or impossible to verify through static analysis. The hardware constraints that can be checked in simulation include memory sequencing, reading uninitialized memory locations, and tri-state bus conflicts.

Since the data bus to the memory is bidirectional, the PE must ensure that it does not begin a write operation before the completion of a read. This constraint is verified within the simulator by checking that the memory read signal is deasserted at least one cycle before the memory write signal is asserted.

The major data buses on the Array Board are bidirectional, relying on the use of tri-state I/O drivers of the FPGAs to prevent conflict. The simulator models these tri-state pins with a four-state logic. The resolution function for the four-state logic detects any attempt to drive a signal to two different logic values simultaneously. When a conflict is found, a warning message is printed and the signal is set to the 'X', or unknown, state.

6.4 COMPILATION

A mix of logic synthesis and standard compilation techniques are used to compile VHDL programs into FPGA configurations. The logic synthesis tools from Synopsys Inc. [3] are used to map the VHDL code into a gate list. A custom peephole optimizer is then applied to the gate list to perform a variety of Xilinx-specific and Splash 2-specific optimizations. The resulting gate list is then mapped into the CLB structures and placed and routed using the Xilinx [4] tool package. The Xilinx tools are also used to extract the detailed timing information from the placed and routed design. This information may be used directly to manually optimize the design, or it may be used to construct a new structural VHDL model for each chip, which may be resimulated by the Splash 2 simulator to provide detailed timing analysis.

6.4.1 Logic Synthesis

In 1991, FPGA technology was still quite new and confined mainly to board-level "glue logic" applications. Consequently, very few commercial CAD tool vendors were targeting FPGAs for logic synthesis. After evaluating the few tools on the market, we chose to base our compiler on the Synopsys Design Compiler. This choice required the development of a custom technology library that allowed the Design Compiler to produce a technology-independent gate list. It was also necessary to write a net list conversion program to translate that generic gate list into a technology-dependent form suitable for the physical mapping tools.

The net list translator, called `edif2xnf`, parsed and flattened the hierarchical `EDIF` net list produced by the Design Compiler, creating another file in Xilinx Netlist Format (XNF). During the translation a number of Xilinx- and Splash 2-specific optimizations were also performed on the design, including:

• Flip-flops on the periphery of the logic were migrated to the I/O frame (IOBs) of the chip wherever possible.

- The board-level program reset and Xilinx Inhibit signals were connected to the internal GSR and GTS signals.

- Hard macro references were identified and marked as such.

- Port names were given specific pin assignments and pad slew-rate options.

- The clock signal was identified and a global buffer inserted in the clock net.

- A pattern-matching algorithm was also used to find opportunities to simplify the logic by exploiting the clock-enable feature of the Configurable Logic Block (CLB) flip-flops.

The output of the optimizer, in Xilinx Netlist Format (XNF), was fed into the Xilinx-provided placement and routing tools and static timing analyzer.

In late 1993 Synopsys released their "FPGA Compiler" product that incorporated much of the functionality of edif2xnf directly into the synthesizer. There were some minor problems, however, in the early releases of the FPGA Compiler, which necessitated our writing another program, xnfer, which was able to manipulate the XNF file. Xnfer inserts the "drop in" logic that connects the internal GSR and GTS signals and moves peripheral flip-flops to the IOBs.

A Unix shell script (vhdl2xnf) presents the user with a simplified interface to the numerous controls of the FPGA Compiler and xnfer. Vhdl2xnf processes a number of command line options and constructs an execution script for the FPGA Compiler. This script, in turn, specifies any elaboration parameters (including the BD_ID and PE_ID), includes port mapping tables, and handles error conditions. The output of vhdl2xnf is an XNF file ready for physical mapping.

6.4.2 Physical Mapping

The physical mapping of the design from XNF to a loadable bitstream is handled by the Xilinx-provided tools. The placement and routing tool, PPR, reads the XNF net list and produces an "LCA" file, which contains all of the configuration information in an ASCII format. The program makebits converts the LCA file into a bitstream format, called a "BIT" file. Makebits also produces an "LL" file that contains a table-mapping CLB and IOB flip-flops to positions in the readback bitstream. Another Unix shell script (xnf2bit) provides a convenient interface to the physical mapping tools and the symbol table creation.

6.4.3 Debugging Support

To support the symbolic capabilities of the runtime debugger, a table is created associating the names of symbols with the location of the corresponding register bit in the readback stream. The information needed to build this table is extracted from the compiled design in two steps. First, the Xilinx tool lca2xnf is used to create an XNF file annotated with the location of each CLB flip-flop and its associated signal name.[2] The location information is then looked up in the LL file produced by makebits to produce an offset into the readback bitstream. A table of symbol names and offsets is then built for use by the debugger.

---

[2]This step is necessary to resolve ambiguities created by PPR through the use of feed-through CLBs.

6.5 RUNTIME SYSTEM

There are two host software interfaces to the Splash 2 system: a C language library that can be linked into an application-specific driving program, and an interactive symbolic debugger. Both interfaces are built upon the same underlying runtime system, and both provide the same basic functionality. The runtime system allows the user to open the Unix device, to map the Splash 2 memory into the host address space, to configure the FPGA devices and crossbar, to establish DMA data streams, and to control the system clock. The clock may be single-stepped, multiply-stepped, or allowed to run free. The user may also read and write various control registers, including the "handshake" registers.

6.5.1 T2: A Symbolic Debugger

To assist in the development of applications on the hardware, an interactive symbolic debugger, T2, was developed. The user interface to T2 is an interpreter executing the Tcl command language [1]. Tcl is a C-like language that provides a variety of control-flow mechanisms and allows the user to extend the command set by writing custom procedures. A set of built-in procedures provides access to the Splash 2 hardware resources and runtime software.

The built-in commands of T2 may be divided into three categories: hardware setup; program execution; and analysis. The setup commands include routines for hardware and software initialization, and configuration of the FPGAs and crossbar. To configure the system, the user specifies a map, which associates Processing Elements (individually or in groups) with bitstream files. The bitstream files for all of the PEs on an Array Board are then merged into a single image called a "raw" file. A given raw file may then be loaded to one or more Array Boards via the ConfigArray command. A raw file may be saved and reloaded on subsequent runs, obviating the need to associate and merge the bitstreams again. The crossbar is initialized from a crossbar configuration file by the ConfigXBar command.

Execution of an application program is controlled by the Step family of commands. There are a variety of these commands that allow the user to specify input and/or output files, file formats, and the interpretation of the "tag": the most significant four bits of the 36-bit data word. For input files the tag may be set to a constant value or it may be taken from the input file. On output the tag is typically used to indicate valid data, so a mask may be provided to control which data are to be written to the output file. All of the Step commands allow the user to specify the number of clock cycles to execute.

The heart of the symbolic debugger is the Xilinx FPGA state readback mechanism. To trace a set of program variables, or symbols, the user issues the AddReadBack command after each Step command. AddReadBack adds the current state information to an internal history buffer. Another set of commands allows the user to inquire about the state of a particular symbol at a particular time. Symbols may be looked up individually, or an alias may be defined to aggregate multiple symbols.

The wave program allows users to view graphically the time-varying behavior of program symbols. The T2 command Trace adds a symbol (or alias) to a trace list. At the end of each clock cycle a readback is performed and the value of every traced signal is written to a file. The `wave` program reads the trace file and paints a waveform display similar to a logic simulator or a hardware logic analyzer.

Finally, T2 provides a set of lower-level routines for reading and writing individual hardware registers. These routines are available for applications that require a level of control not provided by the higher-level interface.

6.5.2 Runtime Library

The Splash 2 runtime library, `libsplash`, which forms the foundation of T2, is also available to be linked into a user-written C program. For every built-in T2 command there is a corresponding entry point into `libsplash` that provides the same functionality. The routine `OpenAndInit` performs the basic hardware and software initialization, including opening the device, allocating and initializing the `Splash` device structure, and mapping the various pages of the physical address space into the user's address space. The `Splash` structure is also initialized with an array of pointers to each of the PE memories in the system. Separate minor devices corresponding to the DMA channels are also opened. The hardware initialization includes loading a passive, or idle, program into all of the FPGAs, setting the clock frequency, and resetting and disabling the DMA channels.

Application programs may be loaded and executed through `libsplash` in the same manner as from T2. Library routines exist to manipulate bitstream files and to create, save, and load raw files. The entire family of `Step` commands is also available as library routines.

In addition to the T2 commands, however, `libsplash` also provides a set of input and output routines based upon the standard Unix system calls `write` and `read`. The `Write` routine is a user-level interface to the `write` system call, which uses the DMA facility to transfer data from the user's address space to the Splash 2 Interface Board and XL. The `Read` routine similarly sets up a DMA transfer from the Interface Board to a buffer in the host memory.

Both `Write` and `Read` are *blocking* operations. That is, once called, these routines do not return control to the user program until the requested operation is completed. To implement two concurrent data streams, one input to Splash 2 and one output from Splash 2, the `WriteRead` routine is provided. `WriteRead` uses the first DMA controller to transfer data from one memory buffer to the Interface Board while simultaneously using the second DMA controller to move data from the Interface Board back to a different host memory buffer. This concurrency is accomplished by spawning a separate Unix process to perform the `Read` while the parent process proceeds with the `Write` operation. Once the `Write` has completed, the parent waits for the `Read` process to complete before returning control to the user program.

Both the output and input memory buffers used by the `WriteRead` routine are in the address space of the user program, but the data received from Splash 2 is in the address space of the `Read` process. Since Unix does not support shared memory very well, it is necessary to copy the received data from the `Read` process back to the address space of the parent process. This copying is accomplished by passing the data from the child back to the parent in a memory-mapped temporary file. The parent process opens a temporary file prior to spawning the child process. The child then maps the file into its address space using the `mmap` system call, and passes it as the target buffer for the Read operation. Upon completion, the parent also memory-maps the temporary file and copies the data to the user's buffer. The temporary file is truncated to zero length prior to closing, to avoid any writes to the disk.

The buffer copying performed by the WriteRead routine can be avoided by forcing the user to manage the memory-mapped temporary files. The WriteReadFD routine allows the user to pass the file descriptors of memory-mapped files in place of the memory buffers. The output data is taken directly from the "write" temporary file, while the input data is written directly to the "read" temporary file.

The user program also has direct access to the various device registers in the Splash 2 system. The register-access commands of T2 are available to the C programmer, but for efficiency reasons a separate set of C macros is also provided. These macros typically accept a symbolic register identifier and a value and perform any necessary data alignment prior to reading or writing a register.

6.5.3 Device Driver

The interface between libsplash and the Splash 2 hardware is handled by the *device driver* [2]. A device driver is a body of code written for a particular physical device which executes within the protected domain of the operating system itself. The Splash 2 driver provides entry points for the various operating system calls such as open, close, mmap, read, and write. The open call reserves a device for use by the user process and typically performs a variety of hardware and software initializations, while close frees the device for use by other processes. The mmap system call is the mechanism by which the operating system makes available to the user some portion of the physical address space of the device. Input to and output from a device are done with the read and write calls. The driver is also responsible for handling system interrupts caused by the device.

The physical address space of the Splash 2 device is composed of several distinct segments corresponding to the registers and memory on the Interface and Array Boards. The register space of each board is further divided into two pieces: user mode space and kernel mode space. User mode space contains those registers which may be mapped directly into the address space of the user program, while kernel mode space contains registers reserved for use strictly within the device driver. As a rule of thumb, access to registers that may adversely affect the operation of the system, such as DMA and interrupt registers, is limited to the "trusted" device driver. The remaining registers and memories may be mapped into user space.

Since the Development Board does not support DMA-controlled input and output or interrupts, the device driver for systems with the Development Board relies entirely upon the mmap call. All the registers on the Development Board are mapped into the user's address space, and a set of user-level library routines is provided to support input and output. The read and write system calls are not supported.

The bank register is managed by the device driver and is transparent to the user program. Whenever a user reference crosses a 24-bit segment boundary, a memory fault is incurred that transfers control to the Splash 2 driver. The driver then unloads the mapping for the previous segment of memory, maps in the new segment, and updates the bank register. No further intervention by the driver is required until the next time a reference falls outside of the current segment.

Since the Processing Element memory is not truly dual-ported, special care must be taken to avoid simultaneous access from the host and from the FPGA. The device driver coordinates access to the memories through the operating system's page fault mechanism. Whenever the Splash 2 system clock is enabled, *all* of the Processing Element memories are unmapped from the user's address space. Therefore, any access to a PE memory from the host causes a fault, transferring control back to the driver. The driver then stops the system clock and unloads the mapping for the clock registers to prevent the user from inadvertently restarting the clock. After the clock has been stopped, the "Xilinx Disable" signal is asserted to passivate the FPGAs, a software timeout interrupt is scheduled for about 10 msec in the future, and the referenced memory segment is mapped in before control is returned to the user program. When either the timeout interrupt or a subsequent user reference to the clock registers occurs, the procedure is reversed by unloading the memory segment, deasserting the Xilinx Disable signal, and restarting the clock.

The device driver for systems containing the Interface Board supports DMA transfers through the `read` and `write` system calls. When a user-level input or output request is made, the driver must perform a variety of software bookkeeping operations before and after the actual data transfer. First, the user's data buffer is mapped into the kernel address space. Next, each page of the buffer is locked into physical memory to prevent the operating system from paging it to disk during the transfer. Then, if the buffer does not begin on a 16-word boundary, the transfer is aligned by manually copying data to or from the DMA channel. Once the buffer has been mapped, locked, and aligned, the DMA transfer is begun. When the transfer is complete, the Interface Board signals the driver by generating a hardware interrupt. The interrupt handler returns control to the driver, which reverses the process, copying any data remaining after the last 16-word block and then unlocking and unmapping the buffer.

The SBus hardware has a peak data bandwidth of nearly 60 MB/sec. Unfortunately, due to the software overhead associated with the DMA transfer, principally mapping the buffer into the kernel space and locking the pages in memory, the best transfer rate a user-level program can expect to achieve is about 23 MB/sec, or about 40 percent of the peak.[3] For small transfers, the software overhead of DMA can completely dominate the time to completion. Therefore, for requests of less than 1024 bytes, the `Read` and `Write` library routines handle the transfer entirely in user mode using slave read and write accesses to the FIFOs.

6.6 DIAGNOSTICS

The suite of diagnostic software for Splash 2 evolved from the need to test and debug the hardware. The diagnostics were originally written to support low-level hardware debugging and system software design, but as the project progressed they took on new roles in the postmanufacture testing of new boards and the routine health

---

[3]These values were empirically determined in our laboratory. A hardware logic analyzer was connected to the LED register and to the SBus grant signal on the Interface Board. A version of the device driver was written that marked events by writing to specific bits of the LED register. The logic analyzer then recorded the time spent in the various phases of the I/O transfer.

checkups of running systems. The principal components of the test suite are the `tsdb` debugger and the `robocop` diagnostic.

Support for the lowest level of hardware debugging is provided by the "trivial SBus debugger," or `tsdb`. This tool is not specific to Splash 2, but rather operates on the physical address space of a given SBus slot. A simple command interpreter allows the user to examine and set locations by specifying an offset within the SBus slot space. Other commands include read and write loops to allow triggering of test equipment. The user can define a set of symbolic names to use in place of numeric values. These symbols can then be used in any command that expects a numeric value such as a physical address.

The main diagnostic program is called `robocop`. Robocop consists of a set of VHDL Processing Element programs and C host routines. The design philosophy of `robocop` is to test the functionality of the system in ever-increasing distance from the host, starting with the SBus interface and proceeding through the Interface Board eventually to the Array Boards. On the Interface Board, `robocop` begins by testing the various status and control registers, then the program and readback memory, the programmable clock, XL and XR, and finally each of the DMA controllers. Once the Interface Board passes all of the tests, `robocop` proceeds to test the Array Boards, starting with the PE memories, the FPGAs, and the Crossbar and data paths. Finally the data path between Array Boards is tested.

A simple menu-driven interface allows users to select tests to perform on individual components or run on the entire system at one of several levels of detail. Any errors discovered are logged on the host by both system name and by individual board serial number.

Robocop may also be configured to run in the background, automatically starting up whenever the Splash 2 system is not in use. This background mode is completely transparent to the user. If the diagnostics are running when a user attempts to start an application, the `OpenAndInit` routine in `libsplash` will send a signal to the `robocop` process causing it to gracefully shut down. Once `robocop` has exited, the `OpenAndInit` call returns control to the application in the normal manner. In addition to the normal error logging, when running in background mode, errors are also reported by sending electronic mail to a list of system maintainers.

REFERENCES

[1] J.K. Ousterhout, *Tcl and the Tk Toolkit*, Addison-Wesley, Reading, Mass., 1994.

[2] J. Stigliani, *Writing SBus Device Drivers*, Sun Microsystems, Inc., Mountain View, Calif., 1990.

[3] Synopsys, Inc., *FPGA Compiler Reference Manual*, Synopsys, Inc., Mountain View, Calif., 1994.

[4] Xilinx, Inc., *The XC4000 Data Book*, Xilinx, Inc., San Jose, Calif., 1994.

A Data Parallel
Programming Model

Maya Gokhale[1]

EDITORS' INTRODUCTION

The following chapter describes an alternative, data parallel, programming model suitable for some of the applications for Splash 2 or for CCMs in general. In the "standard" approach adopted for Splash 2, programmers must design the processor architecture, at least in concept, at the level of a block diagram of comparator boxes, adders, and such, for processing the data, and to a lesser extent for sequencing and control. Given the linear flow of data in many applications, many of the algorithms are most easily viewed as a series of processing boxes connected by lines representing the flow of data (see, for example, Figure 11.12 in Chapter 11). Although the programming of such an algorithm in VHDL in the Splash 2 programming environment is a relatively straightforward programming process, the fact remains that the hard work of determining the data processing steps needed, laying those steps out with the data flow, and partitioning the entire computation into chip-sized pieces has already been done before any programming ever takes place.

It is this process, the design of a processor architecture suitable for a given application, that the dbC approach suggests could be done automatically by the compiler. The underlying idea, at least part of which is certainly not new, is that the programmer is able to write code in a variant of C that supports both bit-oriented data types and massive parallelism of SIMD computation. The compiler then translates the dbC code into assembly language-level instructions and produces as output

---

[1]A version of this appeared as Gokhale and Schott [6] and is used with permission.

the VHDL code necessary to create an instance of a processor architecture capable of executing the specific assembly-level instructions needed for the particular computation at hand. It is in this last step that the Splash 2 dbC work differs from more ordinary SIMD machine computations. In the CM-2, for example, a specific target micro-architecture existed in hardware, and the Paris assembly-level instructions used that micro-architecture. Unlike some other approaches to computing on FPGAs, in which a specific micro-architecture is synthesized and instructions for that micro-architecture are used, with dbC in Splash 2 the architecture is defined by the instructions to be executed, and only as much architecture as is needed is eventually synthesized.

The key issue in the use of CCMs has always been the ability to produce working programs by programmers (rather than hardware engineers) with an expenditure of effort and time consistent with other programming tasks. A dbC approach, if it were to be successful, would go a long way toward resolving that key issue. There were three reasons, however, that precluded the consideration of dbC as the standard method by which Splash 2 was to be programmed.

- In its present form, dbC is suitable only for SIMD applications. Many of the Splash 2 applications simply are not suitable for a SIMD implementation (at least not a SIMD implementation on Splash 2), and it was necessary to have a programming environment that would accommodate those applications.

- The performance of dbC programs on Splash 2 and their use of the still relatively precious FPGA resources is not yet good enough that one could have demonstrated "success" on some important applications.

- Most important, and not unrelated to the previous point, dbC is a research project in its own right and, even now, has not come to closure. What was necessary for the Splash 2 demonstration project was a programming environment in which applications could be developed in a time frame consonant with the rest of the project. Although dbC had existed for other (standard) machines prior to the start of the Splash 2 project, dbC for Splash 2 did not exist and could not be predicted to exist in time for applications development. Further, the degree of risk concomitant with any real research project made the adoption of dbC as "the" programming mode for Splash 2 impractical.

In short, then, we offer this chapter as a suggestion of what the (near) future may hold for the programming of CCMs. Applications have been programmed using dbC, the research continues, and we would expect that future CCMs might rely on dbC or a similar language in a manner from which we were prevented by the sequence of events.

7.1 INTRODUCTION

The standard methodology for programming Splash 1 and Splash 2 was through hardware description languages. Splash 1 was programmed using the Logic Description Generator (LDG) described in Gokhale et al. [5], a textual HDL that facilitated the description of systolic, hierarchical designs. LDG was developed in-house to meet the need for a low-level tool that nonetheless permitted the user to concisely describe a large amount of logic. On Splash 2, we were able to design at a much higher level. Behavioral VHDL approaches the expressive power of a parallel programming language. However, orchestrating a large number of concurrent event-driven loops is complicated, time-consuming, and error-prone. Splash 2 is a complex collection of devices. Although the simulator went a long way in helping to verify the correctness of a Splash 2 design, the programmer had full responsibility for creating the design in the first place, which required working out the timing of a multiplicity of interlocking events across the 17 FPGA chips, memories, FIFOs, crossbar, and host. VHDL programs were required for each distinct FPGA chip design. The crossbar program was in a separate ASCII file. A control program on the host was required to send data and control signals to the array and to read back results.

We knew that raising the conceptual level from hardware design to parallel programming would make Splash 2 (and custom computers in general) accessible to a much wider range of programmers. It would be ideal to write a single parallel program, with some portions executed on the Splash 2 Array Board and others on the host, with communication and coordination between the two (as well as among FPGA computing elements) managed automatically.

It was at this point that a related SRC project was synergistic to the problem of programming Splash 2. Another group at SRC had designed and built the TERASYS SIMD array, composed of custom Processor-in-Memory chips [3]. A new language, data-parallel bit C (dbC), was developed to program TERASYS [12]. Two features of the language and its implementation made it especially appealing for Splash 2.

First, in dbC, bits are first-class parallel objects. Variables of arbitrary bit length can be created, and operations over arbitrary bit length data objects are supported. On Splash 2, this allows us to create and operate with small (1-, 2-, and 4-bit) objects, saving valuable resource on the FPGA. For example, the genetic sequence comparison application uses 4-bit counters to record edit distances. It would not be possible to describe this structure accurately in conventional C, since bitfields are promoted to "`int`" for computation. In dbC, not only is the storage minimized, but the computation is over the actual bit length rather than a standard container size such as 32 bits.

The second enabling aspect of dbC was in its implementation: the dbC "compiler" is actually a translator from the parallel ANSI C superset to ANSI C. The parallel constructs are invoked as function (or macro) calls. For TERASYS, the parallel operations are implemented by a microcode library. For Splash 2, we synthesize logic on a program-by-program basis to support exactly those parallel operations that are required for a given program. The parallel operations are executed on the Array Board, with serial data manipulated on the host. Clock events, FIFOs, the crossbar, and FPGAs disappear from the programming model. A single dbC program controls both Splash 2 and the host. As an added advantage, a dbC simulator had been written for the TERASYS project and could be used by Splash programmers to debug their data parallel programs on a workstation prior to synthesis.

Thus, concurrent with application development in VHDL, we embarked on a research project to build a dbC-to-Splash 2 compiler. We realized at the outset that dbC, which follows the SIMD programming model, would not be suitable for all Splash 2 applications. Many applications are inherently MIMD: different processors perform different tasks. Some applications have real-time constraints, which might not be met through high-level synthesis. Nevertheless, the key issue in the use of CCMs has always been the ability to produce working programs by programmers rather than by hardware designers, with an expenditure of effort and time consistent with other programming tasks. A dbC approach, even with the restricted application domain, would go a long way toward resolving that key issue.

In this chapter, we describe the dbC language and compiler, which translates programs written in a data parallel superset of ANSI C into high-level VHDL for the Splash 2 array of FPGA chips. The next section contains a brief introduction to dbC. Next, we describe the dbC/Splash 2 compiler and illustrate the compilation process with a simple example. Section 4 details how data parallel communication and global reduction operators are mapped onto Splash 2. Optimizations are described in Section 5. We evaluate our system in Section 6 by showing performance on a genetic database search problem coded in dbC. Finally, we summarize and sketch future directions.

7.2 DATA-PARALLEL BIT C

dbC is an ANSI C superset similar to MPL [10] and C* [13]. The programming model is that of a SIMD processor array in which a host processor controls instruction sequencing of many Processing Elements (PEs) (see Figure 7.1). The PEs receive instructions from the host. A PE can be active, in which case it executes the current instruction, or inactive, in which case it ignores the instruction. The active state is controlled by a mask, the *context bit*. Each PE can communicate with its nearest-neighbor in the user-defined virtual topology (a linear topology is illustrated). PEs can also communicate in arbitrary any-to-any patterns through an interconnection network. Global combining operations (also called *reduction operations*) such as global OR, SUM, MAX can be performed over the entire PE array, with the result of the operation being returned to the host.

7.2.1 dbC Overview

The dbC programmer specifies the number of PEs by initializing two predefined variables, DBC_net and DBC_net_shape. DBC_net must be initialized to the number of dimensions in the PE array, and DBC_net_shape is a vector of rank DBC_net, each element of which gives the size of the corresponding PE dimension.

In dbC the programmer designates data which is to reside on the processor array with the attribute *poly*. Figure 7.1 shows a one-dimensional 12-processor array

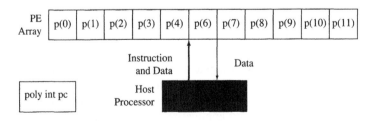

FIGURE 7.1   A SIMD Array

with a `poly int` (P) variable. All of the normal C operators can be used on poly data. In addition, special built-in operators that perform global combining operations are also defined. Processor activity is controlled by parallel control constructs such as "if," "where," or "while." Interprocessor communication is initiated by the programmer with calls to intrinsic functions such as `DBC_net_send` for nearest-neighbor communication, `DBC_send` for arbitrary communication, and `DBC_read_from_proc` (`DBC_write_to_proc`) for PE-host (host-PE) communication.

As noted above, dbC was originally designed for the TERASYS SIMD array. It also runs on the Connection Machine-2. Both of these SIMD arrays have one-bit processors that perform arithmetic bit serially.

7.2.2 dbC Example

We show in Figure 7.2 a dbC program to compute the cross-correlation of two bitstreams. The program compares two bitstreams and accumulates a count of the number of times an individual bit in the bitstreams had the same value. The bitstreams are compared with a delay of zero bits, then with successively larger delays, usually one bit longer for each delay. For each of the delays a counter records the number of matches (see Figure 7.3). The delay is sometimes called a "lag."

In a typical implementation, there are individual cells that perform the correlation between two streams of data for one value of the delay, that is, there is a cell for delay 0, delay 1, and so on. Each cell includes a comparator and a counter. The comparator compares the data in the bitstreams; if they are the same, the counter

```
#include <interproc.hd>
typedef poly unsigned Boolean:1;
Boolean a;
#define N 128
#define NPROC 64
unsigned DBC_net = 1;
poly unsigned int R:16 = 0;
unsigned DBC_net_shape [1] = {NPROC};
int right[1] = {1};
void main()
{
  all {
    int b;
    a = 0;
    for (b=0; b < N; b++) {
      DBC_write_to_proc(&a, 1, 0);
      R += (a ^ (Boolean) b);
      DBC_net_send(&a, a, right);
      printf("%d \n", DBC_read_from_proc(R, (b%NPROC)));
    }
  }
}
```

FIGURE 7.2   dbC Cross-Correlation Program

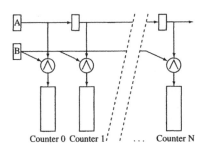

FIGURE 7.3 Bitstream
Cross-Correlation

Counter 0 Counter 1 ... Counter N

is incremented. Comparison of the two bits can be performed with exclusive-or or exclusive-nor. At least one of the bitstream data streams moves from cell to cell, but the counter data is stationary, as shown in Figure 7.3.

In this example, stream a is shifted systolically through the array, while stream b is broadcast to each PE. The counter R accumulates the result of the correlation.

The user specifies the size and shape of the processor array by initializing the predefined variables DBC_net, which gives the number of dimensions, and DBC_net_shape, which gives the rank of each dimension. The dbC/Splash 2 compiler currently supports only linear arrays.

The keyword poly indicates the declaration of parallel variables or data types. Integers and logicals in the parallel domain may have arbitrary user-defined bit length. In the example program, the variable a is a one-bit parallel variable, and the counter R, which holds the result, is a 16-bit unsigned parallel integer. The variable b is a normal C variable that is stored on the host.

The all keyword indicates that all processors are to participate in the body of the compound statement. The body of the all contains an initialization of the parallel variable a and a sequential for statement. Within the for loop, there are three statements. The first statement initiates host-to-processor communication: the host writes a 1 to processor 0's a. The second updates the counter R. On each processor, the result of a XORed with the least-order bit of b is added into R. Finally, each processor in the linear array shifts its value of a to the right. The final statement of the loop simply reads and prints the value of the counter R from a specific processor (b mod 64). This type of register examination has traditionally been very difficult for programmers to design into Splash 2 programs.

7.3 COMPILING FROM dbC TO SPLASH 2

Compiling dbC programs for the Splash 2 system occurs in two phases. First, the dbC translator emits sequential C code with embedded parallel instructions. These parallel instructions are three-address memory-to-memory instructions ("Generic SIMD").

When a dbC program is compiled for a traditional SIMD machine (CM-2 or TERASYS), the generic SIMD instructions are interpreted by microcode libraries (such as the Paris microcode library for the CM-2). These runtime libraries also support intrinsic functions such as DBC_read_from_proc and DBC_net_send.

To compile for Splash 2, an additional compilation phase is invoked. A Splash 2 specific phase focuses on the parallel instructions that were created by the previous phase, and assembles from those parallel instructions a specialized SIMD engine in structural and behavioral VHDL.

The virtual PEs making up this SIMD engine have an instruction set containing all of the generic SIMD instructions appearing in the generated C code. Thus the compiler synthesizes a different instruction set for each different program.

In addition to constructing a custom SIMD engine for the application on Splash 2, the dbC compiler also generates the host program. This program executes the sequential operations of the dbC program on the host and sends parallel instructions to the Splash 2 Array Board in the sequence specified by the dbC program. The compilation steps are enumerated below.

7.3.1 Creating a Specialized SIMD Engine

We demonstrate the steps required to configure Splash 2 as a SIMD machine with the small example of Section 7.2.2.

Phase 1 of the dbC translator does item 1 below. All subsequent steps are performed by the Splash 2 specific phase 2. Starting from the dbC program, the steps are:

1. Generation of the Generic SIMD code.
2. Determination of registers and data movement between registers. The data path, rather than being the generalized data path found in general-purpose computers, is customized on a per-program basis.
3. Determination of the control structure, that is, what decoders for instructions are needed and what those decoders must control. The decoders are also customized for the program.
4. Establishment of inter-PE (and inter-chip) data paths and state machines for nearest-neighbor communication.
5. Establishment of inter-PE (and inter-chip) data paths and state machines for global combining operations. The Xi's, X0, and host must synchronize during a global reduce.
6. Generation of:
   a) VHDL types for the data types;
   b) VHDL SIGNALs for the variables;
   c) VHDL control statements for the instruction decode;
   d) Appropriate VHDL assignment statements for each of the operators;
   e) Port declarations and interconnection to support nearest-neighbor communication and global reduction;
   f) Generation of state machines to sequence the multi-tick operations.
7. Generation of the host program to perform sequential operations and send parallel instructions to the Splash 2 Array Board.
8. Synthesis of VHDL to Xilinx-specific configuration bitstreams, which are downloaded to the chips. This process uses commercial CAD tools.

```
opParMoveZero_1L_a(a.address, 1);
for (b = 0; b < 128; b ++ ) {
  DBC_write_to_proc(a.address, 1, 0, 1);
  opParBxor3c_1L_a(opParAddOffset(_DBC_poly_frame_t_main, 2)
               /* t3:1:2 */, a.address, b, 1);
  opParAdd2_2L_a(R.address,
              opParAddOffset(_DBC_poly_frame_t_main, 2)
               /* t3:1:2 */, 16, 1);
  DBC_net_send(a.address, a, right, 1);
  printf("%d \n", DBC_read_from_proc(R, b%64));
} /* end for */
```

FIGURE 7.4   C + Generic SIMD Code for Correlation

7.3.2 Generic SIMD Code

To begin the process of compiling the correlation program for Splash 2, we translate the dbC to sequential C plus calls to Generic SIMD operators. A fragment of the Generic SIMD code for our correlation program is shown in Figure 7.4. Each "function" call prefaced by opPar is a Generic SIMD instruction.

The instruction name describes both function and parameters. The opPar prefix is followed by the operation, for example, MoveZero in the first instruction. Next, many instructions have a number signifying the number of operands, for example the "3" in the opParBxor3c_1L instruction. If one of the operands is a constant, as in the XOR instruction, a c follows. Next, after the underscore, the number of bit lengths that will follow is specified as a number followed by L. A final suffix _a indicates that the operation is to be performed unconditionally on each PE (even if the context bit is reset).

In our example, the MoveZero instruction clears the single-bit parallel variable a. The intrinsic DBC_write_to_proc writes a 1 into processor 0's a. The Bxor3c instruction performs a Boolean XOR of a and the least-order bit of i^2 into a compiler-generated temporary. Next that temp is added into R in the Add2 instruction. The DBC_net_send shifts a from each PE to its right neighbor. Finally, the DBC_read_from_proc reads R from processor i.

7.3.3 Generating VHDL

In the second phase of compilation to Splash 2, the Generic SIMD code is processed by a specialized backend. The Splash 2 specific Phase 2 generates two chip descriptions, which are VHDL programs for computational chips X1–X16 and the control chip X0, respectively. The computational chips hold the SIMD Processing Elements, while the X0 control chip is used for host-PE communications, global combining, and instruction broadcast.

In Phase 2, we create an instruction set derived from the opPar commands and intrinsic calls generated by Phase 1. The instruction set for this SIMD engine

---

[2]The latter is a variable on the host, and therefore a constant from the point of view of the SIMD array.

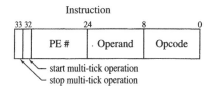

FIGURE 7.5   SIMD Instruction Format

is customized to the specific instruction instance. For example, the Boolean XOR instruction we synthesize expects the operands to be the variable a and the least-order bit of b and the result to go into t3. Thus there is no need for runtime computation of source and destination, a data path to compute and gain access to arbitrary source and destination, or much of the other complexity that comes with a general-purpose instruction set.

The instructions are in a fixed format, shown in Figure 7.5. The least-order eight bits contain the opcode. The next 16 bits, labeled "Operand" in the figure, contain an immediate value, if required by the instruction. For example, our XOR instruction, the opParBxor3c_1L_a, requires a constant to be passed as one of the operands to the operation. In the example (see Figure 7.4), the current value of b is the second operand of the XOR, and thus gets passed to each PE through the Operand field.

The third field of the instruction, PE#, is an optional processor number used for those instructions that are to be executed only by specific single processors. In our cross-correlation program, for example, the DBC_read_from_proc instruction reads the result from a different processor on each iteration of the loop, Processor b. The generated instruction therefore writes the current value of b mod 64 in the PE# field. The final high-order bits are used to synchronize between X0 and the host in multi-tick operations.

Figure 7.6 outlines the interaction between the host and the generated SIMD engine. The controlling program on the host executes a sequence of instructions, some of which are executed locally on the host and some of which are sent as commands to the SIMD engine. In our example, the loop control of the for-loop is done on the

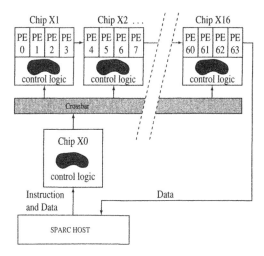

FIGURE 7.6   The Generated SIMD Engine for Cross-Correlation

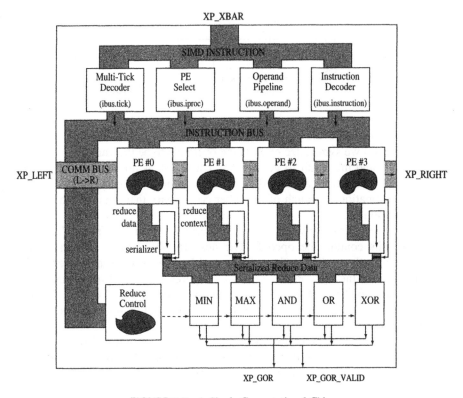

FIGURE 7.7   A Single Computational Chip

host. In the body of the loop, the parallel instructions are broadcast to the SIMD engine, with each PE (0–63) operating independently on its data.

Figure 7.7 shows the layout of each computational chip. Multiple PEs are instantiated on each chip, with the number of PEs per chip being determined by the user-specified size of the processor array. In this example, there are a total of 64 PEs, so four are placed on each of the 16 chips. Instructions are sent through the XL FIFO to X0, which broadcasts them over the crossbar to each chip. At the chip, the instruction is decoded and sent to all the SIMD PEs on the chip, along with the Operand and PE#.

This program contains a call to the intrinsic DBC_read_from_proc, which returns to the host the value of R on a specific PE. We use a special form of the "reduce logic" (see Section 7.4 on Global Operations) to implement this instruction. The figure shows that the SIMD instruction ("ibus") comes into the chip on the XP_XBAR port. There the opcode is decoded, and the decoded opcode, along with the other fields, is passed to each SIMD PE. The SIMD processors contain logic to execute the instructions. In addition, for this correlation program, they are connected to each other linearly through the "communicate bus" over which the value of a is shifted right. The "reduce data" shown flowing out of each SIMD PE is the value of R, which is read from successive PEs and sent to the host. The serializers and reduce logic are explained in Section 7.4. The value of R from the selected PE is sent two bits at a time out the XP_GOR and XP_GOR_VALID lines to X0.

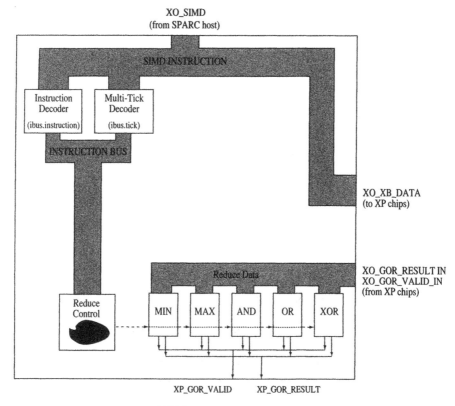

FIGURE 7.8   The Control Chip

Figure 7.8 shows the layout of the control chip X0. The 36-bit instruction word comes in on X0_SIMD from the SPARC host. X0's instruction decoder and multi-tick decoder are identical to those of the computational chips. The reduce logic is similar to that of the computational chips, with the major difference being that the data enters bit-serially on the X0_GOR_RESULT_IN and X0_GOR_VALID_IN lines and goes to the host bit serially on X0_GOR_RESULT and X0_GOR_VALID.

The final step is to generate the host program. Each `opPar` instruction is replaced with a Splash 2 specific instruction, as shown in Figure 7.9. A `SPLASH_INSTRUCTION` simply writes the parameter to the operand field of the SIMD Bus and then steps the clock, which issues the instruction to X0. The `SPLASH_W_INSTRUCTION` writes an 8 to the opcode field, a 1 to operand, and a 0 to the PE# field. The `SPLASH_RP_INSTRUCTION` writes a 3 to opcode, a 16 to operand (the bit length, which is required to control the reduce logic), and the current value of `i` modulo 64 to the PE#. Note that the modular reduction is performed on the host, and the result of the mod is sent to the processor array. The `DBC_net_send` instruction is broken into two parts: the first copies `a` to the communicate output port, and the second copies the communicate input port into `a`. The nearest-neighbor communication is explained further in the next section.

```
SPLASH_INSTRUCTION(9);    /* OPPARMOVEC_1L */
for (i = 0; i < 128; i ++ ) {
  SPLASH_W_INSTRUCTION(8 /* OPPARWRITETOPROC */, 1, 0);
  SPLASH_INSTRUCTION(7);    /* OPPARBXOR3C_1L */
  SPLASH_INSTRUCTION(6);    /* OPPARADD2_2L */
  SPLASH_INSTRUCTION(5);
  SPLASH_INSTRUCTION(5);
  SPLASH_INSTRUCTION(5);    /* OPPARNETSEND1 */
  SPLASH_INSTRUCTION(4);    /* OPPARNETSEND2 */  }
  printf("%d \n", SPLASH_RP_INSTRUCTION(3, 16
       /* OPPARREADFROMPROC */, (i%64)));
}
```

FIGURE 7.9   Final C Program for Correlation

7.4 GLOBAL OPERATIONS

The data parallel model encompasses a number of global operations in which all (active) Processing Elements participate. On Splash 2, we have implemented two classes of data parallel operations,

- DBC_net_send, a nearest-neighbor linear communication pattern in which each PE sends a value to its right neighbor. PE 0 receives its value from the host through the Operand field of the instruction.
- Reduce operators MAX, MIN, AND, OR, and XOR, which perform the indicated operation across the entire virtual PE array and send the result back to the host.

7.4.1 Nearest-Neighbor Communication

Left-to-right communication is accomplished with structural connections between virtual processors. Each PE has a left and right port. The width of the communication ports are defined at compile time. These ports are hard-wired together so that the right port of processor i and the left port of processor i + 1 share a register. An exception to this is on the Xilinx chip boundaries. The Splash 2 linear interconnect is used for chip-to-chip communication. On each chip, the left port of the first virtual processor on the chip and the right port of the last virtual processor on the chip are connected to XP_LEFT and XP_RIGHT, respectively.

Communication of a value from a PE to its neighbor on the same chip requires one cycle. However, the need for inter-chip communication introduces delay. Since we latch data on chip boundaries, the inter-chip communication from the last PE on chip k to the first PE on chip k + 1 requires three cycles.[3]

To accommodate these differences, we separate the net send instruction into two parts, a write and a read. As shown in Figure 7.9, the NETSEND1, which writes the value to the communicate output port, is dispatched three times. Then the NETSEND2 is sent. This instruction latches the input communicate port into the receiving register.

---

[3]A possible alternative, to synchronize the data with a three-cycle pipeline on the internal connections, is too costly in logic.

7.4.2 Reduction Operations

The notion of global combining, having all the PEs work together to produce a single result, is a key component of the SIMD processing model as defined by Hillis [7]. dbC has six primitive global reduction operators: MAX, MIN, SUM, AND, OR, and XOR. There is infix notation for each of these operators. For example, in

```
poly int a,
int b;
b =  >? = a;
```

the operator $>? =$ signifies max reduce.

The programmer can invoke a reduce directly by using the special operators. Combining operators are also generated by the compiler when parallel control constructs such as parallel-if or parallel-while are used [12]. In addition, combining logic is generated for the DBC_read_from_proc intrinsic.

Global combining operations on traditional SIMD machines require a large amount of communication between the processors. This requirement is especially difficult for the Splash 2 implementation in that the crossbar, which could be used for inter-chip communication, is engaged in broadcasting instructions. Any other use of the crossbar interferes with the instruction pipeline. For this reason, we use the GLOBAL_OR lines from each computational chip to X0 and from X0 to the host to compute a "reduce" result bit-serially and send it to the host.

Conceptually, global reduce operations on Splash 2 are performed in two stages. In the first stage, an intermediate result is computed for all of the PEs on a computational chip. These local results are transmitted to the control chip, and the second stage computes the global result, which is transmitted to the host. However, this two-stage computation occurs bit-serially and the stages are heavily pipelined.

When a PE receives a global reduce instruction, the PE sends its register data to a serializer component and its context to a reduce_context signal (refer to Figure 7.7). On the next cycle, the serializer shifts the data to the reduce components at a rate of two bits per cycle. The serial data is masked with the reduce_context signal. Each of the reduce components collects the data from the serializers and performs the appropriate reduction on the bits. The internals of the AND, OR, and XOR are trivial. MIN and MAX are discussed in the next section. The control logic for the reduce components (Reduce Control) selects the 2-bit result from the correct reduce component and sends it to the X0 chip via XP_GOR and XP_GOR_VALID connections.

On the control chip, X0, the 2-bit results from each of the 16 computational chips are collected on X0_GOR_RESULT_IN and X0_GOR_VALID_IN (refer to Figure 7.8). Each of the reduce components collects the data and again performs the appropriate reduction on the bits. The control logic selects the 2-bit result from the correct reduce component and sends it to the host via the X0_GOR_VALID and X0_GOR_RESULT connections.

There are many advantages to performing global combining operations bit-serially on Splash 2. One advantage is that the approach is easy to understand and implement. An obvious bit-serial path is available (and otherwise unused) in the form of the GLOBAL_OR lines. The instruction pipeline is not disturbed in order to perform a global reduction. Another advantage is that the control logic required to drive the reduce is very fast and quite small. Since the same reduce logic is reused every cycle, the speed and size of the logic is largely independent of the size of the registers to be reduced. The size of the logic is a function of the number of PEs per chip and the kinds of reduces to be performed. An unexpected advantage to the bit-serial approach to global combining operations is that the reduce operation takes relatively few cycles to complete. A bit-serial global reduction requires $(w/2)$ + 13 cycles,[4] where w is the width of the destination register in bits. Thus, an 8-bit reduce of 64 processors requires 17 cycles. A 16-bit reduce takes 21 cycles.

The MIN and MAX Global Combining Operations.   A bit-serial approach to MIN and MAX global combining operations requires more thought than the AND, OR, and XOR operations. Nevertheless, the solution becomes evident if the data are processed most-significant-bit (msb) first. All that is required is one bit of state per processor to keep track of which processors are still participating in the computation. Let us first consider the generic problem of finding the maximum value in an array bit-serially.

Bit-serial MAX.   Our method of performing MAX reduce uses an algorithm that computes one binary digit of output per cycle, starting with the most significant bit (msb). The number of cycles is determined by the width of the variable to be reduced. The input at cycle i consists of the ith msb of the register from each of the processors. A mask register (one bit per processor) is maintained to determine which processors should be ignored in subsequent cycles. The algorithm has a few simple steps:

1. The processor mask register is initialized to all 1s.
2. For each bit of the register:
    a) The processor window register contains the ith most significant bit from each processor.
    b) The window and mask registers are ANDed together.
    c) If the result is nonzero, the mask is set to the result and a 1 is output.
    d) Otherwise, the mask is left unchanged and a 0 is output.

Example

The following example traces a four-processor system with 6-bit registers. The processors' registers contain the following values:

Processor	Decimal	Binary representation
p0	6	0 0 0 1 1 0
p1	9	0 0 1 0 0 1
p2	10	0 0 1 0 1 0
p3	11	0 0 1 0 1 1

---

[4]This includes a four-cycle instruction pipeline.

The mask is initialized to all 1s for the first iteration. On subsequent cycles, the Window and Mask registers change as follows:

Cycle	Bit	Window p0 p1 p2 p3	Mask	Window AND Mask	Output
1	5	0 0 0 0	1111	0000	0
2	4	0 0 0 0	1111	0000	0
3	3	0 1 1 1	1111	0111	1
4	2	1 0 0 0	0111	0000	0
5	1	1 0 1 1	0111	0011	1
6	0	0 1 0 1	0011	0001	1

The output bit-serially generated is 001011 (decimal = 11).

Bit-serial MIN.   The algorithm for finding the minimum value bit-serially is virtually identical to finding the maximum value. In essence, we find the maximum value of the one's-complement of the poly register and the one's-complement of the result is the answer. The bit-serial reduce MAX is modified in two simple ways to get reduce MIN: the serial input (window) and the serial output are inverted.

The following example, as in the MAX example, uses the four processor system with 6-bit registers. The processors' registers contain the values 6, 9, 10, and 11.

The mask is initialized to all 1s for the first iteration. On subsequent cycles, the Window and Mask registers change as follows:

Cycle	Bit	Window* p0 p1 p2 p3	Mask	Window AND Mask	Output*
1	5	1 1 1 1	1111	1111	0
2	4	1 1 1 1	1111	1111	0
3	3	1 0 0 0	1000	1000	0
4	2	0 1 1 1	1000	0000	1
5	1	0 1 0 0	1000	0000	1
6	0	1 0 1 0	1000	1000	0

*Note that the bits are simply inverted from the reduce MAX example.

The output bit-serially generated is 000110 (decimal = 6), which is indeed the minimum value.

7.4.3 Host/Processor Communication

Four dbC intrinsics are available for communication between the host and the processor array. DBC_read_from_proc reads a parallel variable from a specific processor. DBC_read_from_all reads a parallel value from each processor into an array in the host. DBC_write_to_proc writes a value from the host to a specific processor. Finally, DBC_write_to_all spreads a host array onto the virtual processor array, one element per processor.

The `DBC_read_from_proc` Operation. The `DBC_read_from_proc` intrinsic is implemented on Splash 2 as a modified reduce OR. The host specifies the PE to be read via the PE# field of the SIMD instruction. The PE Select component compares the PE# field to the processor ID (`iproc`) of each PE (see Figure 7.7). If the `iproc` and PE# are equal, the `pe_selected` signal is set to a 1. The `DBC_read_from_proc` call causes the register to be passed to the serializer, as with any global reduce operation. However, the `reduce_context` signal is set to `pe_selected` in place of the PEs `context` bit. This effectively masks out all PEs except for the PE selected by the host.

This approach to `DBC_read_from_proc` has the advantage that the logic required for the operation is negligible. If a global combining operation such as `or_reduce` is used by the design, that logic is recycled by `DBC_read_from_proc`.

The `DBC_read_from_all` Operation. The `DBC_read_from_all` intrinsic copies all of the values of a poly register held by PEs to an array on the host. This function could be implemented as n iterations of `DBC_read_from_proc` (where n is the number of PEs). However, we chose a more efficient method. The Splash 2 implementation uses n iterations of left-to-right communicate to get the poly registers to the host. The last PE's right port is connected `XP_RIGHT` on the computational chip (refer to Figure 7.7). The `XP_RIGHT` port of the last computational chip in the Splash 2 linear path is connected to the host via the RBUS (see Figure 2.1). As the host issues n iterations of left-to-right net send calls, it reads data from the RBUS. The data appear on the RBUS in reverse order $(n, n-1, n-2, \ldots)$. Consequently, the host fills the destination array backwards. As described in Section 7.4.1, a `DBC_net_send` instruction requires four cycles. Utilizing the net send, the `DBC_read_from_all` intrinsic requires $4n$ cycles to complete. This is much more efficient than n iterations of a 13+ cycle `DBC_read_from_proc`.

Writing to the Processor Array. The `DBC_write_to_proc` implementation on Splash 2 is quite simple due to the fact that both the instruction and the data flow in the same direction, from host to PE array. As described in Section 7.3.3, the SIMD instruction generated by the host has three fields: opcode, operand, and PE#. The operand field contains the data to be written, and the PE# field contains the ID of the destination PE. If the PE# field of the SIMD instruction matches the `iproc` of the processor, the register is assigned the value of the operand field. Otherwise, the instruction is ignored. A `DBC_write_to_proc` call takes only one cycle.

The `DBC_write_to_all` is implemented as a series of n `DBC_write_to_proc` calls, where n is the number of PEs. This operation requires n cycles.

7.5 OPTIMIZATION: MACRO INSTRUCTIONS

Our simple cross-correlation program has approximately 10 instructions. A more realistic application would result in many tens more. It is advantageous to reduce the number of parallel instructions for a variety of reasons. Fewer instructions require a smaller decoder, a savings in logic. By scheduling independent SIMD operations at the same clock, we introduce new instruction-level parallelism within a SIMD PE. Even more compelling, a single powerful multi-tick instruction can be clocked independently at the processor array, allowing the Splash 2 system to run at a faster rate than the host SPARCstation can drive it. Our compiler, therefore, identifies opportunities for multi-tick operations and synthesizes multi-tick instructions, which are activated by a single opcode.

One such category of multi-tick operations is the reduce family of instructions discussed in the previous section. Another category, which we describe here, is parallel basic blocks, from which the compiler creates "macro instructions." A single macro instruction dispatched from the host initiates a multi-tick instruction in which one or more generic SIMD operations occur concurrently on each PE.

7.5.1 Creating a Macro Instruction

A basic block consists of a sequence of computation with a single entry point at the top of the block, a single exit at the bottom, and no branching into or out of the block except through the single entry and exit. Figure 7.10 shows a basic block written in dbC and the corresponding generic SIMD code.

The macro instruction scheduler attempts to schedule all the operations in the block to occur in a single clock tick. This is possible only if there are no interoperation dependencies. For example, instructions (1) and (2) in Figure 7.10 are independent and can safely occur in a single clock tick, but instruction (4) depends on the completion of instruction (3). Only after t3 is registered can the add occur.

```
#define N 16

poly unsigned u:N, v:N, w:N, k:N;

u = DBC_iproc[0 +: N];
v = (poly unsigned:N) (DBC_nproc +1) - DBC_iproc[0 +: N];
k = v - 1;
w = u | v | k;
```

```
(1)  opParMove_1L_a(u.address, opParAddOffset(DBC_iproc.address,
                 (0)), 16);
(2)  opParMovec_1L_a(opParAddOffset(_DBC_poly_frame_t_main, 1)
                 /* t3:16:1 */, (DBC_nproc + 1), 16);
(3)  opParSub3_1L_a(v.address,
                 opParAddOffset(_DBC_poly_frame_t_main, 1)
                 /*t3:16:1 */,
                 opParAddOffset(DBC_iproc.address,
                 (0)), 16);
(4)  opParSub3c_1L_a(k.address, v.address, 1, 16);
(5)  opParBor3_1L_a(opParAddOffset(_DBC_poly_frame_t_main, 1)
                 /* t5:16:1*/, u.address, v.address, 16);
(6)  opParBor3_1L_a(w.address, opParAddOffset
                 (_DBC_poly_frame_t_main, 1)
                 /*t5:16:1 */, k.address, 16);
```

FIGURE 7.10   A Basic Block and Its Translation to Generic SIMD

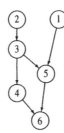

FIGURE 7.11   Dependency Graph

For each basic block, the scheduler constructs a dependency matrix M to reflect the dependencies among parallel instructions. $M[i, j] = 1$ implies that instruction (j) depends on instruction (i). Then, an As Soon As Possible (ASAP) scheduling algorithm is used to sequence the parallel instructions. All instructions j such that $M[*, j] = 0$ can be scheduled in the current tick. Once an instruction j has been scheduled, $M[j, *]$ is set to 0, allowing the instructions that depend on j to be scheduled in the next iteration of the algorithm. Figure 7.11 shows the dependency graph for this example.

The compiler generates a single opcode for the macro instruction. When that opcode is issued, a subinstruction shift register is used to sequence through the subinstructions. For this example, a 4-tick instruction is issued. The sequencing of ticks is controlled by a 4-bit shift register.

7.5.2 Discussion

Our approach differs from more general high-level synthesis systems in two respects. First, since we focus on the SIMD model, control flow is managed by the host. We are concerned only with basic blocks of parallel instructions and need not build and schedule a general control-flow graph as is done by the IBM [2] and similar systems. Second, in contrast to most high-level synthesis systems that synthesize logic for a single chip, we focus on synthesis of the entire FPGA-based parallel computing system. Our efforts are directed toward synthesis for the Splash logic array, of which generating logic for individual chips is one (important) part. We use a commercial FPGA compiler to further optimize the VHDL generated by our system.

7.6 EVALUATION: GENETIC DATABASE SEARCH

Applications involving search for similarity in genome strings have been mapped successfully to Splash 1 [4] and Splash 2 [8]. We have compiled a dbC version of this application for Splash 2. A source stream is stored across the processor array, one 4-bit character per virtual processor. The target stream, of indefinite length, is shifted systolically through the virtual processor array. A dynamic programming algorithm ([9]) is used to correlate similarity of source to target streams. The dbC version runs at 22 million Cell Updates Per Second with one Splash 2 Array Board. By comparison, a SPARC 10/30GX can do 1.2 million CUPS, and an 8K MP-1 can do 32 million. A custom hardware implementation of this algorithm on one Splash 2 Array Board is estimated to achieve 2626 million CUPS [8].

In terms of programming effort, the custom hardware implementation was developed over a period of months. The dbC program was written and debugged in a day.

In comparison to other systems that do high-level synthesis for FPGAs, the Brown University Xilinx FPGA coprocessor achieves a speedup of two to four over the host workstation [1]. The Oxford University Algotronix FPGA array, consisting of eight chips and attached SRAM, performs at twice the speed of the host workstation [11].

7.7 CONCLUSIONS AND FUTURE WORK

dbC was an experiment that is still in progress. We were able to demonstrate with the dbC-to-Splash 2 compiler that for one class of applications, SIMD/systolic, we were able to support a high level of abstraction. The dbC compilation system can map data parallel programs to the Splash 2 reconfigurable logic array. dbC is *not* a hardware description language with C syntax. It is a true procedural data parallel language. Our dbC compiler for Splash 2 can translate programs that

- contain basic arithmetic and logical operations on integers
- use linear nearest-neighbor communication
- do global accumulation operations such as max, min, and Boolean operations
- read and write data from/to individual virtual processors
- read and write data from/to the entire processor array

Application domains that meet these constraints include independent computationally intensive problems, which occasionally compute global state and systolic algorithms such as the genetic database search. On the genome problem, our automatically synthesized SIMD engine runs at 18 times that of a SPARC 10 workstation and about two-thirds the speed of an 8K Maspar MP-1.

Many Splash 2 applications use the off-chip memory. Those applications were not supported by dbC. Our future efforts with the dbC/Splash 2 compiler include adding support for the off-chip memory, which are often used as lookup tables or as storage for results to the host. In addition, we would like to make the technology we have developed of practical use in production applications by supporting a robust interface between the generated SIMD machine and hand-coded custom logic. This would allow, for example, pre- and postprocessing to occur on some of the chips, with the SIMD array on the rest. The preprocessed data could feed the SIMD portion and then be sent from the last virtual processor to a postprocessing chip. As another example, we would like to integrate custom-designed kernels, which require extremely high performance, to appear to the dbC program as a single instruction. The compiler could generate an instruction set that includes this "special" instruction. These tactics can dramatically boost the performance of an application, while still removing most of the programming burden.

REFERENCES

[1]   P.M. Athanas and H.F. Silverman, "Processor Reconfiguration through Instruction Set Metamorphosis: Architecture and Compiler," *Computer*, Vol. 26, No. 3, Mar. 1993, pp. 11–18.

[2]   R. Camposano et al., "The IBM High-Level Synthesis System," R. Camposano and Wayne Wolf, eds., *High Level Synthesis*, Kluwer Academic Publishers, Boston, 1991, pp. 79–104.

[3]   M. Gokhale, W. Holmes, and K. Iobst, "Processing in Memory: "The Terasys Massively Parallel Processor Array," *Computer*, Vol. 28, No. 4, Apr. 1995, pp. 23–31.

[4]   M. Gokhale et al., "Building and Using a Highly Parallel Programmable Logic Array," *Computer*, Vol. 24, No. 1, Jan. 1991, pp. 81–89.

[5]   M. Gokhale et al., "The Logic Description Generator," Tech. Report SRC-TR-90-011, SRC, Bowie, Md., 1990.

[6]   M. Gokhale and B. Schott, "Data Parallel C on a Reconfigurable Logic Array," *J. of Supercomputing*, Vol. 9, 1995, pp. 291–314.

[7]   W.D. Hillis, *The Connection Machine*, MIT Press, Cambridge, Mass., 1986.

[8]   D.T. Hoang, "Searching Genetic Databases on Splash 2," *Proc. IEEE Workshop FPGAs for Custom Computing Machines*, CS Press, Los Alamitos, Calif., 1993, pp. 185–192.

[9]   D.P. Lopresti, *Discounts for Dynamic Programming with Applications in VLSI Processor Arrays*. PhD thesis, Princeton Univ., Princeton, N.J., 1987.

[10] MasPar, Inc., *MasPar Application Language Reference Manual*, MasPar, Inc., Sunnyvale, Calif., 1990.

[11] I. Page and W. Luk, "Compiling Occam in FPGAs," in W. Moore and W. Luk, eds., *FPGAs*, Abingdon EE & CS Books, Abingdon, England, UK, 1991, pp. 271–283.

[12] J. Schlesinger and M. Gokhale, dBC Reference Manual. Tech. Report SRC-TR-92-068, Revision 2, SRC, Bowie, Md., 1993.

[13] Thinking Machines, Inc., *C* Programming Guide*, Thinking Machines, Inc., Cambridge, Mass., 1993.

CHAPTER 8

Searching Genetic Databases on Splash 2

Dzung T. Hoang[1]

8.1 INTRODUCTION

With the onset of the Human Genome Initiative [3] and constant advances in genetic sequencing technology, genetic sequence data are being generated at an ever-increasing rate.[2] As a result, biologists are faced with an influx of new sequences that they would like to classify and study by comparing them to existing databases. The analysis of a newly generated sequence typically involves searching the databases for similar sequences. With the enormous size of the databases, fast methods are needed for comparing sequences [11].

In this chapter, we describe two systolic array architectures for sequence comparison and their implementations on the Splash 2 programmable logic array. One of the systolic arrays was previously implemented on the Princeton Nucleic Acid Comparator P-NAC of Lipton and Lopresti [12], a special-purpose VLSI chip, and later ported to the Splash 1 hardware by Gokhale et al. [4] and by Lopresti [14]. The second systolic array is a new development, improving on the first for database search applications.

---

[1]A version of this chapter appeared as Hoang [6] and is used with permission.

[2]Release 74.0 of GenBank, a database of DNA sequences, contains 97,084 entries with a total of 120,242,234 bases as of December 1992. It is estimated by Lander et al. [10] that by 1999, 1.6 billion base pairs will be sequenced each year.

8.1.1 Edit Distance

In comparing two sequences, it is useful to quantify their similarity in terms of a distance measure. In general, the correspondence between individual elements (characters) of the sequences to be compared is not known in advance. Therefore common distance measures such as Euclidean distance and Hamming distance, in which elements correspond in position and only corresponding elements are compared, may not be appropriate. Biologists have developed several means to characterize the similarity between genetic sequences. One intuitively appealing measure is *edit distance*. The edit distance between two sequences is defined as the minimum cost of transforming one sequence to the other with a sequence of the following operations: deletion of a character, insertion of a character, and substitution of one character for another. No character may take part in more than one operation. Each operation has an associated cost, which is a function of the characters involved in the operation. The cost of a transformation is the sum of the costs of the individual operations.

As an example, Figure 8.1 shows a series of transformations to obtain $GCATAAGC$ from $TCTAGACC$. If we assign a cost of 2 for a substitution, 1 for deletion, and 1 for insertion, the transformation would have a cost of 6. In fact, there are no transformations with lower cost, and therefore the edit distance between $TCTAGACC$ and $GCATAAGC$ is 6.

8.1.2 Dynamic Programming Algorithm

The edit distance can be computed with a well-known dynamic programming algorithm, which has an interesting history of independent discovery as detailed by Sankoff and Kruskal [17]. We use the following formulation.

Let $S = [s_1 s_2 \cdots s_m]$ be the source sequence, $T = [t_1 t_2 \cdots t_n]$ the target sequence, and $d_{i,j}$ the distance between the subsequences $[s_1 s_2 \cdots s_i]$ and $[t_1 t_2 \cdots t_j]$. Then for $1 \le i \le m, 1 \le j \le n$, if $\psi(s_i, \emptyset)$ is the cost of deleting s_i, $\psi(\emptyset, t_j)$ is the cost of inserting t_j, and $\psi(s_i, t_j)$ is the cost of substituting t_j for s_i,

$$
\begin{aligned}
d_{0,0} &= 0, \\
d_{i,0} &= d_{i-1,0} + \psi(s_i, \emptyset), \\
d_{0,j} &= d_{0,j-1} + \psi(\emptyset, t_j),
\end{aligned}
\tag{8.1}
$$

and

$$
d_{i,j} = \min \begin{cases} d_{i-1,j} + \psi(s_i, \emptyset) \\ d_{i,j-1} + \psi(\emptyset, t_j) \\ d_{i-1,j-1} + \psi(s_i, t_j). \end{cases}
\tag{8.2}
$$

The edit distance between S and T is simply $d_{m,n}$.

A cost function often used in the literature assigns a cost of 1 to insertions and deletions, 2 to substitutions, and 0 to matches. We refer to this as the *simple cost function*.

As an example, Figure 8.2 shows the dynamic programming table generated when comparing the sequences $TCTAGACC$ and $GCATAAGC$ with the simple cost function.

A straightforward sequential implementation of the dynamic programming algorithm requires $O(mn)$ time and $O(\min(m, n))$ space to compute the edit distance.

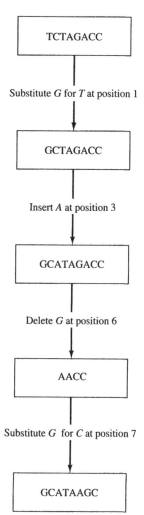

FIGURE 8.1 Listing of Operations to Transform $TCTAGACC$ into $GCATAAGC$. Character matches are assumed to have a cost of 0 and are not shown. Assigning a cost of 2 for a substitution, 1 for deletion, and 1 for insertion, the cost of the transformation is 6.

		G	C	A	T	A	A	G	C
	0	1	2	3	4	5	6	7	8
T	1	2	3	4	3	4	5	6	7
C	2	3	2	3	4	5	6	7	6
T	3	4	3	4	3	4	5	6	7
A	4	5	4	3	4	3	4	5	6
G	5	4	5	4	5	4	5	4	5
A	6	5	6	5	6	5	4	5	6
C	7	6	5	6	7	6	5	6	5
C	8	7	6	7	8	7	6	7	6

FIGURE 8.2 Dynamic Programming Table Generated in Computing the Edit Distance between $TCTAGACC$ and $GCATAAGC$. The lower right-hand entry gives the edit distance, 6 in this example.

FIGURE 8.3   Locality of Computation. Each entry in the dynamic programming table only depends directly on three adjacent entries.

Masek and Patterson [16] give an algorithm with time performance of $O(n^2/\log n)$ for sequences of length n, provided that the sequence alphabet is finite and all costs are integers. However, for a particular implementation, they observe that their algorithm performs faster than the basic dynamic programming algorithm only for sequences of length 262,419 or longer.

Better time performance can be achieved by exploiting the inherent parallelism in Equation (8.2). One notable property of the dynamic programming recurrence is that each entry in the distance matrix depends on adjacent entries, as diagrammed in Figure 8.3. This property has been the basis for many parallel algorithms for computing the edit distance.

8.2 SYSTOLIC SEQUENCE COMPARISON

The locality of reference shown in Figure 8.3 can be exploited to produce systolic algorithms in which communication is limited to adjacent processors.

There are several ways to map the edit distance computation onto a linear systolic array. We describe two such mappings. Both exploit the locality of reference by computing the entries along each antidiagonal in parallel, as shown in Figure 8.4. The two mappings differ primarily in the data movement.

8.2.1 Bidirectional Array

The systolic architecture and data flow shown in Figure 8.5 were used in the design of P-NAC of Lipton and Lopresti [12], a custom VLSI chip for DNA sequence comparison. Each processing element (PE) computes the distances along a particular diagonal of the distance matrix. A block diagram of the PE and a listing of the algorithm it executes are shown in Figures 8.6 and 8.7, respectively.

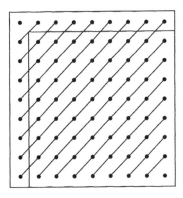

FIGURE 8.4   Parallel Computation of DP Distance Matrix. Entries lying on the same antidiagonal can be computed in parallel. The computation proceeds from the upper-left entry toward the lower-right.

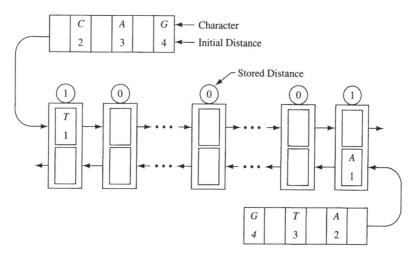

FIGURE 8.5   Data Flow through the Bidirectional Systolic Array. The source and target sequences are streamed through the array in opposite directions. A comparison is performed when a source character and a target character meet in a PE.

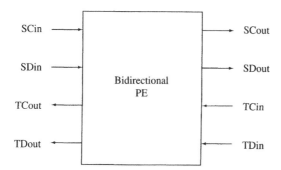

FIGURE 8.6   Processing Element for Bidirectional Array

loop
  if (SCin $\neq \emptyset$) **and** (TCin $\neq \emptyset$) **then**
$$\text{PEDist} \leftarrow \min \begin{cases} \text{PEDist}+\psi(\text{SCin,TCin}), \\ \text{TDin}+\psi(\text{SCin},\emptyset), \\ \text{SDin}+\psi(\emptyset,\text{TCin}) \end{cases}$$
  else-if (SCin $\neq \emptyset$) **then**
    PEDist $\leftarrow$ SDin
  else-if (TCin $\neq \emptyset$) **then**
    PEDist $\leftarrow$ TDin
  endif
  SCout $\leftarrow$ SCin
  TCout $\leftarrow$ TCin
  SDout $\leftarrow$ PEDist
  TDout $\leftarrow$ PEDist
endloop

FIGURE 8.7   Code Executed by Each PE in the Bidirectional Array

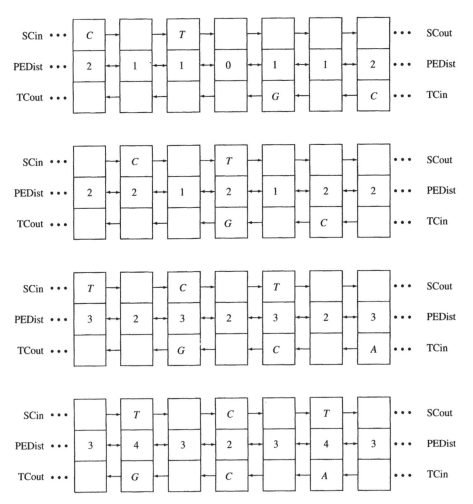

FIGURE 8.8 Trace of Bidirectional Array When Comparing the Sequences *TCTAGACC* and *GCATAAGC*

The source and target sequences enter the array on opposite ends and flow in opposing directions at the same speed. Successive characters in the source and target sequences are separated by a null character for proper timing. In addition, there is one distance stream associated with each character stream.[3] At each step, the contents of the streams represent the characters to be compared and the distances along one of the antidiagonals of the distance matrix. At the end of the computation, the resulting edit distance is transported out of the array on the distance streams.

A partial trace of the bidirectional array when comparing the sequences *TCTAGACC* and *GCATAAGC* is shown in Figure 8.8.

---

[3]In an actual implementation, these two unidirectional distance streams can be combined into one bidirectional stream, using one storage register instead of two. Here we keep the distance streams distinct for clarity.

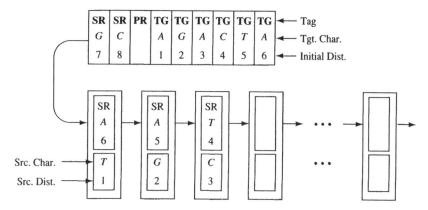

FIGURE 8.9 Data Flow through the Unidirectional Systolic Array. The source sequence is first loaded into the array. The target sequences are then streamed through the array. The tag acts as a simple instruction telling each PE how to process the incoming data. The SR tag instructs an empty PE to load the source character and distance from the input stream. The PR tag marks the end of the source stream. The TG tag signals a target character. Multiple source and target sequences can be carried on the input stream for uninterrupted pipelined processing.

In addition to the original P-NAC implementation, the bidirectional systolic array has been ported to the Splash 1 programmable logic array by Gokhale et al. [4] and Lopresti [14] and now to the Splash 2 programmable logic array. An extension of the bidirectional array to compute an alignment of two sequences in addition to the edit distance is described in Hoang [5] and Hoang and Lopresti [7].

Comparing sequences of lengths m and n requires at least $2\max(m + 1, n + 1)$ processors.[4] The number of steps required to compute the edit distance and to transport it out of the array is proportional to the length of the array.

In a typical database search, the same source sequence is compared against all target sequences in the database. With the bidirectional array, the source sequence must be recycled through the array for each target sequence in the database. At each computational step, at most half of the PEs are active. Also, the source and target sequences are both limited in length to half of the array's length (for one-pass operation). These properties of the bidirectional array lead to inefficiency for database search operations.

8.2.2 Unidirectional Array

We now describe a *unidirectional* systolic array that remedies the shortcomings of the bidirectional array. The architecture and data flow of the unidirectional array are shown in Figure 8.9. As the name suggests, data flows through the unidirectional array in one direction. The source sequence is loaded once and stored in the array starting from the leftmost PE. The target sequences are streamed through the array one at a time, separated by control characters. The tag stream identifies the sequences and

---

[4]With a fixed number of PEs, long sequences can be compared by using multiple passes, each pass computing a submatrix of the dynamic programming distance matrix, as done by Lopresti and Lipton [15].

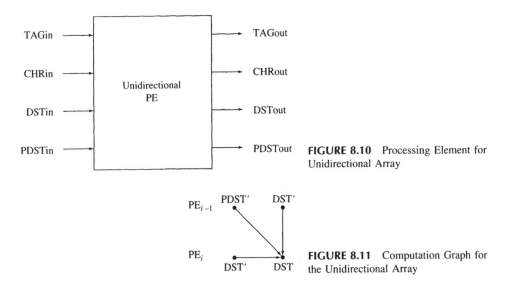

FIGURE 8.10 Processing Element for Unidirectional Array

FIGURE 8.11 Computation Graph for the Unidirectional Array

sends control information to the PEs. With the source sequence loaded and the target sequences streaming through, the array can achieve near 100 percent PE utilization. The length of the array determines the maximum length of the source sequence.[5] The target sequences, however, can be of any length. Together, these properties make the unidirectional array more suitable and efficient than the bidirectional array for database searches.

The unidirectional PE is diagrammed in Figure 8.10. In this configuration, each PE computes the distances in one row of the distance matrix. At each time step, the PEs compute the distances along a single antidiagonal in the distance matrix, as depicted in Figure 8.4. Each PE stores two distances, DST and PDST. Denoting the previously computed value of DST and PDST as DST$'$ and PDST$'$, respectively, the computation graph for the ith PE is shown in Figure 8.11. Compare this to Figure 8.3.

The algorithm executed by each PE in the unidirectional array is listed in Figure 8.12. As shown, the algorithm compares one source sequence to a single target sequence. With some additional code, comparisons can be performed on multiple source and target sequences. A partial trace of the unidirectional array when comparing the sequences $TCTAGACC$ and $GCATAAGC$ is shown in Figure 8.13.

A unidirectional array of length n can compare a source sequence of length at most n to a target sequence of length m in $O(n + m)$ steps.

8.3 IMPLEMENTATION

Both the bidirectional and unidirectional systolic arrays have been implemented on the Splash 2 programmable logic array, with versions for DNA and protein sequences.

---

[5]As with the bidirectional array, a source sequence longer than the array can be compared using multiple passes.

```
loop
  if (TAGin = SR) then
    if (SRCch = ∅) then
      SRCch ← CHRin
      CHRout ← ∅
      DSTout ← PDSTin
    else
      CHRout ← CHRin
    endif
    PDSTout ← PDSTin
  else-if (TAGin = PR) then
    if (SRCch = ∅) then
      DSTout ← PDSTin
    endif
    PDSTout ← DSTin
    CHRout ← CHRin
  else-if (TAGin = TG) then
    if (SRCch ≠ ∅) and (CHRin ≠ ∅) then
                    ⎧ PDSTout+ψ(SRCch,CHRin),
      DSTout ← min  ⎨ DSTin+ψ(SRCch,∅),
                    ⎩ DSTout+ψ(∅,CHRin)
    else-if (SRCch = ∅) then
      DSTout ← DSTin
    endif
    PDSTout ← DSTin
    CHRout ← CHRin
  endif
  TAGout ← TAGin
endloop
```

FIGURE 8.12   Code executed by each PE in the unidirectional array

8.3.1 Modular Encoding

An important optimization used in the implementation of both systolic arrays involves a modular encoding of the distances. With a fixed-length unsigned-integer data structure for the distances, there is a possibility for overflow when comparing long sequences. Lipton and Lopresti [12, 13] use a modular encoding scheme for the distances. In this scheme, only a few of the least significant bits of the distances need be computed. This technique works because the difference between adjacent entries in the dynamic programming matrix is bounded. For DNA sequences, using the simple cost function, only two bits are required for the encoding. For protein sequences, using a more complex cost function, only four bits are needed. The modular scheme reduces the design size, circumvents the overflow problem, and allows for easy scaling of the systolic array. To recover the integer distances, an accumulator, controlled by a simple state machine, is used at the output of the distance stream.

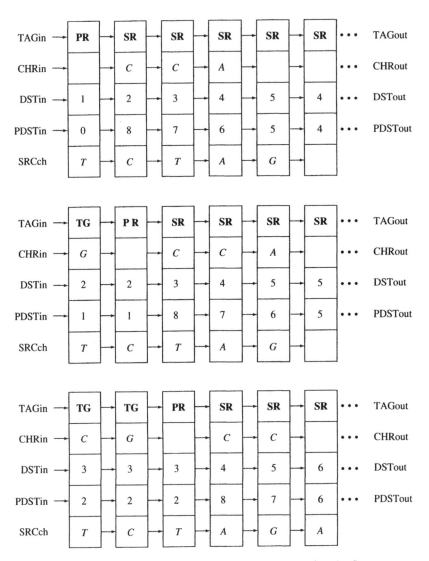

FIGURE 8.13 Trace of Unidirectional Array When Comparing the Sequences *TCTAGACC* and *GCATAAGC*

The accumulator is the only component that may be dependent on the length of the array.

8.3.2 Configurable Parameters

The designs of both systolic arrays are not specific to a particular alphabet or cost function. The sequence alphabet and cost function are defined in an VHDL configuration file and can be customized for a particular sequence comparison application. A change in the parameters, however, would require a recompilation of the VHDL code. Versions for comparing DNA and protein sequences have been implemented.

8.3.3 Bidirectional Array

For the DNA version of the bidirectional array, each of the 16 array FPGAs (X1 to X16) contains 24 PEs, making a total of 384 PEs in a one-board Splash 2 system. The protein version packs 64 PEs into a one-board Splash 2 system. Timing results from XDELAY give a theoretical maximum throughput of 5.5 million characters per second for the DNA version and 3.5 million characters per second for the protein version.

8.3.4 Unidirectional Array

In the DNA version of the unidirectional array, each of the 16 array FPGAs (X1 to X16) holds 14 PEs. In addition, the two interface FPGAs contain 12 PEs each, making a total of 248 PEs in a one-Array-Board Splash 2 system. Timing results from XDELAY give a theoretical maximum throughput of 12 million characters per second for the DNA version and 8 million characters per second for the protein version.

8.4 BENCHMARKS

In order to make a uniform comparison between Splash 2 and implementations of the dynamic programming algorithm on other architectures, we measure the performance of a solution in terms of the number of cells (entries in the DP distance table) updated per second (CUPS). When comparing two sequences of lengths n and m, a total of nm cells needs to be calculated.

The benchmark results for DNA sequence comparison are listed in Table 8.1. The values given for Splash 1 and Splash 2 are peak values, assuming that the length

TABLE 8.1 Benchmark of DNA Sequence Comparison (values are rounded to two decimal places)

Hardware	Specifics	CUPS
Splash 2	unidir; 16 boards	43,000M
Splash 2	bidir; 16 boards	34,000M
Splash 2	unidir; 1 board	3,000M
Splash 2	bidir; 1 board	2,100M
Splash 1	bidir; 746 PEs	370M
CM-2 [9]	64K nodes	150M
CM-5 [9]	32 nodes	33M
MP-1*	8K PEs	32M
Intel iPSC/860 [2]	32 nodes	12M
BSYS [8]	100 PEs	2.9M
SPARC 10/30GX	gcc -O2	1.2M
P-NAC [12]		1.1M
VAX 6620	VMS; CC	1.0M
SPARC 1	gcc -O2	0.87M
486DX-50 PC	DOS; gcc -O2	0.67M

*From personal communication with R.P. Hughey

of the sequences are the maximum for the given configuration and that pipeline delays are ignored. On uniprocessor machines, a straightforward implementation of the dynamic programming algorithm in the C language is used in the benchmark. On multiprocessor machines, a parallel implementation of the dynamic programming algorithm is used. Typically, a run consisting of 1,000 repetitions of a $1,000 \times 1,000$ comparison is used to calculate the CUPS.

8.5 DISCUSSION

From our experience, most of the development time was spent learning about the Splash 2 architecture, learning to program in VHDL, and discovering and taming the idiosyncrasies of the software development system. Overall, the results of the project were well worth the effort. Furthermore, the programmability and reprogrammability of Splash 2 allowed for experimentation and incremental refinements that could not have been afforded on a less flexible system. For example, several variations of the unidirectional PE were implemented, each in a matter of days.[6] In one variation of the unidirectional PE, the cost function is implemented as a lookup table, using the FPGA cells as RAM. The cost function is specified as part of the input stream. In another variation, the edit distance with a linear gap cost function is computed using the coupled recurrences given in Core et al. [1].

8.6 CONCLUSIONS

Two systolic arrays for computing the edit distance between two genetic sequences have been presented and their implementations on Splash 2 described. The bidirectional and unidirectional arrays have maximum throughputs of 5.5 and 12 million characters per second, respectively, for DNA database search. Compared to implementations of the dynamic programming algorithm on several contemporary workstations and minicomputers, the Splash 2 implementations promise to deliver several orders of magnitude better performance.

REFERENCES

[1] N.G. Core et al., "Supercomputers and Biological Sequence Comparison Algorithms," *Computers and Biomedical Research*, Vol. 22, No. 6, 1989, pp. 497–515.

[2] A.S. Deshpande, D.S. Richards, and W.R. Pearson, "A Platform for Biological Sequence Comparison on Parallel Computers," *CABIOS*, Vol. 7, No. 2, April 1991, p. 237.

[3] K.A. Frenkel, "The Human Genome Project and Informatics," *Comm. of the ACM*, Vol. 34, No. 11, 1991, pp. 41–51.

[4] M. Gokhale et al., "Building and Using a Highly Parallel Programmable Logic Array," *Computer*, Vol. 24, No. 1, Jan. 1991, pp. 81–89.

[5] D.T. Hoang, "A Systolic Array for the Sequence Alignment Problem," Tech. Report CS-92-22, Brown Univ., Providence, R.I., 1992.

---

[6]In comparison, the basic unidirectional PE, as described above, took several weeks to design, code, and test.

[6]   D.T. Hoang, "Searching Genetic Databases on Splash 2," *Proc. IEEE Workshop FPGAs for Custom Computing Machines*, CS Press, Los Alamitos, Calif., 1993, pp. 185–192.

[7]   D.T. Hoang and D.P. Lopresti, "FPGA Implementation of Systolic Sequence Alignment," in H. Grünbacher and R.W. Hartenstein, eds., *Field Programmable Gate Arrays: Architectures and Tools for Rapid Prototyping*, Springer-Verlag, Berlin, 1993, pp. 183–191.

[8]   R.P. Hughey, *Programmable Systolic Arrays*, PhD thesis CS-91-34, Brown Univ., Providence, R.I., 1991.

[9]   R. Jones, "Protein Sequence and Structure Comparison on Massively Parallel Computers, *Int'l J. of Supercomputer Applications*, Vol. 6, No. 2, 1992, pp. 138–146.

[10] E.S. Lander, R. Langridge, and D.M. Saccocio, "Computing in Molecular Biology: Mapping and Interpreting Biological Information," *Computer*, Vol. 24, No. 11, Nov. 1991, pp. 6–13.

[11] E.S. Lander, R. Langridge, and D.M. Saccocio, "Mapping and Interpreting Biological Information," *Comm. of the ACM*, Vol. 34, No. 11, 1991, pp. 32–39.

[12] R.J. Lipton and D.P. Lopresti, "A Systolic Array for Rapid String Comparison," *Proc. 1985 Chapel Hill Conf. VLSI*, Computer Science Press, Rockville, Md., 1985, pp. 363–376.

[13] D.P. Lopresti, *Discounts for Dynamic Programming with Applications in VLSI Processor Arrays*, PhD thesis, Princeton Univ., Princeton, N.J., 1987.

[14] D.P. Lopresti, "Rapid Implementation of a Genetic Sequence Comparator Using Field Programmable Logic Arrays," In C.H. Séquin, ed., *Advanced Research in VLSI*, MIT Press, Cambridge, Mass., 1991, pp. 138–152.

[15] D.P. Lopresti and R.J. Lipton, "Comparing Long Strings on a Short Systolic Array," Tech. Report CS-TR-026-86, Princeton Univ., Princeton, N.J., 1986.

[16] W.J. Masek and M.S. Paterson, "How to Compute String-Edit Distances Quickly," in *Time Warps, String Edits, and Macromolecules: The Theory and Practice of Sequence Comparison*, D. Sankoff and J. Kruskal, eds., Addison-Wesley, Reading, Mass., 1983, pp. 337–350.

[17] D. Sankoff and J. Kruskal, eds., *Time Warps, String Edits, and Macromolecules: The Theory and Practice of Sequence Comparison*, Addison-Wesley, Reading, Mass., 1983.

CHAPTER 9

Text Searching on Splash 2

Dan Pryor, Mark Thistle, Nabeel Shirazi[1]

9.1 INTRODUCTION

Very early in the process of designing and building Splash 2, a decision was made to concentrate on applications that emphasized computations or bit manipulations that were not entirely compatible with the processor architecture of traditional computers. The sequence comparison problem of the previous chapter is such a computation. Another, described in this chapter, is a hash-function-based pattern matching.

As the volume of information in the world continues to expand, text searching has become an important and necessary activity, and a fundamental part of text or bibliographic retrieval computations is the ability to recognize that a given keyword or set of keywords appears in a particular body of text. As mentioned by Salton [6], there are a number of commercial services that serve the needs of legal (LEXIS [1]), medical (MEDLARS [3]), and other communities of interest. These commercial services rely on inverted file methods of searching documents and abstracts. For text that is reasonably static or keyword groups that are reasonably static (terms used, for example, by a professional society to describe the subfields within its discipline), the best way to match words against text is indeed to have the text indexed, and this is feasible. For other text search applications, news story data, for example, an index does not exist and a full text search must sometimes be done as shown by Purcell and Mar [5] and Stanfill and Kahle [7].

---

[1]A version of this chapter appeared as Pryor et al. [4] and is used with permission.

As with the DNA sequence comparison problem, several versions of special-purpose hardware, including ASICs, have been manufactured. Inevitably, these provide a higher processing performance than an FPGA-based system as described here. However, as with any special-purpose machine, flexibility or adaptability of the hardware can be a serious issue. Our computation is hash-based, and the success is probabilistic depending both on the hash functions and on the text data. Thus, one could expect to want to vary the hash function depending on the data to be searched. With the Splash 2 implementation described here, this is relatively easy; with an ASIC, this could be much harder. Further, the cost of developing an ASIC may not be justifiable if the number of planned units is relatively small.

Our text searching application tests a stream of words for inclusion and/or exclusion in a dictionary, a predetermined list of keywords. In the Splash 2 implementation, words are streamed through a series of FPGAs, each configured to implement a different hash function. These hash functions are set up to use a single bit on each attached memory module to represent the inclusion of a word in the search list. The 2^{22} bits of memory attached to each FPGA are quite sufficient for many uses. The English language, for example, has about 2^{18} words, which would allow a sparse scattering of words throughout the memory address space. The sparser the representation of the keyword list in the memory, the lower the probability of a false hit. Cascading the independent hash functions multiplies these low probabilities, resulting in an extremely low probability that a word not in the keyword list is reported as a match.

Two approaches are studied, one that sends a single byte of text through the system on each clock tick and one that sends two bytes per tick. In both of these algorithms, the Splash 2 system is used as a linear array (no use is made of the crossbar) in which the data is pipelined from the Interface Board through each chip in the Splash board and back to the Interface Board. The results of the hash function evaluations are successively AND-ed into an indicator bit as the data travels through the array. The indicator bit at the end of the array denotes success (a hit) or failure of the search for the corresponding word. The locations of the hits in the data stream are recorded by the final FPGA on the Interface Board.

9.2 THE TEXT SEARCHING ALGORITHM

The original motivation behind implementing a dictionary search algorithm on Splash 1 was that the predicted performance on a Splash-based system matched requirements of real-world problems and exceeded general-purpose solutions. The Splash 1 implementation was I/O bound and ran at 4 megacharacters/second. Due to the improved I/O performance on Splash 2, a Splash 2 8-bit implementation has been created and demonstrated. This section describes the algorithm used and the first of two approaches implemented.

The text processing in the Splash 2 system can be thought of as a pipelined operation on a stream of characters (bytes). There are three major stages to the pipeline, with the middle stage divided into a series of nearly identical substages. The first stage of the algorithm takes place in FPGA XL on the Interface Board. (See Figures 2.3, 2.4, and 2.5.) In this FPGA, the data is read in, one 32-bit word per clock tick, and sent out over the SIMD Bus at the rate of one 8-bit byte per tick. The job of XL is to coordinate the splitting of the data words into characters that are fed through the Array Board one at a time, as well as to set tag bits to perform whatever bookkeeping is required with respect to end-of-data conditions, and such. Each data byte is assumed to be part of a valid dictionary word, and XL sets a tag bit to indicate this assumption. As the byte progresses through the Array Board, this condition may be modified by successive hash function evaluations.

The second stage of the algorithm takes place on the Array Board, where the bulk of the work is done. This stage is made up of a series of nearly identical stages, each occupying a separate FPGA, with the communication between them being in pipeline fashion. Upon receiving a data character from its leftward neighbor, the jth FPGA Xj first detects an end-of-word condition by deciding whether the character is alphabetic or nonalphabetic. If the received character is alphabetic, the hash function is updated using this character. If the character is nonalphabetic, and if the previous character was alphabetic, an end-of-word condition has occurred and a zero in the memory bit pointed to by the hash register indicates the word is not in the dictionary. When the memory is read, the hash register is reset to all zeros to get ready for the next word, which begins when the next alphabetic character is received. When the memory is read, the bit indicating a hit or miss is AND-ed to the corresponding bit passed from $X(j-1)$ and passed on to $X(j+1)$ as one of the tag bits. In this way, the tag bit indicates whether all hash functions produced a hit, or whether at least one of them resulted in a miss. A word is declared to be in the dictionary only if all hash function evaluations result in hits.

The final stage of the algorithm takes place in the FPGA labeled XR on the Interface Board. This FPGA contains a 32-bit counter that counts the number of characters processed and decoder logic that determines when to write out the value of the counter. A block diagram of this implementation is shown in Figure 9.1.

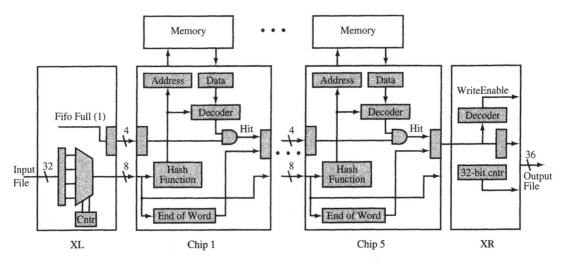

FIGURE 9.1 Text Matching Implementation

9.3 DESCRIPTION OF THE SINGLE-BYTE SPLASH PROGRAM

The design reads 8-bit ASCII characters from an input file until the end of the file. The word boundaries are then found by detecting the nonalphabetic characters within the input stream. Each word is compared to a user dictionary and is marked as a hit, meaning the word is present in the dictionary, or a miss, meaning the word is not in the dictionary. The word's location is then recorded along with the corresponding hit/miss flag to an output file. Instead of doing a direct comparison of the input word to the user dictionary, a series of hashing functions is used to do the comparison. The hashing function maps each word to a pseudo-random value that is then used to reference a lookup table, indicating if a given word is in the user dictionary. The lookup tables are generated by passing the user dictionary through the same hashing functions that are used at runtime. This is a one-time operation and does not necessarily have to be performed on the Array Board.

The algorithm used is similar to the Splash 1 version implemented by McHenry [2]. First, a hash table is produced for each function and then loaded into the Array Board's memories. The memories are 256K × 16 bits, and each of the four megabits is used to indicate a hit or a miss. A 22-bit hashing function value, which is generated in an FPGA, is used to address the four megabits of the FPGA's memory. During runtime a hash function value is determined for each word of the input stream. For example, in Figure 9.2 the word "the" is passed through the hash function, and the resulting hash value is shown.

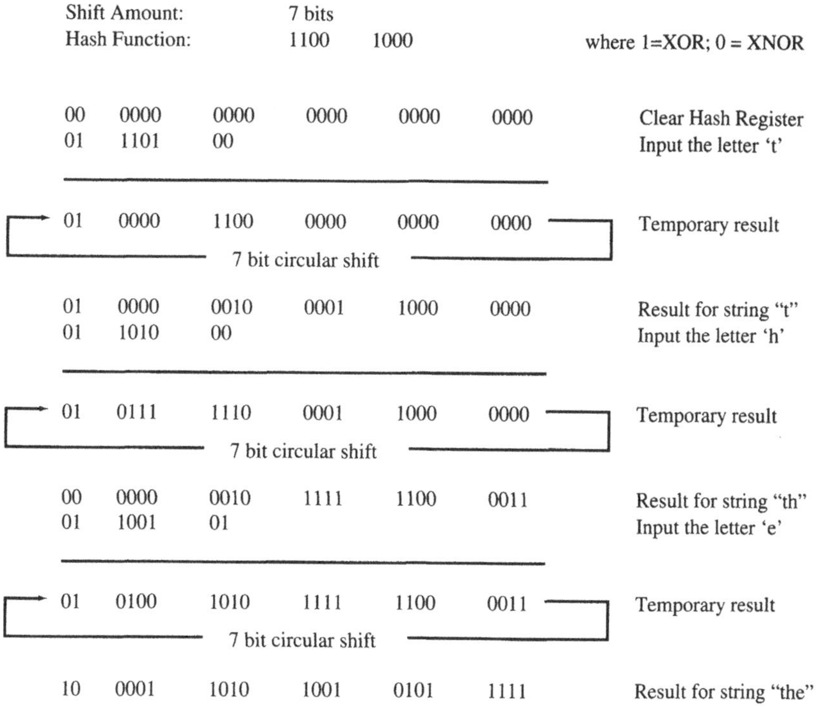

```
Shift Amount:              7 bits
Hash Function:             1100    1000            where 1=XOR; 0 = XNOR


      00   0000   0000   0000   0000   0000        Clear Hash Register
      01   1101   00                               Input the letter 't'
     ┌───────────────────────────────────────┐
  ┌─ 01   0000   1100   0000   0000   0000 ──┐    Temporary result
  │   └──────────── 7 bit circular shift ────┘
  │
      01   0000   0010   0001   1000   0000        Result for string "t"
      01   1010   00                               Input the letter 'h'
     ┌───────────────────────────────────────┐
  ┌─ 01   0111   1110   0001   1000   0000 ──┐    Temporary result
  │   └──────────── 7 bit circular shift ────┘
  │
      00   0000   0010   1111   1100   0011        Result for string "th"
      01   1001   01                               Input the letter 'e'
     ┌───────────────────────────────────────┐
  ┌─ 01   0100   1010   1111   1100   0011 ──┐    Temporary result
  │   └──────────── 7 bit circular shift ────┘
  │
      10   0001   1010   1001   0101   1111        Result for string "the"
```

FIGURE 9.2   22-Bit Hashing Example

TABLE 9.1   Hashing Functions Used

Function Number	Shift	Mask	Splash 1	%	Splash 2	%
1	7	C8	1138	4.5	1127	4.5
2	5	A5	771	3.1	422	1.7
3	3	8C	1636	6.5	1461	5.8
4	4	AE	1035	4.1	654	2.6
5	5	C8	924	3.7	507	2.0

The five hashing functions used are listed in Table 9.1. The shift and mask values of these hash functions were chosen by picking a shift value that is relatively prime to 22 and a mask value that has approximately the same number of ones as zeros. These functions were then checked for randomness by hashing a 25,261-word dictionary and recording the number of duplicate hits. A comparison of duplicate hits produced by a 20-bit hash function (used in the Splash 1 version) versus a 22-bit hash function (used in the Splash 2 version) was performed, and the results are shown in Table 9.1.

This algorithm was implemented and tested on Splash 2. The XL chip of the Interface Board is designed to read in a 32-bit word on every fourth clock cycle. The 32-bit word is then divided into four 8-bit values and passed onto the first FPGA of the Array Board. FPGAs X1 through X5 on the Array Board compute the hash functions and access their memory to check if the word is in its lookup table. FPGAs X6 through X16 of the array are essentially unused, passing data from the left side of the FPGA to the right side. From FPGA X16 of the array, the data are passed into FPGA XR of the Interface Board. This FPGA contains a 32-bit counter that counts the number of characters processed and decoder logic that determines when to write out the value of the counter.

9.4 TIMINGS, DISCUSSION

The text search program was functionally debugged using the Splash system simulator. The functionally correct design was then synthesized to determine the timing information for each chip. Due to the simplicity of the XL chip design, when this chip was synthesized, the maximum clock rate was found to be 25 MHz. The XR chip design includes a 32-bit counter, and this was the primary reason why the chip could run at only 14 MHz after synthesizing the first time. This problem was fixed by using two 16-bit Hard Macro Counters provided by Xilinx, and the new version of the design now has a maximum clock speed of 17 MHz. The chips that perform the hashing function are the slowest, and thus dictate the clock speed of the entire application. The maximum clock rate for FPGAs X1 through X5 was 16 MHz. Since the I/O speed into the Splash 2 system is faster than 4 megawords/second, this application can process data at 16 megacharacters/second.

9.5 OUTLINE OF THE 16-BIT APPROACH

Since the Splash 2 system is capable of receiving more than a single byte of data per clock tick, we decided to investigate the possibility of extending the algorithm discussed above to one that processed 16 bits per tick. In order to use the hash functions in the Array Board in a way similar to the method of the single-byte algorithm, we need to have some concept of a nonalphabetic 16-bit "superbyte" that signals the time to do the memory access and reset the hash function. But in general, nonalphabetic characters do not come two at a time and on two-byte boundaries. Viewing 16 bits at a time, or two consecutive characters from the text stream, therefore involves considering a number of cases that are not seen in the single-byte algorithm. And in order that the pipeline nature of the algorithm for the FPGAs on the Array Board be preserved, we condition the data stream on the Interface Board using the XL chip. In some cases, a 16-bit zero must be inserted into the outgoing stream in order to play the role played by the single nonalphabetic character in the 8-bit algorithm. That is, the FPGAs on the Array Board must receive a 16-bit superbyte that is easily tested for, contains no important data, and signals the end of the accumulated word of text. The distinct cases that must be considered by XL for each new byte pair received are:

1. The new pair consists of two alphabetic characters, and the preceding character was alphabetic. In this case, the data stream is in the middle of a word, so this byte pair is passed on to the Array Board without special action. This is the case that is most similar to the 8-bit case described in Section 4.
2. The new pair consists of a nonalphabetic character followed by an alphabetic character. This case splits into two subcases: the preceding superbyte sent was zero, and the preceding superbyte was nonzero. If zero, then the end of the previous text word has already been signaled by the sending of the zero superbyte. Therefore the nonalphabetic character is changed to an 8-bit zero and sent to the Array Board. If the last superbyte sent to the Array Board was nonzero, then XL must insert a zero superbyte into the Array Board data stream to indicate the end of a text word before sending the new byte pair.
3. The new pair consists of an alphabetic character followed by a nonalphabetic character. In this case, we have an end-of-word condition and must send out first the new pair and then a 16-bit zero to signal the end-of-word.
4. The new pair consists of two nonalphabetic characters. Both bytes are replaced by zero bytes and sent to the Array Board, since the Array Board must receive something on each clock tick, even if it contains no useful data.

Because a text word can begin at either an odd or an even position in the data stream, and the hash functions can only be evaluated 16 bits at a time, there must be two versions of each dictionary word represented in the hash table. For text words with an odd number of characters, we have chosen to represent the two versions by appending either a leading blank character or a trailing blank character to the word. Dictionary words having an even number of characters are represented first by including only the characters in the word and second by attaching both a leading blank and a trailing blank. Thus, a further task that must be performed is the substitution of nonalphabetic characters with blank characters.

This effective doubling of the dictionary size also means that either our probability of a false hit will increase or that we will have to use more FPGAs in the design. For normal English text, this is not a serious problem, as we have, say, 2^{18} dictionary words (making $\approx 2^{19}$ 1s in each hash table). Hence the probability of a false hit in any one hash table will be about $2^{19}/2^{22} = 2^{-3}$. With 16 FPGAs, this yields a false hit probability of about 2^{-48}, or about 10^{-15}—not as low as that of the single-byte method, but certainly acceptable for many situations.

Since the bulk of the workload was shifted from the Array Board to the Interface Board, in particular to the XL chip, it is no surprise to see that the timing of this application is now limited by the timing of XL. Our XL design has been analyzed and processed by the placement and routing programs to determine a clock speed of 13.6 MHz. This is almost as fast as the single-byte method, but would not produce a near doubling of throughput, since we must adjust our timing estimates to account for the insertion of zero superbytes into the text stream. For example, ordinary English text averages about 4.7 characters per word [6]. So, with this figure as a guideline, it is safe to expect that this design could process around 20 million characters of text data per second.

9.6 CONCLUSIONS

We have presented two versions of a dictionary search application on the Splash 2 system. These results are encouraging in that they show the Splash 2 design to be quite fast as well as relatively easy to program. We believe that there are many other applications where Splash or a system similar to Splash can be exploited for its cost/performance benefits over large general-purpose machines and for its flexibility advantages over conventional special-purpose (ASIC-based) devices. We believe that, while Splash-like architectures will certainly never replace general-purpose or special-purpose machines, they do provide effective solutions in selected application areas.

REFERENCES

[1] Mead Data Central, *LEXIS Quick Reference*, Mead Data Central, New York, 1976.

[2] J.T. McHenry and A. Kopser, "Keyword Searching on Splash," tech. report, SRC, Bowie, Md., 1991.

[3] Nat'l Library of Medicine, *MEDLARS, The Computerized Literature Retrieval Services of the Nat'l Library of Medicine*, Publication NIH 79-1286, U.S. Dept. of Health, Education, and Welfare, Washington, D.C., 1979.

[4] D.V. Pryor, M.R. Thistle, and N. Shirazi, "Text Searching on Splash 2," *Proc. IEEE Workshop FPGAs for Custom Computing Machines*, CS Press, Los Alamitos, Calif., 1993, pp. 172–178.

[5] G. Purcell and D. Mar, "SCOUT: Information Retrieval from Full-Text Medical Literature," Knowledge Systems Lab. Report KSL-92-35, Stanford Univ., Palo Alto, Calif., 1992.

[6] G. Salton, *Automatic Text Processing*, Addison-Wesley, Reading, Mass., 1989.

[7] C. Stanfill and B. Kahle, "Parallel Free-Text Search on the Connection Machine System," *Comm. of the ACM*, Vol. 29, No. 12, 1986, pp. 1229–1239.

CHAPTER 10

Fingerprint Matching on Splash 2

Nalini K. Ratha, Anil K. Jain, & Diane T. Rover

10.1 INTRODUCTION

Fingerprint-based identification is the most popular biometric technique used in automatic personal identification [7]. Law enforcement agencies use it routinely for criminal identification. Now, it is also being used in several other applications such as access control for high-security installations, credit card usage verification, and employee identification [7]. The main reason for the popularity of fingerprints as a form of identification is that the fingerprint of a person is unique and remains invariant through age. The law enforcement agencies have developed a standardized method for manually matching rolled fingerprints and latent or partial fingerprints (lifted from the scene of a crime). However, the manual matching of fingerprints is a highly tedious task for the following reasons. As the features used for matching are rather small compared to the image size, a human expert often has to use a magnifying glass to get a better view of the fingerprint impression. The matching complexity is a function of the size of the fingerprint database, and a typical database contains a very large number (the order of millions) of fingerprint records. Even though the standard Henry formula [6] for fingerprint recognition can be used to reduce the search, manual matching can take several days in some cases. These problems can be easily overcome by automating the fingerprint-based identification process.

A fingerprint is characterized by ridges and valleys. The ridges and valleys alternate, flowing locally in a constant direction (see Figure 10.1). A closer analysis of the fingerprint reveals that the ridges (or the valleys) exhibit anomalies of various kinds, such as ridge bifurcations, ridge endings, short ridges, and ridge crossovers.

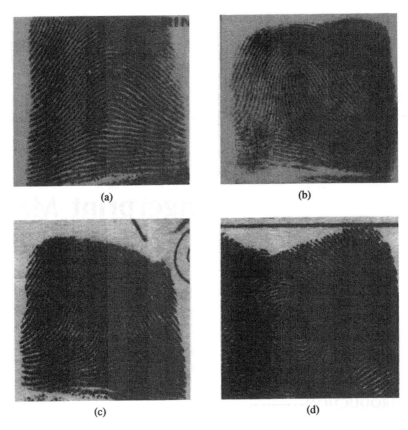

FIGURE 10.1 Gray-level Fingerprint Images of Different Types of Patterns: (a) Arch; (b) Left loop; (c) Right loop; (d) Whorl

Eighteen different types of fingerprint features have been enumerated in the booklet prepared by the Federal Bureau of Investigation [2]. Collectively, these features are called *minutiae*. For automatic feature extraction and matching, the set of fingerprint features is restricted to two types of minutiae: ridge endings and ridge bifurcations. Ridge endings and bifurcations are shown in Figure 10.2. We do not make any distinction between these two feature types because data acquisition conditions such as inking, finger pressure, and lighting can easily change one type of feature into another. More complex fingerprint features can be expressed as a combination of these two basic features. For example, an enclosure can be considered as a collection of two bifurcations, and a short ridge can be considered as a collection of a pair of ridge endings. These features are shown in Figure 10.3.

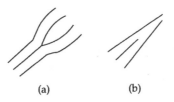

FIGURE 10.2 Two Commonly Used Fingerprint Features: (a) Ridge bifurcation; (b) Ridge ending

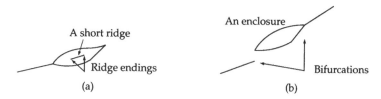

FIGURE 10.3   Complex Fingerprint Features as a Combination of Simple Features:
(a) Short ridge; (b) Enclosure

In the area of criminal identification, there are two types of fingerprint matching requirements: rolled fingerprint matching and latent fingerprint matching. These are characterized by the information available for matching. In the case of rolled fingerprint matching, the suspect is cooperative and all of the suspect's fingerprints (called rolled fingerprints) are used for identification. The objective is to verify the suspect's identity. In the second case, latent fingerprints, lifted from the scene of a crime, are characterized by smudgy, unclear, and partial impressions. Obviously, matching of latent fingerprints is more difficult. For rolled fingerprints, the Henry classification scheme is used, whereas for latent fingerprints, Batley's formula [4] is used. In both cases, a (human) fingerprint expert performs the detailed matching.

In the last three decades, substantial efforts have been made to automate fingerprint identification. These efforts can be grouped into the following two categories.

- *Semi-automatic*
  The computer is used to match the Henry formula of the fingerprints containing minor variations in ridge counts. A list of records that have similar Henry formula is obtained. However, due to the limitations of the Henry formula in disambiguating a large collection of records, this system is not very popular.

- *Automatic*
  An image processing system is used to automatically extract features from a digital image of the fingerprint. A query fingerprint is matched to a stored database of fingerprints based on the extracted features.

A survey of commercially available automatic fingerprint identification systems (AFIS) is available in the book edited by Lee and Gaensslen [6]. Well-known manufacturers of automatic fingerprint identification systems include NEC Information Systems, De La Rue Printrak, North American Morpho, and Logica.

The high computational requirement of matching is primarily due to the following three factors: (i) a query fingerprint is usually of poor quality; (ii) the fingerprint database is very large; and (iii) structural distortion of the fingerprint images requires complex matching algorithms.

We consider the task of matching rolled fingerprints against a database of rolled fingerprints. Typically, the number of records with which a query fingerprint image needs to be matched is very large ($\approx 10^6$). The matching process is repeated over the records in the database. It is also not uncommon to have hundreds of match queries per day, which need to be answered within a short (say, a few hours) time period. This imposes a heavy computational load on the matching system. Even if a single match takes, say, one millisecond of CPU time, matching against a database of one million fingerprints would require a total of 10^3 seconds of CPU time. If we have to process 100 queries per day, we would need 10^5 seconds or 27.78 hours of CPU time alone, not including the I/O time in reading the fingerprints from the database.

In order to provide a reasonable response time for each query, commercial systems use dedicated hardware accelerators or application-specific integrated circuits (ASICs). While application-specific architectures and ASICs have been designed to meet the computing requirements of complex image processing tasks, such designs have the following two major limitations: (i) once fabricated, they are difficult to modify; and (ii) the cost of building special-purpose application accelerators is very expensive for low-volume applications. Both of these limitations have been the driving force behind the design of custom computing machines (CCMs) using reconfigurable logic arrays known as field-programmable gate arrays (FPGAs). An attached processor built with FPGAs can overcome the two limitations noted above. High performance is achieved with FPGAs by exploiting an important principle: most of the processing time of a compute-intensive job is spent within a small portion of its execution code [3], and if an architecture can provide efficient execution support for the frequently executed code, then the overall performance can be improved substantially. Portions of the matching algorithm have been identified for implementation on Splash 2, leaving the remainder to be implemented using software on the host.

The goal of this chapter is threefold. First, it describes a successful application using Splash 2. Second, we demonstrate that a suitable mapping of an algorithm to a given architecture results in excellent performance. Third, we illustrate how FPGAs can facilitate this mapping process without sacrificing speed and flexibility. In fact, FPGAs offer greater flexibilty since the hardware is customized to meet the requirements of the algorithm.

This chapter is organized as follows. In Section 2, a brief introduction to pattern recognition systems is given, followed by definition of the terminology used in fingerprint matching, and introduction of various stages in an AFIS. Section 3 briefly reviews the Splash 2 architecture and its programming paradigm. The fingerprint matching algorithm and its computational requirement are briefly presented in Section 4. The hardware-software design is presented in Section 5. The hardware component of the parallel algorithm has been simulated using the Splash simulator. The results of simulation and synthesis are discussed in Section 6. The synthesized logic has been executed on a set of actual fingerprints. For measuring execution speed, a synthetic database of 10,000 fingerprints has been created from 100 real fingerprints. The execution speed of the matching module is analyzed in Section 7, followed by conclusions in Section 8.

10.2 BACKGROUND

This section is devoted to an introduction to pattern recognition systems, some basic definitions with respect to fingerprints, and automatic fingerprint identification systems (AFIS).

10.2.1 Pattern Recognition Systems

Pattern recognition techniques are used to classify or describe complex patterns or objects by means of some measured properties or features. A pattern is an entity, vaguely defined, that could be given a name. A speech waveform, a person's face, and a piston head are examples of patterns. The goals of pattern recognition are to (i) assign a pattern to a heretofore unknown class of patterns (clustering) or (ii) identify a pattern as a member of an already known class (classification). Two examples of the recognition problem are identifying a suspect in a criminal case based on fingerprints, and finding defects in a printed circuit board.

A pattern recognition system (PRS) classifies an object into one of several predefined classes. The input to a PRS is a set of N measurements represented by an N-dimensional vector called a pattern vector. A PRS can be used to completely automate the decision-making process without any human intervention. A PRS requires data acquisition via some sensors, data representation, and data analysis or classification. The data are usually either in the form of pictures, as in the case of fingerprint matching, or one-dimensional time signals, as in the case of speech recognition. Although these images or signals can be interpreted, analyzed, or classified by trained human operators, pattern recognition systems can provide more reliable and faster analysis, often at a lower cost.

The design of a PRS involves the following three steps:

- Sensing
- Representation
- Decision making

The problem domain influences the choice of sensor, representation, and decision making model. An ideal representation is characterized by the following desirable properties; it is

1. Provided with discriminatory information at several levels of resolution (detail)
2. Easily computable
3. Amenable to automated matching algorithms
4. Stable and invariant to noise and distortions
5. Efficient and compact

The compactness property of a representation often constrains its discriminating power.

The pattern recognition problem is difficult because various sources of noise distort the patterns, and often there exists a substantial amount of variability among the patterns belonging to the same category [5]. For example, the character 'A' written by different people looks different, though we assign the same class label 'A' to all of them. Hence, it is not appropriate to use the raw pattern vector for classification. Invariant features that characterize a set of patterns are used to represent a class of patterns. Several issues arise, such as what features should be used and how they should be extracted reliably. The features of a pattern are the input to a classification stage. The challenge in designing a recognition system is in extraction of features that can tolerate the intra-class variations and still possess the inter-class discriminating power. If the extracted features have sufficient discriminating power, then the decision making stage is simple. Conversely, a sophisticated decision making stage can compensate for an unreliable feature extraction stage. In practice, we never have a noiseless input pattern, an ideal representation, perfect feature extraction, or robust decision maker. Imperfections in any of these stages may result in classification error. The goal of a pattern recognition system is to minimize the classification error. Many successful pattern recognition systems have been built in the area of document analysis, medical diagnosis, and fingerprint identification. A large number of books and survey papers have been written on pattern recognition. Readers interested in more details are referred to [5].

10.2.2 Terminology

The structural features that are commonly extracted from the gray-level input fingerprint image are ridge bifurcations and ridge endings. Each of the features has three components, namely, the x-coordinate, the y-coordinate, and the local ridge direction at the feature location, as shown in Figure 10.4. Many other features that have been used for fingerprint matching are derived from this basic three-dimensional feature vector [1].

Definitions of some relevant fingerprint-related terms are given below. Readers interested in more details are referred to [2].

- Fingerprint image: A digitized image of a fingerprint impression usually containing 512×512 pixels and 256 gray levels.
- Fingerprint card: A paper card with a provision to record impressions of all 10 fingers of a person, including other textual details (such as name, sex, and age) useful for identification.

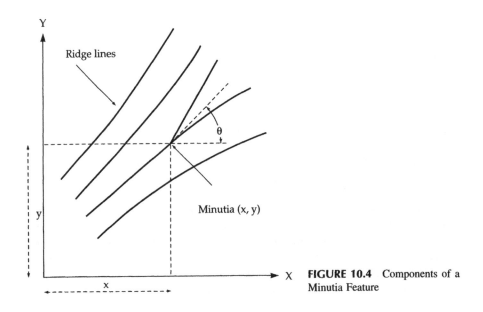

FIGURE 10.4 Components of a Minutia Feature

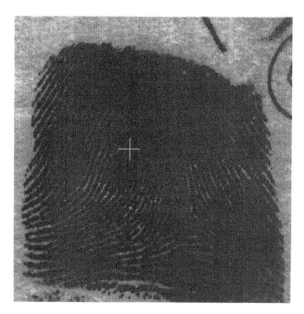

FIGURE 10.5   A Core Point Marked on a Gray-level Fingerprint

- Pattern area: The area of the image where the fingerprint pattern is located.
- Ridge: A black line in a fingerprint image. See Figure 10.1.
- Valley: A white line in a fingerprint image. See Figure 10.1.
- Ridge bifurcation point: A point where a ridge branches into two ridges. See Figure 10.2(a).
- Ridge end point: A point where a ridge stops flowing. See Figure 10.2(b).
- Minutia: A ridge ending or bifurcation point.
- Classification: Based on the ridge flow type, the process of categorizing fingerprints into one of the following five classes: (i) arch, (ii) loop, (iii) whorl, (iv) double loop, and (v) accidental. The first three fingerprint classes are shown in Figure 10.1.
- Matching: The process of comparing a pair of fingerprints based on their minutiae feature sets. The AFIS systems usually determine a list of probables (possible matches) from the database, often sorted on a matching score that indicates the degree of match.
- Core point: For whorls, loops, and double loops, the core point is defined as the topmost point on the innermost ridge, assuming the fingerprint is oriented. See Figure 10.5.

10.2.3 Stages in AFIS

An AFIS is a pattern recognition system for fingerprint matching. A typical AFIS consists of various processing stages as shown in Figure 10.6. For the purpose of automation, a suitable representation of fingerprints is essential. Clearly, the raw digital image (set of pixels) of a fingerprint itself does not meet the requirements of an ideal representation described earlier. Hence, high-level structural features are extracted from the fingerprint image for the purpose of representation and matching.

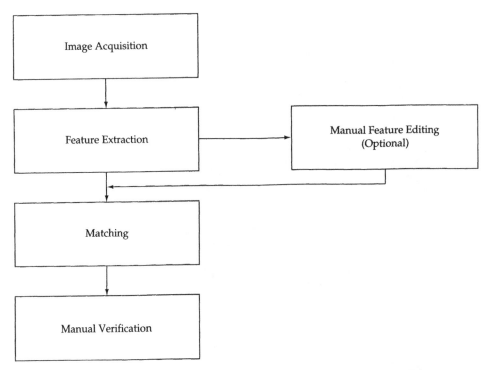

FIGURE 10.6   Stages in an Automatic Fingerprint Identification System (AFIS)

The commercially available fingerprint systems typically use ridge bifurcations and ridge endings as features (see Figure 10.2). Because of the large size of the fingerprint database and the noisy fingerprints encountered in practice, it is very difficult to achieve a reliable one-to-one matching in all test cases. Therefore, the commercial systems provide a ranked list of possible matches (usually the top 10 matches) that are then verified by a human expert. The matching stage uses the position and orientation of these features and the total number of such features. As a result, the accuracy of feature extraction has a strong impact on the overall accuracy of fingerprint matching. Reliable and robust features can simplify the matching algorithm and obviate the manual verification stage.

One of the main problems in extracting structural features is the presence of noise in the fingerprint image. Commonly used methods for taking fingerprint impressions involve applying a uniform layer of ink on the finger and rolling the finger on paper. This leads to the following problems. Smudgy areas in the image are created by overinked areas of the finger, while breaks in ridges are created by underinked areas. Additionally, the elastic nature of the skin can change the positional characteristics of the fingerprint features depending on the pressure applied on the fingers. Though inkless methods for taking fingerprint impressions are now available, these methods still suffer from the positional shifting caused by the skin elasticity. The AFIS used for criminal identification poses yet another problem. A noncooperative attitude of suspects or criminals in providing the impressions leads to smearing parts of the fingerprint impression. Thus, noisy features are inevitable in real fingerprint images.

The matching module must be robust to overcome the noisy features generated by the feature extraction module.

The functioning of an AFIS can be described starting with the input stage. A gray-scale fingerprint image is obtained using a scanner or a camera. Recently, inkless methods have been used for this stage [7]. The input image needs enhancement before further processing can be done. This stage involves image processing techniques to minimize noise and enhance image contrast. A feature extraction stage locates the minutiae points in the enhanced image. Often, it is difficult to extract minutiae reliably from noisy inputs. In such cases, a human fingerprint expert interactively updates the location of the minutiae. The set of minutiae forms the input to a matcher. The matcher reads fingerprint features from the database and matches these with the query fingerprint feature set. It outputs a list of probables from the database in order of their degree of match. The system output is verified by the human expert to arrive at the final decision for each query fingerprint.

10.3 SPLASH 2 ARCHITECTURE AND PROGRAMMING MODELS

We review the major components of the Splash 2 system that are used by our fingerprint matching algorithm. (For details, refer to the chapters on Splash 2 architecture and programming.)

Each Splash 2 processing board has 16 Xilinx 4010s as Processing Elements (PEs X1–X16) in addition to a seventeenth Xilinx 4010 (X0) that controls the data flow into the processor board. Each PE has 512 KB of memory. The Sun SPARC-station host can read/write this memory. The PEs are connected through a crossbar that is programmed by X0. There is a 36-bit linear data path (SIMD Bus) running through all the PEs. The PEs can read data either from their respective memory or from any other PE. A broadcast path also exists by suitably programming X0.

The Splash 2 system supports several models of computation, including PEs executing a single instruction on multiple data (SIMD mode) and PEs executing multiple instructions on multiple data (MIMD mode). It can also execute the same or different instructions on single data by receiving data through the global broadcast bus. The most common mode of operation is systolic, in which the SIMD Bus is used for data transfer. Also, individual memory available with each PE is used to conveniently store temporary results and tables.

To program Splash 2, we need to program each of the PEs (X1–X16), the crossbar, and the host interface. The crossbar sets the communication paths for any arbitrary pattern of communication between PEs. In case the crossbar is used, X0 needs to be programmed. The host interface handles data transfers in and out of the Splash 2 board.

10.4 FINGERPRINT MATCHING ALGORITHM

The feature extraction process takes the input fingerprint gray-level image and extracts the minutiae features described in Section 1, making no efforts to distinguish between the two categories (ridge endings and ridge bifurcations). Figure 10.7 shows

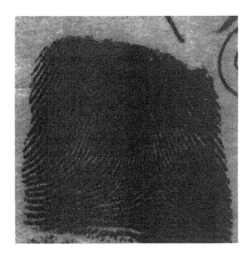 

FIGURE 10.7 Feature Extraction. (a) A gray-scale image of a fingerprint; (b) its skeleton with features

a gray-scale fingerprint image and its skeleton image where these features are marked. In this section, an algorithm for matching rolled fingerprints against a database of rolled fingerprints is presented. A query fingerprint is matched with every fingerprint in the database, discarding candidates whose matching scores are below a user-specified threshold. Rolled fingerprints usually contain a large number of minutiae (between 50 and 100). Since the main focus of this chapter is on parallelizing the matching algorithm, we assume that the features have been extracted from the fingerprint images and the important information is available. In particular, we assume that the core point of the fingerprint is known and that the fingerprints are oriented properly.

10.4.1 Minutia Matching

Matching a query and database fingerprint is equivalent to matching their minutiae sets. Each query fingerprint minutia is examined to determine whether there is a corresponding database fingerprint minutia. Two minutiae are said to be *paired* or *matched* if their components (x, y, θ) are equal within some tolerance after registration, which is the process of aligning the two sets of minutiae along a common core point (see section 4.2 for precise definitions). Three situations arise as shown in Figure 10.8.

1. A database fingerprint minutia matches the query fingerprint minutia in all the components (paired minutiae);
2. A database fingerprint minutia matches the query fingerprint minutia in the x and y coordinates, but does not match in the direction (minutiae with unmatched angle);
3. No database fingerprint minutia matches the query fingerprint minutia (unmatched minutia).

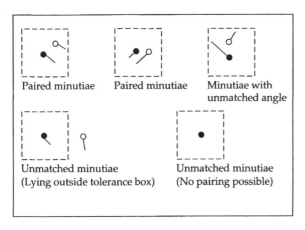

Paired minutiae   Paired minutiae   Minutiae with
                                       unmatched angle

Unmatched minutiae   Unmatched minutiae
(Lying outside tolerance box)   (No pairing possible)

⌐¬ Tolerance box
● Query fingerprint minutiae
○ Database fingerprint minutiae

FIGURE 10.8 Different Situations in
Minutia Matching

Of the three cases described above, only in the first case are the minutiae said to be paired.

10.4.2 Matching Algorithm

The following notation is used in the sequential and parallel algorithms described below. Let the query fingerprint be represented as an n-dimensional feature vector $\mathbf{f}^q = (\mathbf{f}_1^q, \mathbf{f}_2^q, \ldots, \mathbf{f}_n^q)$. Note that each of the n elements is a feature vector corresponding to one minutia, and the ith feature vector contains three components, $\mathbf{f_i} = (f_i(x), f_i(y), f_i(\theta))$.

The components of a feature vector are shown geometrically in Figure 10.4. The query fingerprint core point is located at (C_x^q, C_y^q). Similarly, let the rth reference (database) fingerprint be represented as an m_r-dimensional feature vector $\mathbf{f}^r = (\mathbf{f}_1^r, \mathbf{f}_2^r, \ldots, \mathbf{f}_{m_r}^r)$, and the reference fingerprint core point is located at (C_x^r, C_y^r).

Let (x_q^t, y_q^t) and (x_q^b, y_q^b) define the bounding box for the query fingerprint, where x_q^t is the x-coordinate of the top-left corner of the box and x_q^b is the x-coordinate of the bottom-right corner of the box. Quantities y_q^t and y_q^b are defined similarly. A bounding box is the smallest rectangle that encloses all the feature points. Note that the query fingerprint $\mathbf{f}^q$ may or may not belong to the fingerprint database $\mathbf{f}^D$. The fingerprints are assumed to be registered with a known orientation. Hence, there is no need of normalization for rotation.

The matching algorithm is based on finding the number of paired minutiae between each database fingerprint and the query fingerprint. It uses the concept of minutiae matching described in Section 4.1. A tolerance box is shown graphically in Figure 10.9. In order to reduce the amount of computation, the matching algorithm takes into account only those minutiae that fall within a common bounding box.

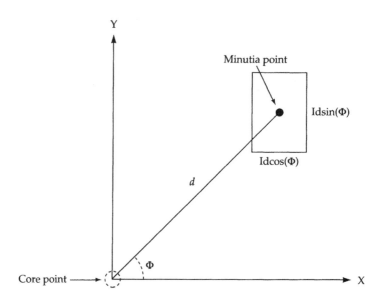

FIGURE 10.9　Tolerance Box for X- and Y-components of a Minutia Point

The common bounding box is the intersection of the bounding box for query and reference (database) fingerprints. Once the count of matching minutiae is obtained, a matching score is computed. The matching score is used for deciding the degree of match. Finally, a set of top-scoring reference fingerprints is obtained as a result of matching.

In order to accommodate the shift in the minutia features, a tolerance box is created around each feature. The size of the box depends on the ridge widths and distance from the core point in the fingerprint.

The sequential matching algorithm is described in Figure 10.10. In the sequential algorithm, the tolerance box (shown in Figure 10.9 with respect to a query fingerprint minutia) is calculated for the reference (database) fingerprint minutia. In the parallel algorithm described in the next section, it is calculated for the query fingerprint (as in Figure 10.9). A similar sequential matching algorithm is described by Wegstein [9]. Depending on the desired accuracy, more than one finger could be used in matching. In that case, a composite score is computed for each set.

10.5 PARALLEL MATCHING ALGORITHM

We parallelize the matching algorithm so that it utilizes the specific characteristics of the Splash 2 architecture. While performing this mapping, we need to take into account the limitations of the available FPGA technology. This is consistent with the approaches taken in hardware-software codesign. Any preprocessing needed on the query minutiae set is a one-time operation, whereas reference fingerprint minutiae matching is a repetitive operation. Computing the matching score involves floating-point division. The floating-point operations and one-time operations are performed in software on the host, whereas the repetitive operations are delegated to the FPGA-based PEs of Splash 2. The parallel version of the algorithm involves operations on

Input: Query fingerprint n-dimensional feature vector $\mathbf{f^q}$ and the rolled fingerprint database $\mathbf{f^D} = \{\mathbf{f^r}\}_{r=1}^{N}$.
The rth database fingerprint is represented as an m_r-dimensional featurevector.
Output: A list of top ten records from the database with matching score > T.
Begin

    For $r = 1$ to N do

      1. Register the database fingerprint with respect to the core point (C_x^q, C_y^q) of the query fingerprint:

        For $i = 1$ to m_r do

$$f_i^r(x) = f_i^r(x) - C_x^q$$
$$f_i^r(y) = f_i^r(y) - C_y^q$$

      2. Compute the common bounding box for the query and reference fingerprints:

        Let (x_q^t, y_q^t) and (x_q^b, y_q^b) define the bounding box for the query fingerprint.

        Let (x_r^t, y_r^t) and (x_r^b, y_r^b) define the bounding box for the rth reference fingerprint.

        The intersection of these two boxes is the common bounding box.

        Let the query print have M_e^q and reference print have N_e^r minutiae in this box.

      3. Compute the tolerance vector for ith feature vector f_i^r:

        If the distance from the reference core point to the current reference feature is less than K then

$$t_i^r(x) = l d \cos(\phi),$$
$$t_i^r(y) = l d \sin(\phi), \text{ and}$$
$$t_i^r(\emptyset) = k_3,$$

        else

$$t_i^r(x) = k_1,$$
$$t_i^r(y) = k_2, \text{ and}$$
$$t_i^r(\emptyset) = k_3,$$

        where l, k_1, k_2 and k_3 are prespecified constants determined empirically based on the average ridge width,

        ϕ is the angle of the line joining the core point and the ith feature with the x-axis, and d is the distance of the feature from the core point.

        Tolerance box is shown geometrically in Figure 10.9.

      4. Match minutiae:

        Two minutiae $\mathbf{f_i^r}$ and $\mathbf{f_j^q}$ are said to match if the following conditions are satisfied:

$$f_j^q(x) - t_i^r(x) \le f_i^r(x) \le f_j^q(x) + t_i^r(x),$$
$$f_j^q(y) - t_i^r(y) \le f_i^r(y) \le f_j^q(y) + t_i^r(y), \text{ and}$$
$$f_j^q - t_i^r(\theta) \le f_i^r(\theta) \le f_j^q(\theta) + t_i^r(\theta),$$

        where $t_i^r = (t_i^r(x), t_i^r(y), t_i^r(\theta))$ is the tolerance vector.

      Set the number of paired features, $m_p^r = 0$;

      For all query features $\mathbf{f_j^q}$, $j = 1, 2, \ldots M_e^q$, do

        If $\mathbf{f_j^q}$ matches with any feature in $\mathbf{f_i^r}$, $i = 1, 2, \ldots, N_e^r$, then increment m_p^r.

        Mark the corresponding feature in $\mathbf{f^r}$ as paired.

      5. Compute the matching score (MS (q,r)):

$$MS(q, r) = \frac{m_p^r * m_p^r}{(M_e^q * N_e^r)}.$$

    Sort the database fingerprints and obtain top 10 scoring database fingerprints.

End

FIGURE 10.10   Sequential Fingerprint Matching Algorithm

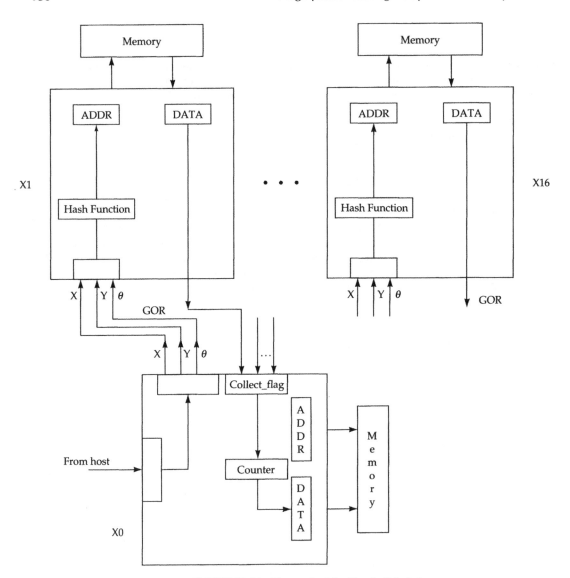

FIGURE 10.11   Fingerprint Matching in Splash 2

the host, on X0, and on each PE. The schematic of fingerprint matching algorithm using Splash 2 is shown in Figure 10.11.

One of the main constructs of the parallel algorithm is a lookup table. The lookup table consists of all possible points within the tolerance box that a feature may be mapped to. The Splash 2 data paths for the parallel algorithm are shown in Figure 10.12.

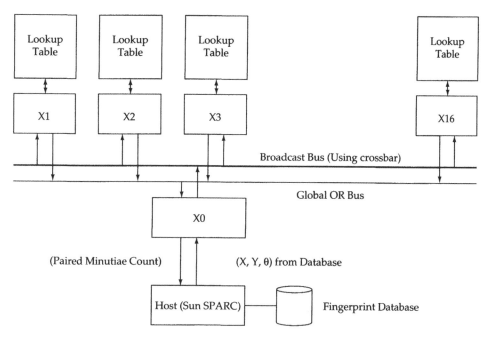

FIGURE 10.12   Data Flow in Parallel Matching Algorithm

10.5.1 Preprocessing on the Host

The host processes the query and database fingerprints as follows. The query finger-print is read first and the following preprocessing is done:

1. The core point is assumed to be available. For each query feature $\mathbf{f_j^q}$, $j = 1, 2,$ $\ldots n$, generate a tolerance box. Enumerate a total of $(t_x \times t_y \times t_\theta)$ grid points in this box, where t_x is the tolerance in x, t_y is the tolerance in y and t_θ is tolerance in θ.

2. Allocate each feature to one PE in Splash 2. Repeat this cyclically, that is, features 1–16 are allocated to PEs X1 to X16, features 17–32 are allocated to PEs X1 to X16, and so on.

3. Initialize the lookup tables by loading the grid points within each tolerance box in step (1) into the memory.

In this algorithm, the tolerance box is computed with respect to the query fingerprint features. The host then reads the database of fingerprints and sends their feature vectors for matching to the Splash 2 board.

For each database fingerprint, the host performs the following operations:

1. Read the feature vectors.

2. Register the features as described in step (1) of the sequential algorithm in Figure 10.10.

3. Send each of the feature vectors over the broadcast bus to all PEs if it is within the bounding box of the query fingerprint.

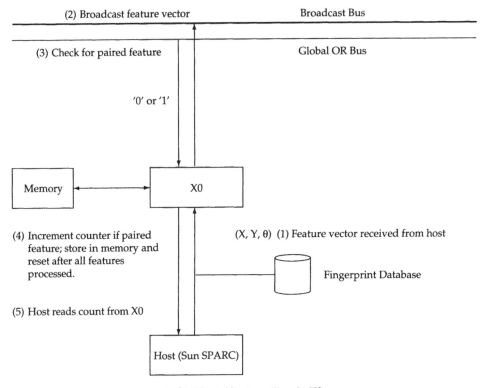

FIGURE 10.13   Data Flow in X0

For each database fingerprint, the host then reads the number of paired features m_p^r that was computed by the Splash 2 system, $r = 1, \ldots N$. Finally, the matching score is computed as in the sequential method.

10.5.2 Computations on Splash

The computations carried out on each PE of Splash 2 are described below. As mentioned earlier, X0 plays a special role in controlling the crossbar in Splash 2.

1. Operations on X0:
   Each database feature vector received from the host is broadcast to all PEs. If it is matched with a feature in a lookup table, the PE drives the Global OR bus high. When the OR bus is high, X0 increments a counter. The host reads this counter value (m_p^r) after all the feature vectors for the current database fingerprint have been processed. Operations on X0 are highlighted in Figure 10.13.

2. Operations on each PE:
   On receiving the broadcasted feature, a PE computes its address in the lookup table through a hashing function. If the data at the computed address is a '1', then the feature is paired, and the PE drives the Global OR bus high. Operations on a PE are highlighted in Figure 10.14.

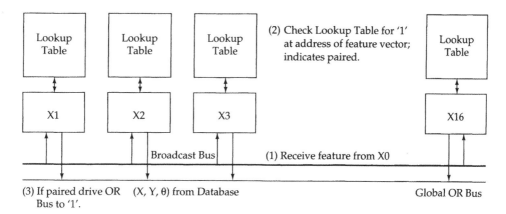

FIGURE 10.14   Data Flow in a PE

10.5.3 VHDL Specification for X0

We illustrate how the operations on X0 are customized by describing segments of its VHDL code. The tasks carried out by the other PEs are relatively simpler. The following functions are carried out by X0:

1. Broadcast feature vector to all PEs
2. Update a counter if at least one of the bits of the Global OR bus is '1', and
3. Reset the counter after all the minutiae of a database fingerprint are processed and the result is updated in X0 memory.

Five segments of VHDL code are shown in Figure 10.15 and are briefly described here. Segment 1 (lines 1.1–1.7) shows the signal declarations. The hardware buses have been directly mapped to bit vectors in VHDL. Some of the program variables have been tailored for the range needed based on the application requirement (such as *count, features*). Segment 2 describes the padding instructions. Note that because of using input-output pads, there is a delay in a signal reaching all the PEs after it has been seen by X0. The delay is accounted for by using a data pipeline of suitable length (in our case the pipeline is 6 stages deep). The code in line 1.7 combined with code segment 5 (line 5.1) show the use of the pipeline. X0 maintains this pipeline by writing data into the pipeline and flushing out the last data sets by writing zeros. The code in X0 looks at the end of the pipeline. Thus, the data is seen by X0 code when it would have reached other PEs.

By setting suitable configuration parameters, X0 can be set to broadcast the contents of the SIMD Bus to all PEs. To set this mode, code segment 3 is used.

In code segment 4, the collection of OR flags from all 16 PEs (PE X1 through X16) is being checked for any possible match by comparing with a bit vector of all 0's. If any of the bits is a '1', we increment the counter *count*.

If the input for a new database record is initiated, indicated by the 33rd bit of the SIMD bus, then the final paired count and the number of features for the previous record is stored in memory. The two counters *count* and *features* are reset to zero. These activities are carried out in code segment 5.

—   Signal declarations — (Segment 1)

```
1.1–  SIGNAL   Data          :        Bit_Vector(15 downto 0);
1.2–  SIGNAL   Address       :        Bit_Vector(17 downto 0);
1.3–  SIGNAL   count         :        natural range 0 to 255 := 0;
1.4–  SIGNAL   features      :        natural range 0 to 255 := 0;
1.5–  SIGNAL   SIMD          :        Bit_Vector(35 downto 0);
1.6–  SIGNAL   Collect_flag  :        Bit_Vector(15 downto 0);
1.7–  SIGNAL feat_pipeline   pipeline;
```

—   Connections to I/O pads — (Segment 2)

```
2.1–  pad_output  (X0_Mem_A, Address);
2.2–  pad_output  (X0_Mem_D, Data);
2.3–  pad_Input   (X0_SIMD, SIMD);
2.4–  pad_Output  (X0_XB_Data, Xbar_Out);
2.5–  pad_Input   (X0_GOR_Result_in, Collect_flag);
```

—   Setting X0 to be the crossbar master — (Segment 3)

```
3.1–  X0_Xbar_En_L  <= '0';
3.2–  X0_X16_Disable <= '1';
3.3–  X0_Xbar_Send  <= '1';
```

— ..... — (Segment 4)

```
4.1–  IF (Collect_flag /= itobv(0,16)) THEN
4.2–              count <= count + 1;
4.3–  END IF;
```

— .....
— New person record, store present counters and then reset — (Segment 5)

```
5.1–  IF (feat_pipeline(0)(32) = '1') THEN
5.2–              Data(7 downto 0) <= itobv(count,8);
5.3–              Data(15 downto 8) <= itobv(features,8);
5.4–              count <= 0;
5.5–              features <= 0;
5.6–              Address <= itobv(bvtoi(Address) + 1,18);
5.7–  END IF;
```

FIGURE 10.15   VHDL Specification Segments for X0

10.6 SIMULATION AND SYNTHESIS RESULTS

The VHDL behavioral modeling code for PEs X0–X16 has been tested using the Splash simulation environment. The simulation environment loads the lookup tables and crossbar configuration file into the simulator. Note that the Splash simulator runs independently of the Splash 2 hardware and runs on the host. The input data are read from a specified file, and the data on each of the signals declared in the VHDL code can be traced as a function of time. A sample output of simulation using test inputs

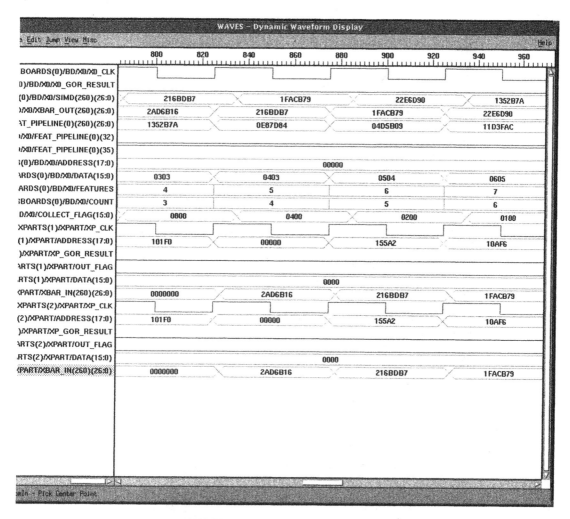

FIGURE 10.16   Simulation Waveforms for Test Data

is shown in Figure 10.16. The waveforms show the changes in signals with respect to the system clock on each of the PEs of Splash 2. For example, on X0, the signals *count* and *features* (11th and 10th lines, respectively) show the number of minutiae paired and the number of minutiae sent for matching to all the PEs, respectively.

The synthesis process starts by translating the VHDL code to a Xilinx net list format (XNF). The vendor-specific 'ppr' utility (in our case Xilinx) generates placement, partitioning, and routing information from the XNF net list. The final bitstream file is generated using the utility 'xnf2bit'. The 'timing' utility produces a graphical histogram of the speed at which the logic can be executed. The output of the 'timing' utility is shown in Figure 10.17. The logic synthesized for X0 can run at a clock rate of 17.1 MHz, and the logic for the PEs X1 to X16 can run at 33.8 MHz. Observe that these clock rates correspond to the longest delay (critical) paths, even though most of the logic could be driven at higher rates. Increased processing speed may be possible by optimizing the critical path.

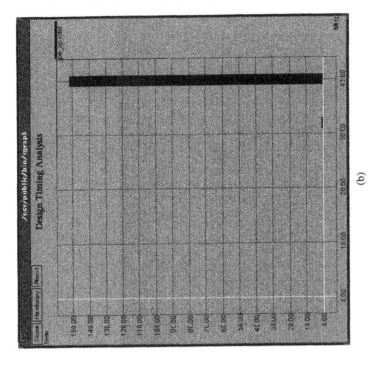

(a)

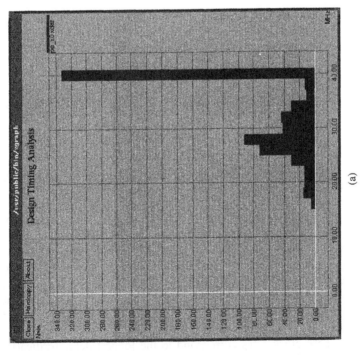

(b)

FIGURE 10.17 Timing Results. (a) for PE X0; (b) for PE X_i

136

10.7 EXECUTION ON SPLASH 2

The bitstream files for Splash 2 are generated from the VHDL code. Using the C interface for Splash 2, a host version of the fingerprint matching application is generated. The host version reads the fingerprint database from the disk and obtains the final list of candidates after matching.

10.7.1 User Interface

An interactive user interface to the fingerprint matching application has been developed using the X Window System. The interface provides pull-down menus for selecting a query fingerprint for matching and for invoking tasks of feature extraction, matching, and verification. The graphical user interface is shown in Figure 10.18. The matching menu can select either the host or Splash 2 to perform the computations during matching. The speed of matching is computed by obtaining the elapsed time for the number of fingerprints in the database.

10.7.2 Performance Analysis

The sequential algorithm, described in Section 4.2, executed on a Sun SPARC-station 10, performs at the rate of 70 matches per second on database and query fingerprints that have approximately 65 features. A match is the process of determining the matching score between a query and a reference fingerprint. The Splash 2 implementation should perform matching at the rate of 2.6×10^5 matches per second. This matching speed is obtained from the 'timing' utility. The host interface part can run at 17.1 MHz and each PE can run at 33.8 MHz (as shown in Figure 10.17). Hence, the entire fingerprint matching will run at the slower of the two speeds, that is, 17.1 MHz. Assuming 65 minutiae, on an average, in a database fingerprint, the matching speed is estimated at 2.6×10^5 matches per second. We evaluated the matching speed using a database of 10,000 fingerprints created from 100 real fingerprints by randomly dropping, adding, and perturbing minutiae in a given set of minutiae. The measured speed on a Splash 2 system running at 1 MHz is of the order of 6,300 matches per second on this database. The experimental Splash 2 system has not been run at higher clock rates. Assuming a linear scaling of performance with an increase in clock rate, we would achieve approximately 110,000 matches per second. We feel that the disparity in the projected and achieved speeds (2.6×10^5 versus 1.1×10^5) is due to different tasks being timed. The time to load the data buffers onto Splash 2 has not been taken into account in the projected speed, whereas this time is included in the time measured by the host in an actual run. We are in the process of timing only the matching component of the code on the system.

The main advantage of the Splash 2 implementation is the higher performance compared to the sequential implementation. The Splash 2 implementation is over 1,500 times faster than a sequential implementation on a SPARCstation 10. Another advantage of the parallel implementation on Splash 2 is that the matching speed is independent of the number of minutiae in the query fingerprint. The number of minutiae affects only the lookup table initialization, which is done as preprocessing by the host, and this time is amortized over a large number of database records.

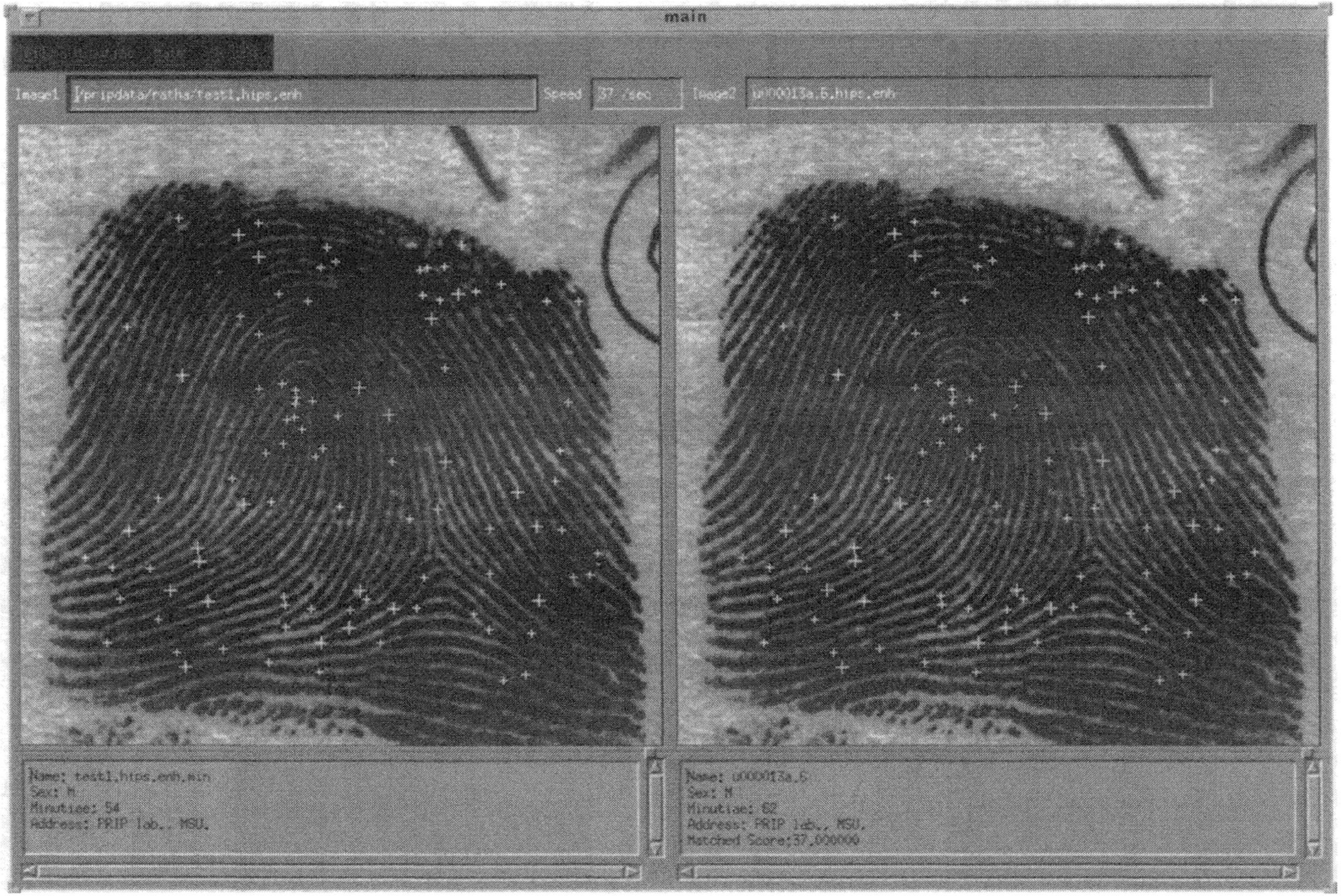

FIGURE 10.18 GUI Used in Fingerprint Analysis

The matching algorithm can scale well as the number of Splash 2 boards on the system is increased. Multiple query fingerprints can be loaded on different Splash 2 boards, each matching against the database records as they are transferred from the host. This would result in a higher throughput from the system.

The processing speed can be further improved by replacing some of the soft macros on the host interface part (X0) by hard macros. To sustain the matching rate, the data throughput should be at a rate of over 250,000 fingerprint records per second (with an average of 65 minutiae per record). This may be a bottleneck for the I/O subsystem.

10.8 CONCLUSIONS

The Splash 2 architecture is highly suitable for rolled fingerprint matching. The parallel algorithm has been designed to match the Splash 2 architecture, thereby resulting in substantially better performance. The algorithm applies a hardware-software design approach to maximize the performance of the overall system.

We will be coding our matching algorithm in dbC to evaluate the performance of such a high-level language to express low-level parallelism. This effort will also enable us to compare the development time needed to program Splash 2 using VHDL versus dbC. In the next phase of the project, we plan to implement a minutiae extraction algorithm and a latent fingerprint matching algorithm on Splash 2. Both of these algorithms appear promising for achieving performance gains on the Splash 2 architecture. The minutiae extraction process involves two-dimensional convolution, which has been successfully implemented on Splash 2 [8].

ACKNOWLEDGMENT

We would like to thank Duncan Buell, Jeff Arnold, and Brian Schott of Supercomputing Research Center, Bowie, Maryland, for their help and suggestions. This research was supported by a research contract from the Institute for Defense Analyses, Alexandria, Virginia.

REFERENCES

[1] "Application Briefs: Computer Graphics in the Detective Business," *IEEE Computer Graphics and Applications*, Apr. 1985, pp. 14–17.

[2] Federal Bureau of Investigation, *The Science of Fingerprints: Classification and Uses*, U.S. Govt. Printing Office, Washington, D.C., 1984.

[3] J.H. Hennessy and D.A. Patterson, *Computer Architecture: A Quantitative Approach*, Morgan Kauffmann Publishers, San Mateo, Calif., 1990.

[4] Sir W.J. Herschel, *The Origin of Fingerprinting*, AMS Press, New York, 1974.

[5] A.K. Jain, "Advances in Statistical Pattern Recognition," in *Pattern Recognition Theory and Applications*, P.A. Devijer and J. Kittler, eds., Springer-Verlag, New York, 1987, pp. 1–19.

[6] H.C. Lee and R.E. Gaensslen, *Advances in Fingerprint Technology*, Elsevier, New York, 1991.

[7] B. Miller, "Vital Signs of Identity," *IEEE Spectrum*, Vol. 31, No. 2, Feb. 1994, pp. 22–30.

[8] N.K. Ratha, A.K. Jain, and D.T. Rover, "Convolution on Splash 2," *Proc. IEEE Symp. FPGAs for Custom Computing Machines*, CS Press, Los Alamitos, Calif., 1995, pp. 204–213.

[9] J.H. Wegstein, *An Automated Fingerprint Identification System*, Special Publication 500–89, Nat'l Bureau of Standards, Washington, D.C., 1982.

CHAPTER 11

High-Speed Image
Processing with Splash 2

Peter M. Athanas and A. Lynn Abbott

11.1 INTRODUCTION

Image processing is the problem of extracting useful information from an image or from a sequence of images. Although images can be produced by many different sources (including x-ray sensors, tomographic scanners, acoustic imagers, and computer-graphics programs), the video camera is of particular interest because it generates images that are easily interpreted by a human observer. Unfortunately, the amount of data that is present in a single image is very large, and the methods that are used in biological vision are not well understood. The challenge of image-processing research is therefore to develop computational approaches—both algorithms and hardware—that can accept images and produce useful results at high speed.

Conventional von Neumann machines are commonly used for image processing tasks, but their performance does not begin to approach real-time rates. The usual alternative is to employ special-purpose architectures that have been designed specifically for image processing. These systems can perform at sufficiently high speeds, but at the expense of flexibility; they can perform *only* the tasks that they have been designed to do. Splash 2 represents a third alternative. Custom computing platforms such as Splash 2 are sufficiently flexible that new algorithms can be implemented on existing hardware, and are fast enough that real-time or near-real-time operation is possible.

This chapter describes a real-time image processing system that is based on the Splash 2 general-purpose custom computing platform. Even though Splash 2 was not designed specifically for image processing, this platform possesses architectural properties that make it well suited for the computation and data transfer rates that are characteristic of this class of problems. Furthermore, the price/performance of this system makes it a competitive alternative to conventional real-time image processing systems.

Other important factors for using Splash 2 are prototyping and design verification. The typical hardware design process requires extensive behavioral testing of a new concept before proceeding with a hardware implementation. For any image processing task of reasonable complexity, simulation of a VHDL model with a representative data set on a workstation is prohibitive because of the enormous simulation time required. Days, or even weeks, of processing time are commonly needed to simulate the processing of a single image. Because of this, the designer is often forced into a trade-off as to how much testing can be afforded versus an acceptable risk of allowing an iteration in silicon. The Splash 2 approach permits an automated (or near-automated) transformation of a structural or behavioral VHDL representation into a real-time hardware implementation. The Splash 2 platform can therefore serve not only as a means to evaluate the performance of an experimental algorithm/architecture, but also as a working component in the development and testing of a much larger system.

The next section describes VTSPLASH, a laboratory system based on Splash 2 that has been developed at Virginia Tech [4]. Section 11.3 presents an overview of image-processing fundamentals, and discusses architectural considerations for high-speed operation. Sections 11.4 and 11.5 present two case studies in the development of image processing tasks: a median filter, and Laplacian pyramid generation. Section 11.6 discusses performance issues. Finally, Section 11.7 summarizes the chapter.

11.2 THE VTSPLASH SYSTEM

The adaptive nature of the Splash 2 architecture makes it well suited for the computational demands of image processing. In addition, Splash 2 features a flexible interface design that facilitates customized I/O for situations that cannot be accommodated by the host workstation. A real-time image processing custom computing system (referred to as VTSPLASH) has been constructed based on Splash 2; this is depicted in Figure 11.1.

A video camera or a VCR is used to create a standard RS-170 video stream. The signal produced from the camera is digitized with a custom-built frame grabber card. This board not only captures images, but also performs any needed sequencing or simple pixel operations before the data are presented to Splash 2. The frame grabber card was built with a parallel interface that can be connected directly to the input data stream of the Splash 2 processor. Two processor Array Boards are used in the VTSPLASH laboratory system. The output data produced by Splash 2, which may be a real-time video data stream, image overlay data, or some other form of information, is first presented to another custom board for converting the data to an appropriate format (if necessary). Once formatted, the data are then presented to a commercial image acquisition/display card, which presents the images to a color video monitor. A Sun SPARCstation serves as the Splash 2 host, and is responsible for configuring the Splash 2 arrays and sending runtime commands intermixed with the video stream if needed. The laboratory system can be rapidly reconfigured from one task to another in just a few seconds.

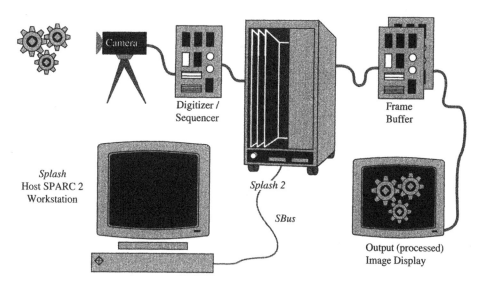

FIGURE 11.1 Components in the VTSᴘʟᴀsʜ Laboratory System

Although Splash 2 was not specifically designed for image processing, it is a suitable testbed for implementing a wide range of image processing tasks, including those requiring temporal processing. A single Splash 2 processor Array Board contains slightly more than 69 megabits[1] of memory—enough for 32 frames of image data [27]. Not all of this storage is necessarily available to applications in a convenient form; the actual available storage is dependent upon how individual applications are constructed.

11.3 IMAGE PROCESSING TERMINOLOGY AND ARCHITECTURAL ISSUES

A digitized image can be represented as a rectangular array $I(r, c)$, where r and c refer to the row and column location of a picture element, or *pixel*, in the image. For a standard monochrome (black and white) video camera, common image sizes are 512×512 and 480×640 pixels (rows × columns), where each pixel is an 8-bit quantity representing the light intensity at one point. Since the standard video rate is 30 images per second, even simple tasks represent a significant computational challenge because of the sheer quantity of data: 7.5 MB/s for images of size 512×512. Storage and I/O are also especially significant when real-time operation is required.

The goal of many image processing tasks is to produce an output image I_{out} that is an enhanced or filtered version of an input image I_{in}. One way to accomplish this is to apply a linear filter, $I_{out}(r, c) = \sum_i \sum_j I_{in}(r + i, c + j) \cdot h(i, j)$, where h is the filter and where the summations are performed over a neighborhood determined

[1]This number is based upon seventeen 256K (16 static RAM devices plus 12,800 bits of storage (maximum) in each of the seventeen Xilinx 4010 chips.

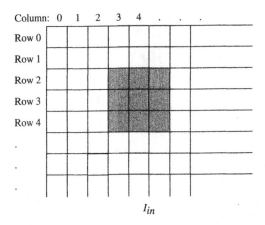

I_{in}

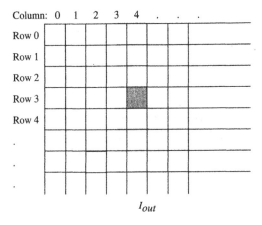

I_{out}

FIGURE 11.2 Example Image Arrays. Each cell represents one pixel, which is commonly 8 bits for a monochrome image. The shaded area at the top indicates a 3×3 neighborhood centered about pixel (3, 4). The result of the neighborhood operation is placed in the shaded location at the bottom.

by the extent of h. For example, a smoothed image I_{out} is produced if we define

$$h(i, j) = \begin{cases} \frac{1}{9} & \text{for } -1 \leq i \leq 1 \text{ and } -1 \leq j \leq 1 \\ 0 & \text{otherwise} \end{cases}.$$

This is equivalent to averaging the pixels within a 3×3 neighborhood of I_{in} to produce a single output pixel of I_{out}. This same low-pass filter can be represented as follows:

$$h = 1/9 \times \begin{array}{|c|c|c|} \hline 1 & 1 & 1 \\ \hline 1 & 1 & 1 \\ \hline 1 & 1 & 1 \\ \hline \end{array}$$

Conceptually, this template (often called a *mask* or *operator*) passes over I_{in}, producing an output pixel at each discrete step as illustrated in Figure 11.2. For the linear case, "applying" the template at a given location in I_{in} means to multiply each template value by the associated underlying pixel value, and then to compute the sum of the products. This sum is the pixel value for I_{out}, and may no longer be an 8-bit quantity. It is assumed that $h = 0$ outside the specified grid. Special rules may be needed for pixels near the image borders.

Other linear filters can be implemented by changing the weights in such a template. For example, the following high-pass filters are commonly used to enhance intensity edges, which result from sharp changes in pixel values. Known as *Sobel operators*, h_1 and h_2 can be used to detect vertical and horizontal intensity gradients, respectively.

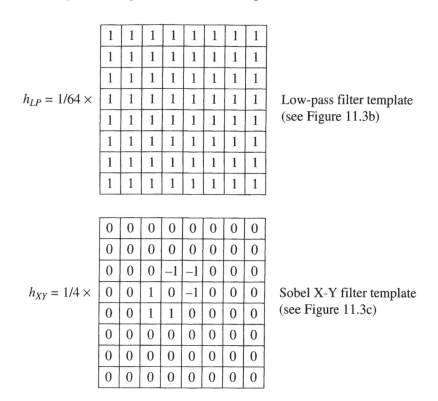

Larger templates are also possible, as illustrated below. Examples of images produced using these templates are shown in Figure 11.3.

Low-pass filter template (see Figure 11.3b)

Sobel X-Y filter template (see Figure 11.3c)

After an image has been appropriately low-pass filtered, the image can be subsampled without fear of violating the Nyquist criterion. If an image is recursively filtered and subsampled, the resulting set of images can be considered a single unit and is called a *pyramid*. This data structure facilitates image analysis at different scales. Processing at the lower-resolution portion of the pyramid can be used to guide processing at higher-resolution levels. For some tasks (such as surveillance and road following) this approach can greatly reduce the overall amount of processing required.

In addition to low-pass pyramids, it is possible to generate band-pass pyramids, in which each level of the pyramid contains information from a single frequency band. A popular technique for generating these pyramids (known as Gaussian and

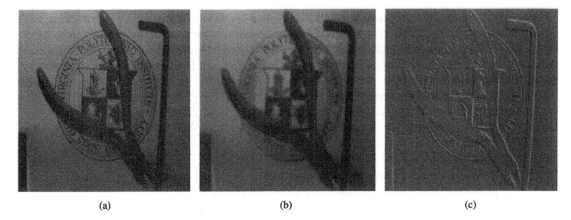

(a)   (b)   (c)

FIGURE 11.3   Example of Filtering Operations. (a) Original image. (b) Smoothed image, created by applying a low-pass filter to the original image. (c) Edge image, created by applying a Sobel XY filter. All of these images are 512 × 512 in size. The output images were obtained using 8 × 8 templates on VTSPLASH.

Laplacian pyramids) is described in [6]. A VTSPLASH implementation of a low-pass and a band-pass pyramid generator will be presented in a later section.

Neighborhood operations are not necessarily linear. For example, the output pixel value could be chosen as the *median* of the neighborhood in the input image. This nonlinear filtering operation can be expressed as follows:

$$I(r, c) = \text{median}\{ \quad \begin{matrix} I(r-1, c-1), & I(r-1, c), & I(r-1, c+1), \\ I(r, c-1), & I(r, c), & I(r, c+1), \\ I(r+1, c-1), & I(r+1, c), & I(r+1, c+1)\} \end{matrix}$$

One advantage of this operation is reduced blurring, as compared with linear filtering. The design of a median filtering system using VTSPLASH is also described in detail in Section 11.4.

The remainder of this section presents a brief description of image processing operations that have been implemented on VTSPLASH. For example, other nonlinear operations can be implemented using the ideas of *mathematical morphology* [20, 2]. This is an algebra that uses multiplication, addition (subtraction), and maximum (minimum) operations to produce output pixels. The fundamental operations are called dilation and erosion, which cause image regions to expand and shrink, respectively. The gray-scale dilation of an image I_{in} by the structuring element h is defined as

$$I_{out} = (I_{in} \oplus h)(r, c) \equiv \max_{i,j}\{I_{in}(r-i, c-j) + h(i, j)\},$$

and erosion by h is defined as

$$I_{out} = (I_{in} \ominus h)(r, c) \equiv \min_{i,j}\{I_{in}(r+i, c+j) - h(i, j)\}.$$

These operations can be pipelined, and often serve as building blocks for higher-level processing.

Another operation that has been implemented on VTSPLASH is the 2-D discrete Fourier transform (DFT). For an $M \times N$ image, this is defined as

$$I_{out}(r, c) = \frac{1}{MN} \sum_{k=0}^{M-1} \sum_{l=0}^{N-1} I_{in}(k, l) \exp\left[-j2\pi\left(\frac{lr}{M} + \frac{lc}{N}\right)\right]$$

where I_{out} is composed of real and imaginary components. This can be rewritten as follows,

$$I_{out}(r, c) = \frac{1}{M} \sum_{k=0}^{M-1} \left\{ \frac{1}{N} \sum_{l=0}^{N-1} I_{in}(k, l) \exp\left[-j2\pi\left(\frac{lc}{N}\right)\right] \right\} \exp\left[-j2\pi\left(\frac{lr}{M}\right)\right],$$

which illustrates the fact that the 2-D DFT can be implemented as a sequence of 1-D DFTs. For example, the DFT of a 512×512 image can be obtained by first computing 512 independent 1-D DFTs (one for each row), and then computing 512 1-D DFTs of the resulting columns. This has been implemented on VTSPLASH using floating-point arithmetic [22].

The *Hough transform* [10, 13] is a technique that can be used to detect lines in an image. Assume that intensity edges have been detected, so that the Hough algorithm processes only foreground (edge) or background values. The procedure begins by initializing all values in an accumulator array to zero. For each edge point, a parametric curve is traced through the accumulator array, and each array element on the curve is incremented. Effectively, each edge point "votes" for all possible lines that pass through that point.

Referring to Figure 11.4, assume that a line is parameterized by $d = r\cos\theta + c\sin\theta$, where (r, c) represents an image location. The Hough transform is implemented as follows:

Algorithm Hough
Initialize all elements of accumulator array A to 0
for $r = 0$ to $M - 1$
      for $c = 0$ to $N - 1$
            if $I_{in}(r, c)$ is an edge point
                 for $\theta = 0$ to 2π in steps of $\Delta\theta$
                     $d := $ (round) $(r\cos\theta + c\sin\theta)$
                     $A[d, \theta] := A[d, \theta] + 1$
                 end for
            end if
        end for
    end for
end Hough

This produces the accumulator array, and has been implemented on Splash [11, 1]. The next step is to detect peaks in the array. Each local maximum represents one line in the image I_{in}. This procedure can be generalized to detect other parametric shapes, such as ellipses and polygons.

The image processing operations described above can be broadly classified into four generic classes [26]. An operation in the *combination* class takes two images

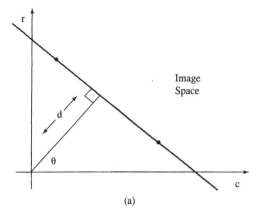

(a)

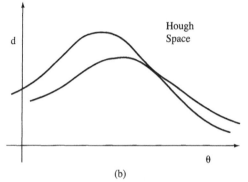

(b)

FIGURE 11.4 The Hough Transformation to Parameter Space. Edge points (r_i, c_i) in the image (a) map to sinusoids in the d-θ parameter space (b). In this example, the two sinusoids intersect at the values d and which determine the line that passes through (r_1, c_1) and (r_2, c_2).

and produces a new image of the same type. This is accomplished by combining each pair of elements from the input images into a new element. The *transformation* class accepts an image from a given class, and produces a new image in the same class. The *measurement* class reduces an image of a given type into a scalar or vector. The *conversion* class refers to those operations that take an image of a given type, and convert it into a new class.[2] Examples from each of these categories have been modeled and synthesized using the VTSPLASH system, as summarized in Table 11.1. Further descriptions of these and other image processing tasks are described in [14, 17], and [19].

These image processing tasks represent a considerable computational challenge if near-real-time operation is needed. Image pixels are typically produced and conveyed in *raster order*—pixels are presented serially, left-to-right for each image row, beginning with the top row. Consider again the 3×3 filtering operations discussed above. Although the nine neighboring pixels are spatially localized in the actual image, they are widely separated in the pixel stream from the camera. This is illustrated in Figure 11.5. For processing purposes, the straightforward approach is to store the entire input image into local memory, and then access pixels as needed

---

[2]Another class of operations that does not require an input image is the *generation* class, which produces a new image from scratch. This class of operations is not considered here.

TABLE 11.1   A Representative List of Image Processing Categories and Example Tasks

Class	Example image task	Description
Transformation	Convolution	Linear filtering operation.
	Median filtering	Nonlinear filter which can be used to eliminate "salt and pepper" noise.
	Morphological filtering	Nonlinear operations that alter region shapes in an image. Gray-scale *erosion* and *dilation* operations have been implemented.
Combination	Laplacian Pyramid generation	Produces an image hierarchy of decreasing image size and spatial resolution. The image for each pyramid level is formed by taking the difference of two blurred versions of the original image.
Measurement	Histogram generation	Statistical operation for computing intensity distribution of pixels in an image.
Conversion	Fast Fourier Transform	Converts an image from the spatial domain to the frequency domain.
	Hough Transform	A voting scheme that detects the presence of lines (or parametric curves) from a set of points in an image.
	Region detection and labeling	Finds connected regions in an image, and assigns a unique label to each.

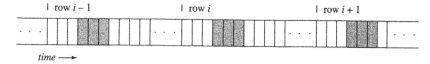

FIGURE 11.5   Example Image in Raster Order. Pixels are produced serially in row-major order. The highlighted pixels represent a single 3×3 image neighborhood.

to produce the output image. However, this approach introduces a latency of at least an entire image frame before the processor can begin to generate output pixels. This latency can be reduced to less than the time of n rows (for an $n \times n$ template) if the architecture is carefully designed to interleave memory reads and writes, effectively utilizing memory as a delay line. Splash 2 has been used to implement both of these processing methods. More discussion of image processing architectures can be found in [9, 16], and [24].

The default image size that is used on VTSPLASH is 512×512, with a pixel clock of 10 MHz. Although the rest of this chapter will discuss images in terms of monochrome light intensities, the same ideas also apply to other image types. Examples are range images, for which each pixel represents a distance value; x-ray images, where each pixel depends on object density; and computed tomography (CT) images, where each 2-D image represents a reconstructed slice of density information within a 3-D array of data.

11.4 CASE STUDY: MEDIAN FILTERING

Median filtering is a common approach for reducing noise in images [26]. Median filtering is a computational operation that replaces each picture element, or pixel, of an input image with the median value of several neighboring pixels in the image. The result is an output image that is a smoothed version of the input. Compared with traditional linear filtering, the median filter is more effective at removing impulsive noise and at smoothing an image without blurring intensity edges. Unfortunately, median filtering requires considerably more computations per pixel than linear filtering for a given neighborhood size. This is a significant problem because of the large number of pixels associated with a single image.

Rank-order filters such as the median filter are widely used for reducing noise and periodic interference patterns in images, and are useful for cleaning impulsive noise without blurring sharp edges. Implementing a median filter is computationally costly on a general-purpose platform because of the need to sort a large number of sets of pixel values repeatedly.

The median filtering operation may be stated mathematically in the following manner. Let $f_0, f_1, \ldots, f_{N-1}$ represent the intensity values for input image I_{in} within an N-point neighborhood about the point (r, c) in the image. These values are ordered so that $f_K \leq f_{K+1}$. The output image I_{out} is determined as:

$$I_{out}(r, c) = f_{(N-1)/2} \qquad \text{for odd } N$$
$$I_{out}(r, c) = \tfrac{1}{2}[f_{(N/2)-1} + f_{(N/2)}] \qquad \text{for even } N$$

In most image processing applications, rectangular neighborhoods are assumed. Conceptually, a median-filtered image is created by passing a small template over a source image. At each location of the template, the median of the image values covered by the template is selected as the corresponding value for the new image. Median filtering is therefore a neighborhood operation, characterized by repeated comparisons of neighboring pixel values.

Figure 11.6 illustrates again the concept of a 3×3 neighborhood operation. The shaded 3×3 window is assumed to "slide" over I_{in} producing an output value

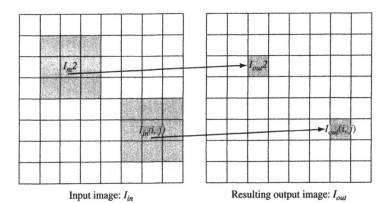

| Input image: I_{in} | Resulting output image: I_{out} |

FIGURE 11.6   Concept of a 3×3 Window-Based Operation. For the median filter, the value of $I_{out}(i, j)$ is the median of the nine pixels of I_{in} which lie within the 3×3 window with center at $I_{in}(r, c)$.

for I_{out} at each location of the window. For median filtering, the value of the pixel at any location in I_{out} is the median of the nine values in the 3×3 window with center at that position in I_{in}. Two window positions are shown in the figure, with corresponding positions highlighted in I_{out}. For an input image of size 512×512, approximately 262,144 nine-point median values need to be extracted to produce I_{out}.

The median filter does a good job of estimating the true pixel values in situations where the underlying neighborhood trend is flat or monotonic and the noise distribution has flat tails. It is effective for removing impulsive noise. However, when the neighborhood contains fine detail such as thin lines, they are distorted or lost. Corners can be clipped. It can produce regions of constant or nearly constant values that are perceived as patches, streaks, or amorphous blotches. Such artifacts may suggest boundaries that really do not exist. In spite of these problems, median filtering is often an attractive alternative to traditional linear filtering. Unfortunately, the computational complexity of median filtering is much higher.

The median filter has been implemented on Splash 2 as a single-board design [23]. The design and data flow within the Splash 2 processor Array Board are shown in Figure 11.7. The design makes available all the pixels in a 3×3 window simultaneously so that a combinational sort can be performed on them. The median is then chosen from the sorted values.

Input image pixels are presented to VTSPLASH in raster order (left to right for the first image row, then repeating for each subsequent row). Pixels are presented to the first Splash 2 Processing Element at a rate of 10 MHz. The task of storing the input image is so divided that six Processing Elements are required for the purpose. Each receives the input pixel stream at the same time. This requires the input pixels to be rearranged such that every four consecutive input pixels are packed together to form a 32-bit data word. This packing of input pixels, and transferring the resulting data stream to the crossbar, is done by Processing Elements PE-1 and PE-2. The packed input data is broadcast to PE-3 through PE-8, once every four clock cycles. The effective input data rate remains unaltered.

Processing Elements PE-3 through PE-8 are responsible for storing and retrieving the image pixels in local memory. This storage is organized such that all the

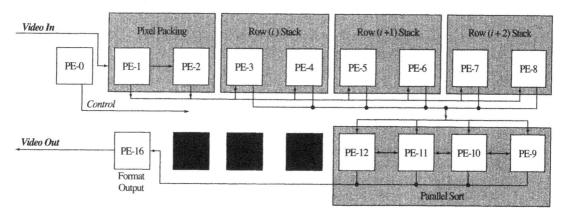

FIGURE 11.7 Communication Structure and Processing Element Layout for a Single Processor Array Board Implementation. Note that solid blocks denote unused PEs.

pixels within a 3×3 window may be accessed simultaneously. Let $I(i, j)$ represent the pixel value stored at row i and column j. Pixels are presented left to right for each row ($j = 0$ to 511), and top to bottom ($i = 0$ to 511). The first four pixels, $I(0, 0), I(0, 1), I(0, 2), I(0, 3)$ are directed by PE-2 simultaneously to PE-3 and PE-4. $I(0, 0)$ and $I(0, 1)$ are stored in the first location of PE-3's memory while $I(0, 2)$ and $I(0, 3)$ are stored in the first location of PE-4's memory. Two pixels are packed into each 16-bit memory location. The next four pixels $I(0, 4)$–$I(0, 7)$ are stored in similar fashion in the second locations of PE-3 and PE-4.

The second row of the image is stored similarly into the local memory of PE-5 and PE-6. The third row is stored in the memory of PE-7 and PE-8. This sequence repeats, with the fourth row being stored in memories of PE-3 and PE-4, the fifth in PE-5 and PE-6, the sixth in PE-7 and PE-8, and so on, until the entire image has been captured.

The retrieval of the stored pixels begins as soon as three rows have been received. As soon as the first three rows are stored in the memory of PE-3 through PE-8, all six PEs (PE-3–PE-8) perform a read operation from the first location of their local memory. With two pixels packed within each memory location, the six PEs are capable of concurrently accessing a total of 12 pixels. At this point, data corresponding to a 3×4 window is available for processing. The 3×4 window referred to here lies within the range $i = 0$ to 2 and $j = 0$ to 3. Two complete 3×3 windows lie within this 3×4 window and may therefore be processed at once.

The two rightmost columns of data in the window ($j = 2$ and 3) are stored in registers internal to the FPGAs. This storage helps create two additional 3×3 windows every time a 3×4 window is formed.

In the subsequent read cycle, four new pixels for each of the first three rows ($j = 4$ to 7) are read from memory. Since two columns have been stored in internal FPGA registers, the effective window size is 3×6 instead of 3×4. Four 3×3 windows may be formed from this window and thus four median values may be computed simultaneously.

This process continues with the 3×4 window sliding four pixels to the right in every read operation. Once the window reaches the extreme-right border of the image ($j = 488$ to 511), it "wraps" around in a "snake-like" fashion such that it moves one row to the bottom and starts from the leftmost border. The process of sliding right is resumed. This procedure continues for the entire frame and the pixels within each window are delivered to PE-9 through PE-12, which process them to compute a median value.

The design does not require the entire image to be stored in memory. Only three rows are sufficient at any point of time. The latency between the input and output frames is approximately three rows—a latency that is typically achieved by dedicated image processing hardware. A substantial number of data transfers are required between the Processing Elements on the Array Board, and this requires switching the crossbar configuration every clock cycle. This switching is controlled by the Xilinx element PE-0. PE-0 is programmed such that in every clock cycle, it switches to one of the three possible crossbar configurations, which are user-specified.

This design has been tested using the image shown in Figure 11.8. Noise was artificially introduced into the input image, and has been removed in the filtered image produced by Splash 2. Also, careful observation reveals contours or regions of small plateaus formed in the resulting image. This is another result that is expected

(a)   (b)

FIGURE 11.8   (a) Input test image for median filtering. This is a 512×512 gray-scale image that is presented to Splash 2. To demonstrate the noise-cleaning effect of median filtering, noise is deliberately introduced in the image. This is seen as black and white spots. (b) Median-filtered image obtained from Splash 2. The noise that was introduced in the original image has been filtered out. This demonstrates the noise-cleaning property of the median filter.

by median filtering. The image obtained by simulation using a C program compares well with the result image obtained from Splash 2, differing only in the pixel values at the frame edges. This difference arises because the border effect is ignored in the Splash 2 design.

With a 10 MHz clock on VTSPLASH (the video pixel rate), the time to process one frame is 0.027 seconds. The same task, written in C, and compiled with the appropriate optimizations, requires 8.0 seconds on a SPARCstation-2 and 3.75 seconds on a SPARCstation-10. The implementation presented here performs a number of arithmetic and memory operations in parallel. Although this is difficult to quantify, there are roughly 39 arithmetic/logical operations performed each clock cycle,[3] and effectively three memory operations per clock cycle. Based on these factors alone, this application effectively performs 420 million operations per second.

11.5 CASE STUDY: IMAGE PYRAMID GENERATION

Multiresolution and multirate image processing techniques have become increasingly popular over the past decade because of the advantages of processing image data at different scales. A basic data structure used in multiresolution and multirate processing is the image pyramid, which is a complete image representation at different

---

[3]In a hardware implementation, the process of identifying "operations" that correspond to instructions found in typical microprocessors is somewhat subjective. In this approximation, only major "word"-wise operations (such as *add* or *shift*) were considered.

levels of resolution. An image pyramid is constructed by recursively applying two basic operations—filtering and subsampling—to an image, creating a set of images of decreasing size and spatial resolution. Filtering is performed to convolve the input image with a family of local, symmetric smoothing functions. Subsampling then produces samples for the images at the next-higher scale. The two most common image pyramids are the Gaussian (low-pass) and the Laplacian (band-pass) pyramids [6].

11.5.1 Gaussian Pyramid

The sequence of images $g_0, g_1, \ldots, g_{k-1}$ as shown in Figure 11.9a is called a Gaussian pyramid. A weighting function that resembles the Gaussian probability distribution is applied to each pixel neighborhood of the original video image g_0 to generate the lower-resolution image g_1, which is used in turn to generate g_2, and so on. The level-to-level filtering and resampling can be expressed as a function REDUCE as shown below:

$$g_k = \text{REDUCE}(g_{k-1}) \tag{11.1}$$

where each pixel value in g_k is obtained by a weighted sum of pixels from g_{k-1}, computed over a 5×5 neighborhood as follows [18]:

$$g_k(i, j) = \sum_{m=-2}^{2} \sum_{n=-2}^{2} \omega(m, n) g_{k-1}(2i - m, 2j - n) \tag{11.2}$$

To simplify the computational requirements, the 5×5 weighting function ω is often chosen to be separable into two one-dimensional filters: $\omega(m, n) = \omega_x(m)\omega(n)$.

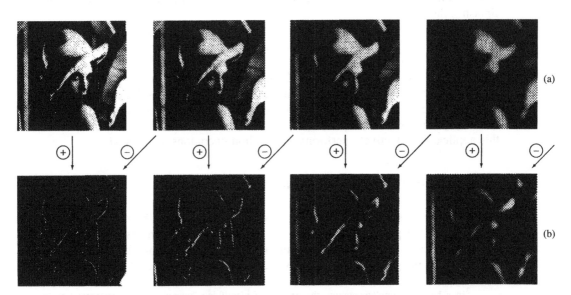

(a)

(b)

FIGURE 11.9 Example Data Produced from (a) a Gaussian Pyramid, and (b) a Laplacian Pyramid (from [27]).

The function REDUCE in Equation (11.2) is then split into two functions, REDUCEX and REDUCEY:

$$g_{k,x}(i, j) = \text{REDUCEX}(g_{k-1}) = \sum_{m=-2}^{2} \omega_x(m)g_{k-1}(2i - m, j)$$

$$g_k(i, j) = \text{REDUCEY}(g_{k,x}) = \sum_{m=-2}^{2} \omega_x(n)g_{k,x}(i, 2j - n)$$

(11.3)

The 1-D weighting function in the vertical direction, ω_y, is usually the transpose of the function in the horizontal direction, ω_x. The functions ω_x and ω_y are constructed so that it is normalized ($\sum_{i=-2}^{2} \omega(i) = 1$), symmetric ($\omega(i) = \omega(-i)$), and the equal contribution rule [25] which requires that $a + 2c = 2b$, where $a = \omega(0)$, $b = \omega(-1) = \omega(1)$, and $c = \omega(-2) = \omega(2)$. Although other solutions are possible, these three constraints are satisfied when $\omega(0) = a$, $\omega(1) = 1/4$, and $\omega(2) = 1/4 - a/2$. The equivalent weighting function is particularly Gaussian-like when a is around 0.4. For implementation in digital logic, it is convenient to choose $a = 3/8$, $b = 1/16$, and $c = 1/4$.

Since the denominators of all weighting factors are powers of two, the multiplication of image pixels by the weighting factors can be simply implemented using binary shift operations. For instance, a pixel multiplied by 3/8 is the sum of the value shifted two places to the right plus the original value, all shifted three places to the right.

To maintain numerical accuracy, the summation elements have been expanded to 12 bits each. Four bits with values of 0 are appended to the right of each image pixel value before computation. The eight most significant bits of the final result are maintained.

11.5.2 Two Implementations for Gaussian Pyramid on Splash 2

Figure 11.10a shows the block diagram of a five-chip pyramid generation architecture that has been developed for Splash 2 [1, 7]. This implementation is based on the recirculating pipeline structure, and is designed to produce five levels of pyramids (g_0 through g_5). Although compact, this architecture is capable of converting only every other image frame into pyramid form (15 frames per second). The Control Element PE-0 buffers image pixels, and passes the data to Processing Element PE-1 through the crossbar. The processing steps of this architecture are horizontal convolution by ω_x (Processing Element PE-1), vertical convolution by ω_y (Processing Elements PE-2 and PE-3), and recirculating and output image production (Processing Element PE-4).

The Control Element PE-0 broadcasts image pixels, representing g_0, through the crossbar to Processing Elements PE-1 through PE-3, which compute the first level of the Gaussian pyramid, g_1. Image data is recirculated through the crossbar to PE-1, and processed through the same path to form the higher pyramid levels. Two different crossbar configurations are used to multiplex the original image data and feedback pyramid data. PE-0 controls the crossbar configuration, which is used during processing.

Device PE-1 receives image data from either PE-0 or PE-4 through the crossbar, computes the convolution by ω_x, and passes the result to PE-2. Resampling in

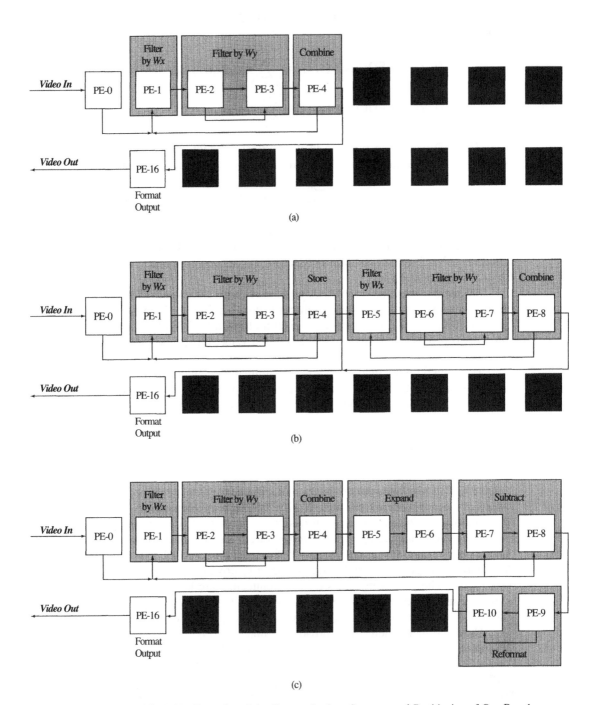

FIGURE 11.10 Examples of the Communications Structure and Partitioning of One-Board Pyramid Applications. a) simple five-level Gaussian Pyramid generator, b) Gaussian Pyramid generator using the hybrid pipeline architecture, and c) five-level Laplacian Pyramid generator.

the horizontal dimension is performed during the convolution to eliminate half of the computations. The image data that is passed to PE-2 has half of the pixels per image row.

The image data is presented into Splash 2 one row at a time in raster order. The 8-bit image pixels that are presented to PE-1 are grouped so that four pixels are passed simultaneously on the crossbar. Four control bits on this data path are appended to indicate data validity and the pyramid level.

PE-2 and PE-3 together implement the convolution by ω_y. Unlike the convolution in the horizontal direction, the five pixels required by each computation are not presented in the same image row, but in five consecutive rows. The image data, therefore, needs to be stored in a delay line, which is implemented using the external RAMs. One memory write and four memory reads are needed for sequencing the data for each 5×1 convolution. Only one memory write and two memory reads are allowed in four Splash 2 cycles because of access constraints. PE-2 computes three of the five partial sums, and passes the 12-bit partial result directly to PE-3. PE-3 performs the remaining three partial sums, and passes the rounded 8-bit value to PE-4.

PE-4 resamples the image data in the vertical dimension to reduce the number of pixels per image-column by half. The data are then recirculated to PE-1 through the crossbar to form the next level of the pyramid. Each pyramid level is also made available to the next Processing Element, PE-5, for further analysis.

11.5.3 The Hybrid Pipeline Gaussian Pyramid Structure

The block diagram of a nine-chip hybrid structure of a Gaussian pyramid generator is shown in Figure 11.10b. The original image pixel (g_0) are passed to PE-1 directly from the input stream, and are processed through Processing Elements PE-1 through PE-4 to form the first-level Gaussian pyramid, g_1. Processing Elements PE-5 through PE-8 generate the remaining four levels of the pyramid. PE-9 takes data from PE-4 and PE-8 to form the resulting pyramids.

The hybrid implementation requires five more PEs than the recalculating implementation. The two stages comprised of PE-1 through PE-4 and PE-5 through PE-8 are very similar in structure. The key advantage of this algorithm (at the cost of four additional PEs) is that it is capable of generating Gaussian pyramids in real time (30 frames per second).

11.5.4 The Laplacian Pyramid

The Laplacian pyramid as illustrated in Figure 11.9b is a sequence of difference images, in which each image is the difference between two successive Gaussian levels. Two types of Laplacian pyramids are in common use: the filter-subtract-decimate (FSD) structure and the reduce-expand (RE) structure [6].

The FSD Laplacian is formed by subtracting a filtered image of the next-higher Gaussian pyramid level from the same level of the pyramid image. The kth level of the FSD Laplacian pyramid can be expressed as,

$$L_k^{FSD}(i, j) = g_k(i, j) - g_{k+1}^F(i, j) \tag{11.4}$$

where g_{k+1}^F is the $(k+1)$th level of the filtered Gaussian image before subsampling.

The RE pyramid generation structure includes two basic operations: image expansion and image subtraction. The EXPAND operation can be regarded as the reverse of the REDUCE function in Gaussian pyramid generation. First, the image size is doubled by inserting a pixel with a gray level of '0' between two successive pixels in every row and column. The expanded image is then convolved by the same Gaussian-like weighting function. As was done for the REDUCE function, the EXPAND operation is split into two 1-D identical convolutions applied to the image in both horizontal and vertical direction. The 1-D operation can be expressed as below:

$$g^i(x) = 2 \sum_{m=-2}^{2} \omega(m) g^e(x - m) \tag{11.5}$$

and

$$g^e(x) = \begin{cases} g\left(\frac{x}{2}\right) & \text{if } x \text{ is even} \\ 0 & \text{if } x \text{ is odd} \end{cases} \tag{11.6}$$

where $g(x)$ is the Gaussian pyramid image, and $g^i(x)$ and $g^e(x)$ are the 1-D interpolated and expanded image, respectively. The above equations can also be represented in a more explicit way:

$$g^i(x) = \begin{cases} 2 \times \left[\omega(-2) \times g\left(\frac{x}{2}+1\right) + \omega(0) \times g\left(\frac{x}{2}\right) + \omega(2) \times g\left(\frac{x}{2}-1\right)\right], & \text{if } x \text{ is even} \\ 2 \times \left[\omega(-1) \times g\left(\frac{x+1}{2}\right) + \omega(1) \times g\left(\frac{x-1}{2}\right)\right], & \text{if } x \text{ is odd} \end{cases} \tag{11.7}$$

Replacing the weighting factors $(\omega(-2), \ldots, \omega(2))$ with their values $\left[\frac{1}{16}, \frac{1}{4}, \frac{3}{8}, \frac{1}{4}, \frac{1}{16}\right]$, the equation can be simplified as follows:

$$g^i(x) = \begin{cases} \frac{1}{8} \times \left[g\left(\frac{x}{2}+1\right) + g\left(\frac{x}{2}-1\right)\right] + \frac{3}{4} \times g\left(\frac{x}{2}\right), & \text{if } x \text{ is even} \\ \frac{1}{2} \times \left[g\left(\frac{x+1}{2}\right) + g\left(\frac{x-1}{2}\right)\right], & \text{if } x \text{ is odd} \end{cases} \tag{11.8}$$

The odd-numbered pixel of the expanded image is equal to the weighted sum of two pixels in the Gaussian pyramid, and the even-numbered pixel is the weighted sum of three pixels, for instance pixels 1 and 4. The 1-D EXPAND operation can be considered as functions of 2-by-1 convolutions and 3-by-1 convolutions, with weighting functions of $\left[\frac{1}{2}, \frac{1}{2}\right]$ and $\left[\frac{1}{8}, \frac{3}{4}, \frac{1}{8}\right]$, respectively. Both weighting functions are normalized and symmetric as well. The edge pixels 0, 8, and 9 are not defined in Equation (11.4). In this design, the first and last calculated values, pixels 1 and 7, are duplicated to form the edge.

Once the pyramid is expanded to have the same size as the next-higher resolution pyramid, the *subtraction* operation is applied to obtain one Laplacian pyramid level. The function is expressed as:

$$L_k^{RE}(i, j) = g_k(i, j) - g_{k+1}^{int}(i, j) \tag{11.9}$$

where g^{int} is the interpolated image constructed from g^e.

11.5.5 Implementation of the Laplacian Pyramid on Splash 2

The Laplacian pyramid-generation system consists of two major parts: Gaussian pyramid generation, and image subtraction. The system uses the recirculating pipeline structure, as presented in the previous section, to generate a Gaussian image pyramid. After the Gaussian pyramid is generated from Processing Elements PE-0 through PE-4, the Laplacian pyramid is computed by Processing Elements PE-5 through PE-10, as shown in Figure 5.2. The data is passed directly to Processing Element PE-5, and to PE-7 and PE-8 through the crossbar. Devices PE-5 and PE-6 implement the EXPAND operation in the horizontal and vertical directions, respectively. The pixel-by-pixel SUBTRACTION operation is then implemented in chips PE-7 and PE-8 to generate a difference image. PE-9 and PE-10 reformat the images for output.

As described in the previous section, the data output from PE-4 to PE-5 is the image data directly from the "XP_Right" port of device PE-3. The 36-bit-wide bus carries only 20 bits of useful information: two 8-bit image pixels and four control bits. Since PE-3 does not perform the subsampling function in the vertical direction, the even-numbered rows of the image data are ignored in future data processing. A depiction of this implementation is given in Figure 11.10c.

11.6 PERFORMANCE

This section provides a quantitative summary of the performance of VTSPLASH for the operations discussed in the previous section. The computational properties, communications architectures, and required resources vary significantly from one application to the next. All of these examples operate at the pixel clock rate of 10 MHz with 512×512 images. Many of the applications presented here have been implemented using a pipeline architecture. The pipeline accepts digitized image data in raster order, often directly from a camera, and, in most cases, produces output data at the same rate, possibly with some latency. Many of these applications can be chained together to form higher-level image processing functions.

Simplified block diagrams illustrating the partitioning and communication architecture for selected tasks are shown in Figure 11.11. For example, Figure 11.11a shows the architecture for a region detection and labeling application [18]. This application analyzes an image to distinguish foreground objects from background through thresholding, and then for each foreground image, a unique label is assigned. This task is a useful front end for applications such as recognition, industrial inspection, and tracking. After the image is appropriately thresholded, an initial estimate is made of the disjoint regions in the image by the block labeled *Pass 1 Labeling*. It may be subsequently discovered that regions that were initially disjoint are actually contiguous. Such regions need to be merged and assigned the same label. This is accomplished in the following two blocks, *Pass 2 Merging (EVEN)* and *Pass 2 Merging (ODD)*.

Conventional performance-benchmarking techniques are at best awkward when applied to custom computing machinery. Figure 11.12 illustrates graphically the computational performance of each of these tasks executing on the VTSPLASH platform. In the figure, the application name is listed to the left of the graph. The

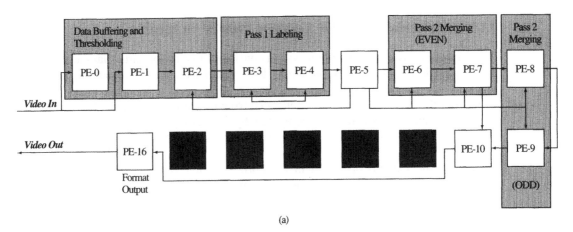

(a)

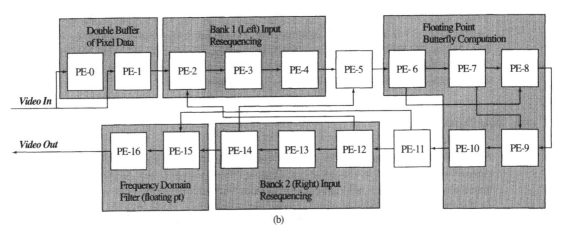

(b)

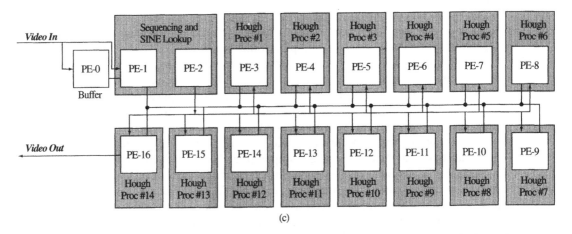

(c)

FIGURE 11.11   Examples of the Communications Structure and Partitioning for Examples that Use Only One Splash 2 Processor Array. a) region detection and labeling, b) FFT (forward transform), and c) Hough transform. Solid squares at Processing Element sites denote unused Processing Elements.

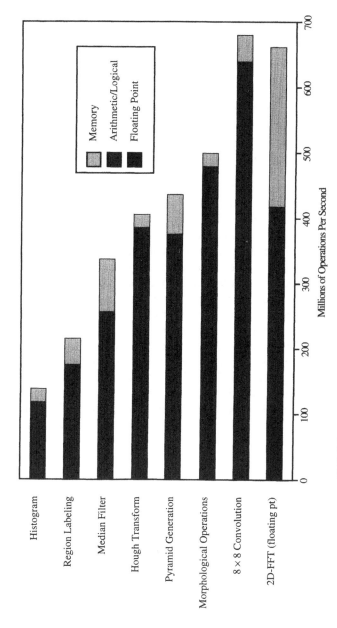

FIGURE 11.12 Approximate Performance of Image Processing Tasks

performance bar associated with each task consists of two or three components. The first component (*arithmetic/logical*) is an appraisal of the number of general-purpose operations performed, on average, per second. (These are operations that are likely to be found in the repertory of common RISC processors, such as MULTIPLY, XOR, or COMPARE.) This number, when divided by the pixel clock frequency of 10 MHz, gives an indication of the average number of the easily discernible arithmetic and logic function units (word parallel) that are active in each task. The second component of the performance bar provides an estimate of the number of storage references (memory accesses) performed by the task per second. The third component represents the number of floating-point operations. All of the tasks, except for the 2D-FFT application, use fixed-point operators. The pixel calculations for the 2D-FFT task utilize custom-designed floating-point arithmetic. The combination of these three components provides a basis for quantifying the computational load of each of the tasks, and provides a rough estimate of the number of operations performed each second.

The operating speed for an application is under the control of the designer, and depends upon critical path delays in the implementation. The Splash 2 processor features a programmable system clock that can be varied under software control from zero to 40 MHz. The tasks developed in this project were made to satisfy the *minimum* criteria of operating at the pixel data rate of 10 MHz. Because of limitations of the image data source, the listed applications were tested only at this rate. It is feasible that some of these tasks operate well beyond this clock frequency.

In addition to quantifying the number of operations per second, it is useful to consider how fast computations are performed relative to the input image frame rate of 30 Hz. Some of the tasks are completed during one frame time (histogramming, median filtering, Gaussian pyramid generation, and gray-scale morphological operations). Others require two image frame times (region labeling, 8×8 convolution, and Laplacian pyramid generation). The FFT implementation can completely process two 512×512 images per second (or 128×128 images at 30 frames per second) [21]. The time to complete the Hough transform is image-dependent; the implementation shown in Figure 11.11c distributes equal portions of an input image to separate PEs that process in parallel.

Another method of benchmarking the performance is to compare with contemporary machines. Comparisons were made with a general-purpose workstation (a Sun SPARCstation-10). The VTSPLASH applications run between 10 to 100 times faster than the same application written in C and executed on the SPARC workstation. A number of commercial machines exist that have been designed specifically for image processing. The Datacube MaxVideo 200 [8], for example, consists of several functional units that have been carefully tuned to perform common image-processing tasks. In most cases, for the specific tasks that are implemented by the application-specific hardware, the VTSPLASH system is outperformed. For example, the MaxVideo 200 can perform 8×8 convolution four times faster than the existing VTSPLASH implementation. The motivation of the custom-computing approach, therefore, is *not* to provide the fastest possible performance for a given task. As illustrated by VTSPLASH, the strength of this approach is the ability of the system to be reconfigured to provide high performance for a wide range of tasks. The performance of application-specific systems diminishes quickly for tasks that are not directly supported in hardware.

11.7 SUMMARY

Reconfigurable computing platforms, such as Splash 2, can readily adapt to meet the communication and computational requirements of a wide variety of applications. With the addition of input/output hardware, we have demonstrated that general-purpose custom computing machines are well suited for many meaningful image processing tasks. Such platforms are excellent testbeds for prototyping high-performance algorithms. The custom computing platform can be viewed not only as a general-purpose computing engine, but also as:

- a medium for hardware/software codesign
- a VHDL accelerator
- a testbed for rapid prototyping

Furthermore, the platform is multi-use since it can be reconfigured from one task to another by downloading a hardware-personalization database.

Applications operational on the VTSPLASH laboratory system include:

- 2-D Fast Fourier Transform (using floating point)
- Expandable 8×8 convolver (with on-line filter adjustment)
- Pan and zoom
- Median filtering
- Morphologic operators
- Histogram and graphical display
- Region detection and labeling

Splash is representative of the state of the art in custom computing processors—both in hardware capabilities and software support—yet it requires a substantial time investment to develop an application. To make this class of machinery more widely accepted and cost-effective, methods must be developed to reduce application development time. There are several promising endeavors that focus on this issue [3, 5, 12, 15].

ACKNOWLEDGMENTS

This project has been a success only because of the hard work of the entire VTSPLASH team at Virginia Tech. The team has included several graduate students, some of whom have graduated and taken leave for broader horizons. The major players have been Luna Chen, Robert Elliott, Brad Fross, Jeff Nevits, James Peterson, Ramana Rachakonda, Nabeel Shirazi, Adit Tarmaster, and Al Walters. The authors also gratefully acknowledge support and guidance from Jeffrey Arnold and Duncan Buell from the Supercomputing Research Center, and John McHenry.

REFERENCES

[1]   L. Abbott et al., "Finding Lines and Building Pyramids with Splash-2," *Proc. IEEE Workshop FPGAs for Custom Computing*, CS Press, Los Alamitos, Calif., 1994, pp. 155–163.

[2]   A.L. Abbott, R.M. Haralick, and X. Zhuang, "Pipeline Architectures for Morphologic Image Analysis," *Machine Vision and Applications*, Vol. 1, No. 1, 1988, pp. 23–40.

[3]   L. Agarwal, M. Wazlowski, and S. Ghosh, "An Asynchronous Approach to Efficient Execution of Programs on Adaptive Architectures Utilizing FPGAs," *Proc. IEEE Workshop FPGAs for Custom Computing*, CS Press, Los Alamitos, Calif., 1994, pp. 111–119.

[4]   P.M. Athanas and A.L. Abbott, "Processing Images in Real Time on a Custom Computing Platform," in R.W. Hartenstein and M.Z. Servít, eds., *Field-Programmable Logic: Architectures, Synthesis, and Applications*, Springer-Verlag, Berlin, 1994, pp. 156–167.

[5]   P. Athanas and H. Silverman, "Processor Reconfiguration through Instruction-Set Metamorphosis: Architecture and Compiler," *Computer*, Vol. 26, No. 3, Mar. 1993, pp. 11–18.

[6]   P.J. Burt and E.H. Adelson, "The Laplacian Pyramid as a Compact Image Code," *IEEE Trans. Comm.*, Vol. COM-31, No. 4, Apr. 1983, pp. 532–540.

[7]   L. Chen, "Fast Generation of Gaussian and Laplacian Image Pyramids Using an FPGA-based Custom Computing Platform," master's thesis, Virginia Polytechnic Inst., Blacksburg, Va., 1994.

[8]   Datacube, Inc., The MaxVideo 200 Reference Manual, Datacube, Inc., Danvers, Mass., 1994.

[9]   P.M. Dew, R.A. Earnshaw, and T.R. Heywood, eds., *Parallel Processing for Computer Vision and Display*, Addison-Wesley, Reading, Mass., 1989.

[10] R.O. Duda and P.E. Hart, "Use of the Hough Transform to Detect Lines and Curves in Pictures," *Comm. of the ACM*, Vol. 15, 1972, pp. 11–15.

[11] R. Elliott, "Hardware Implementation of a Straight Line Detector for Image Processing," master's thesis, Virginia Polytechnic Inst., Blacksburg, Va., 1993.

[12] M. Gokhale and R. Minnich, "FPGA Computing in a Data Parallel C," *Proc. IEEE Workshop FPGAs for Custom Computing*, CS Press, Los Alamitos, Calif., 1993, pp. 94–101.

[13] P.V.C. Hough, "A Method and Means for Recognizing Complex Patterns," U.S. Patent No. 3,069,654, 1962.

[14] B. Jahne, *Digital Image Processing*, Springer-Verlag, New York, 1991.

[15] Q. Motiwala, "Optimizations for Acyclic Dataflow Graphs for Hardware-Software Codesign," master's thesis, Virginia Polytechnic Inst., Blacksburg, Va., 1994.

[16] R.J. Offen, *VLSI Image Processing*, McGraw-Hill, New York, 1985.

[17] W.K. Pratt, *Digital Image Processing*, Wiley, New York, 1978.

[18] R. Rachakonda, "Region Detection and Labeling in Real-time Using a Custom Computing Platform," master's thesis, Virginia Polytechnic Inst., Blacksburg, Va., 1994.

[19] A. Rosenfeld and A. Kak, *Digital Picture Processing*, 2nd ed., Academic Press, New York, 1982.

[20] J. Serra, *Image Analysis and Mathematical Morphology*, Academic Press, London, 1982.

[21] N. Shirazi, "Implementation of a 2-D Fast Fourier Transform on an FPGA-based Computing Platform," master's thesis, Virginia Polytechnic Inst., 1995.

[22] N. Shirazi, A. Walters, and P. Athanas, "Quantitative Analysis of Floating-Point Arithmetic on FPGA-based Custom Computing Machines," *Proc. IEEE Symp. FPGAs for Custom Computing*, CS Press, Los Alamitos, Calif., 1995, pp. 155–162.

[23] A. Tarmaster, "Median and Morphological Filtering of Images in Real Time Using an FPGA-based Custom Computing Platform," master's thesis, Virginia Polytechnic Inst., Blacksburg, Va., 1994.

[24] L. Uhr, ed., *Parallel Computer Vision*, Academic Press, New York, 1987.

[25] G. VanDerWal and P. Burt, "A VLSI Pyramid Chip for Multiresolution Image Analysis," *Int'l J. of Computer Vision*, Vol. 8, No. 3, 1992, pp. 177–189.

[26] R. Vogt, *Automatic Generation of Morphological Set Recognition Algorithms*, Springer-Verlag, New York, 1989.

[27] Xilinx, Inc., *The Programmable Gate Array Data Book*, Xilinx, Inc., San Jose, Calif., 1994.

CHAPTER 12

The Promise and the Problems

Duncan A. Buell and Jeffrey M. Arnold

The time has come to reflect upon what we have done. The soldering irons have grown cold on the workbenches, the celebration cake has long been eaten, and even the T-shirts are fading from too many launderings. What have we learned? Where did we go right? Where did we go wrong? Have suppositions been confirmed as facts or debunked as myths? Most important, for it is the whole basis for research, what from our experience might prove valuable to the next builders of such hardware?

12.1 SOME BOTTOM-LINE CONCLUSIONS

12.1.1 High Bandwidth I/O Is a Must

This will come as no surprise to anyone in the traditional high-performance computing business, but in our situation, the rationale is slightly different. We have, in a CCM, relatively little state that can be retained in the processor portion of the machine. To achieve high performance, then, one must have an application that requires extensive computation localized on a very small amount of data or a computation that requires relatively little state but is "compute-intensive" because it must be done to a relatively large volume of data. The RSA encryption/decryption algorithm done by Shand et al. [3] at the DEC Paris lab—modular exponentiation of 512-bit integers with 512-bit exponents—is an example of the former kind of application but we have found such applications, in general, to be rare. The latter category of applications, including signal processing, image processing, data compression, and the like, appear to predominate. To handle such applications, it must be possible to get data to the CCM at a rate that permits the FPGAs to demonstrate their computational superiority.

Another issue that contributes to the desire to operate on large sets or continuous streams of data is the relatively high cost of loading an application "program" onto the FPGA. A Xilinx XC4010 takes about 22 msec to configure (180, 000 bits at 8 MHz). With system overhead from a workstation disk, this can approach 100 msec. At a clock speed of 20 MHz, 100 msec is 2 million cycles lost to reconfiguration. If each configuration of the FPGA ran for as many as 2 million cycles, the CCM would be utilized only half the time; to achieve 90 percent utilization, each configuration would need to execute on the order of 18 million cycles.

A corollary of the conclusion that I/O bandwidth is important is that I/O from the CCM to the outside world, and not just to the host computer, is essential. The 4 Mbytes per second or so that can be delivered from a SCSI disk is not enough. In the world of supercomputers, it is often observed that one of the few attributes distinguishing a supercomputer from a high-performance workstation is the speed at which data can be delivered from disk to processor. CCMs are unlikely to be designed to connect to supercomputers, if only because the small number of supercomputers makes it difficult for a commercial CCM industry to develop around them. We believe, therefore, that for CCMs to become commercially successful there must be a model of data flow and control similar to that of Splash 2: in addition to the usual programming and control lines to the host (workstation), there must be an ability to take data from some other source at rates much higher than workstation disks allow. We remark that our conclusion here seems to be consistent with the thoughts behind and design of the DEC systems.

12.1.2 Memory Is a Must

We have reasoned that a CCM like Splash 2 needs high I/O bandwidth because the computations must be relatively simple and must require relatively little state. Therefore, in order to be useful, the CCM must process a large volume of data. Our conclusion that it is important to have as much memory as possible as close to the FPGAs as possible stems from a similar line of reasoning. The Processing Elements one designs into the FPGAs must be relatively simple; the FPGAs are not yet large enough to accommodate complex objects, and they operate at speeds that are slow by microprocessor standards, so multiple-tick state machines are not going to provide a performance advantage unless significant pipelining is possible. It has been our experience that including memory for lookup tables and similar augmentations of processor state is absolutely vital to obtaining high performance. Memory is essential, and the more memory the better, because it permits, among other things, a fast horizontal encoding that requires little logic to implement, instead of a vertical encoding that takes either more complex logic or more pipeline steps.

We point out here, as was mentioned once before, that some of the lookup tables one might want to use would be much larger than could reasonably be implemented in any system. A lookup table for an 8-bit by 8-bit multiplier requires only $\frac{1}{8}$ Mbyte of memory, for example, but an only slightly less modest 12-bit by 12-bit multiplier requires 48 Mbytes. We further mention that the memory *structure* can also be important. We were pin-limited in Splash 2 and coupled one memory to one FPGA. As FPGAs accommodate larger and larger designs on a single chip, the probability will grow that more than one part of a given chip's design will need to access memory in the same clock period. The data stream-oriented computations on Splash 2 tended to have many small computational units in a pipeline. It can easily happen that each of these needs its own lookup table but more than one exists on a single FPGA, making a single memory port the bottleneck.

To some extent our conclusion here differs from what one might deduce from the work at DEC, but we remain skeptical of designs in which the FPGAs and the memories lie in separate clusters. There has been work and there seems to be continuing interest in single chips or in multi-chip modules that closely couple programmable logic and memory. Either arrangement would enlarge the processor state without continuing the current limitations, faced by Splash 2 and all other present systems, of insufficient pins for the memory bandwidth desired plus the inherent loss of speed in having to go off-chip for memory references. The disadvantage of this approach (at least the single-chip approach) is that the amount of memory that can be integrated with the processor is severely limited. This implies the need for a hierarchical memory, that is, a larger external backing store in addition to the on-chip memory, which would now function much as a cache functions in traditional processor architectures.

12.1.3 Programming Is Possible, and Becoming More So

We began Splash 2 with the firm belief that it would be possible to program Splash 2 from a high-level language, but without any clear notion of exactly *how* this would be accomplished. Our belief has not turned out to be a delusion, and the clear ideas of how to accomplish the desired ends came to us as we progressed in the project. There were questions about whether an appropriate subset of VHDL could be identified as the high-level "programming language." There were questions about whether the VHDL environment provided by vendors would provide the support we needed and, if not, whether our own augmentations could be made. There were a number of questions about the ability to sequence the vendors' tools into a compilation process. In part due to our sponsorship of work on the Synopsys FPGA Compiler and in part as a consequence of more general interest in CCMs, the path from high-level VHDL to Xilinx bitstream files is much smoother than it was three years ago. Xilinx, on the one hand, has raised the level at which their software supports design—the XBLOX tool allows circuit designers to use much larger building blocks of registers, sequencers, and the like, instead of constructing them individually from CLBs. From the top down, Synopsys has made a serious commitment to target the architecture of FPGAs in the technology-mapping phase of logic synthesis so that the resources of Xilinx (and other) FPGAs can be used efficiently and achieve performance closer to that attainable with handcrafted designs. There is now a reasonably smooth process from VHDL to Xilinx chips that yields acceptably high performance, and the situation will no doubt continue to improve in the future.

12.1.4 The Programming Environment Is Crucial

We have asserted that programming of CCMs is in fact possible. We now maintain further that the great effort we expended to create a complete programming environment has been crucial to users' acceptance of the fact that a CCM is to be viewed as a "computer."

Users of modern computer systems expect an interactive programming environment. They expect to be able to compile programs quickly, test them on sample data, step them through a debugger, and examine the resulting output. With many experimental hardware systems, performing these tasks on the hardware itself can be quite difficult. Complicating the usual problems of dealing with experimental hardware (which one might imagine to be of questionable reliability) is the very significant problem for Splash 2 and for similar CCMs of the time required for logic synthesis and the placement and routing of the netlist onto the Xilinx chips. In the absence of the simulation environment that allowed programs to be written and debugged until they were functionally correct, we doubt that many of our applications would have been completed. Certainly we feel that none of the "users" (as distinct from the "true believers") would have been willing to follow through to a completed application without the full panoply of simulation and development tools available to them.

A further reason to stress this point is that although, on the one hand a solid programming environment is an obvious desideratum, its achievement requires the cooperation of vendors. In order for T2 to be successful in a debugging mode, it was necessary that T2 be able to associate with the objects of the synthesis process the VHDL objects named within the program; otherwise, it would not be possible for T2 to examine the state in the FPGAs for debugging purposes. Similarly, although users need not ordinarily be concerned with information at the bitstream file level, those who would write system software and programming development tools may have occasion to need some of this information, at least the placement or mapping of flip-flops to CLBs and the ability to extract the flip-flop state from the chip in readback mode for debugging. Certainly, if one is to envision a CCM acting as a closely connected coprocessor instead of as an attached processor "at cable's length" like Splash 2, some details are also necessary. One concept being explored is the idea of swapping parts of a design on an FPGA in and out, in the way that code is swapped in and out of virtual memory. This will require that the systems software writer have access to information about the location of the portions of the design to be swapped out, and the I/O paths in and out of those regions of the FPGA. Swapping hardware also implies the need to constrain the physical mapping phase of compilation to lay the logic out in particular shapes, or use only particular portions of the chip.

12.2 TO WHERE FROM HERE?

Throughout the Splash 2 project, we were asked the obvious question, "Will there be a Splash 3?" That question has always been answered in the negative. There have never been plans to do a third-version system, largely because Splash 2 is, if anything, already too complex and contains too many features.

This is not a statement that Splash 2 is flawed in its design, but rather the simple admission that it would make a poor "product" in its present form, something that has been recognized by the commercial licensees—none of the commercial versions contains all the features of the original Splash 2 system. Splash 2 was designed to be large enough to deliver high performance through parallelism, and yet few applications really used anything like the full complement of hardware that could be assembled. It was designed with a rich interconnect structure, and yet many applications use only a small part of the interconnect.

In general, we find that while all the features of the system have been used at one time or another, any single application uses only a subset of the features. And, given that we are on the edge of what can reasonably be put on a board or in a system, the cost of the features is not linear with their number. If we had to do it all over again, there are certainly some things we would change. With more pins on a Xilinx chip, we could have a 32-bit data path to memory instead of only 16. With the newer, larger, Xilinx FPGAs, we could get more logic on a chip and board and achieve higher performance. We have an extra address pin left over, and we would certainly like to double the memory attached to each FPGA. But these possibilities, intriguing as they are, represent incremental changes in the hardware to the inevitable progress of technology. What should concern us more is not the moving target of state-of-the-art technology but the broader choices of architecture, programming style, and applications for which a Custom Computing Machine makes sense.

It is within this broader framework that we realize that no good follow-on to Splash 2 exists because the major goals of the research effort have been met. Splash 2 was largely a research prototype, although some of the requirements for "real work" to be done go beyond those normally expected of such a prototype. The major goals were to build the attached processor, to demonstrate its computational effectiveness, and to demonstrate that it could be programmed. These have been met, and although there are many research questions to be addressed, none of these require the building of a "bigger and better" next version of *this* machine.

This is not to say that Splash 2 is "the last word" in CCMs. Rather, it is to say that the benefits to be gained from building a Splash 2-like machine for *research* purposes probably do not outweigh the costs. If one had real applications and real customers for a similar machine, the conclusion on costs and benefits might be different, but the decision for research purposes seems clear. A bigger machine does not seem warranted. Splash 2 was extensible in terms of number of Array Boards beyond what we found we had applications to support, and although one could now build, with flat-pack FPGAs, a board with more compute power on it, it does not seem clear that research conclusions could be drawn from the new system that could not be drawn by extrapolation from Splash 2.

The Array Board architecture similarly seems, if not optimal, at least sufficiently general yet capable of high performance, such that variations within its genre are unjustified. The two basic modes of data flow—linear and broadcast—are well supported and augmented by a crossbar whose full range of capabilities was never needed. Here, as elsewhere, we believe the research value of this part of the design space has been adequately explored. We can easily imagine a worthwhile machine produced for a niche market that resembles Splash 2. We can easily imagine other architectures (a richer hierarchical machine, for example, with clusters of FPGAs at each level of a tree structure). We can easily imagine that changes in or improvements to FPGA technology (for example, greater on-board memory, perhaps content-addressable memory, incorporation of higher-level functions, incorporation of FPGAs onto multi-chip modules) might introduce new reasons to engineer a Splash 2-like machine. But absent these justifications, we do not feel that research conducted in the building of another Splash 2-like machine is likely to lead to conclusions that could not readily be predicted from studies on Splash 2.

It is worth mentioning one major architectural feature that one would want to change in a next-generation machine. Splash 2 was oriented toward computations in which the data streamed past processing elements. The 36-bit-wide data path allows both parallel single-bit streams or wider, word-oriented streams. On a given Array Board, substantial interconnect allows for adjustments in time of the data stream. Similarly, when programmed as a SIMD machine, extensive broadcast capability exists, as well as an efficient back door for removal of a result stream. Looked at this way, the next architectural step is obvious, and almost impossible. One would like to provide, at a board-to-board level, the rich interconnect that exists on the individual boards. This is the problem we dealt with in Chapter 4 in discussing the evolution of the Splash 2 architecture. Providing the same level of interconnect among the boards that the FPGAs have on each board is a complicated matter, however, and one must ask whether the payoff justifies the expense. The answer, in terms of good applications that were made impossible due only to insufficient board-to-board communication, is no.

The problem of board-to-board communication is not unique to Splash 2 and its orientation toward a linear data stream. The DEC PeRLe PAM, with its Xilinx chips arranged in a two-dimensional grid, suffers from the same problem—at some point, an application might outgrow a single board and require substantial communication from one board to another. Fortunately, however, with Splash 2 we seem to win on both fronts. Not only does it appear that most reasonable computations can be done with at most a small number of boards requiring little communication among them (and we are sincere in our belief that we have not begged the question here), the omnipresent march of technology makes it possible to put more and more onto a single board, so that the problem should be getting less, rather than more, pronounced with time.

In retrospect, the most problematic feature of the Splash 2 architecture—the crossbar[1]—was perhaps not worth the effort, although there was no way to predict the events that occurred. The features of the crossbar—multiple configurations, dynamic choice of configuration, one-tick latency—were all used in one application or another, but each can be obtained (at some cost) by means of other switch chips or architectures.

12.3 IF NOT SPLASH 3, THEN WHAT?

Having decided that Splash 3 is not in the offing, it is reasonable to ask what sort of future research does make sense. We do not feel that the end of the CCM idea has been reached, and we expect that, in addition to other machines independently designed, several variations on our general theme (Splash 2α, Splash 2β, ... , if you will) will appear.

What we have claimed in the previous section is that the Splash 2 line of research machines for demonstration purposes is (at least temporarily) at an end, with strongly positive conclusions: sufficient compute power exists in an attached processor to obtain high performance, data can be delivered at a rate high enough to keep the processor busy and meet real-world constraints, and the machine can in fact

---

[1]The reader should consult Appendix A for the saga of the crossbar chips.

be programmed. What we see as future work is an elaboration of the hardware and software ideas for CCMs, now that we know that such elaboration could be worthwhile: not only must existence precede essence, but in the real world of engineering design the existence of follow-on machines must be justified by the success of their predecessors. We present some thoughts, then, on areas ripe for further work.

12.3.1 Architectures

There are strong arguments in favor of a trend toward physically smaller rather than larger systems. It is difficult to justify the price of very large systems, and such systems, with the added cabinet, backplane, interfacing, and such, are inherently more cumbersome to build. Also, as systems get physically larger, it becomes more difficult to keep propagation delays down. CCMs tend to get much of their performance advantage from tightly pipelined and carefully, explicitly, synchronized computations; these become more difficult to achieve in a system in which the propagation delays, which must be taken into account, have more than one value.

Mitigating the problem of justifying large systems is the fact that as technology advances, small systems tend more and more to deliver the processing capability of large systems. A further advantage that comes with making systems smaller and therefore cheaper is that they can be specialized to a particular collection of applications. These CCMs are inherently things that need not be single-purpose but are not likely in the near future to be general-purpose; one clear trend is toward programmable systems within a particular market. For example, there have been several designs from commercial vendors that combine DSP chips and FPGAs on a single board, aimed at signal-processing tasks of various kinds. None of these of which we are aware are "programmable" yet in the sense that Splash 2 is programmable—applications are still designed using CAD tools. But with the success of Splash 2 and of the DEC PeRLe systems and the growing awareness of the ability to make detailed circuit design unnecessary by the use of higher-level tools, we have no doubt that programming of such systems will come in the near future.

If physically smaller systems seem to be the trend, the following is, we feel, an argument against *logically* smaller systems. For the foreseeable future, CCMs will be one to two generations behind general-purpose machines, since commodity microprocessors and not FPGAs drive the technology and the market. In terms of logic performance (that is, clock rate), general-purpose machines start with about an order of magnitude advantage over CCMs. A CCM must overcome this disadvantage just to break even. Then, in order to cover the additional costs of hardware and software, download time, and such, one can argue that the CCM needs another order of magnitude in performance improvement to be considered a serious competitor. These performance advantages are presumably to be made up through parallelism in the application running on the CCM, but how small can one make a CCM and still obtain at least 100-fold parallelism? For the next several years at least, we would argue that systems with only a small number of FPGAs simply will not have the compute power to be competitive.

Although it is not technically our province to comment on the architecture of FPGAs themselves, at this point we discuss aspects of chip architecture that directly affect their use in CCMs. In this discussion, although two competing themes emerge, we do have a preference. At the grossest level and with the greatest of oversimplifications, there are two extant architectures in FPGAs. A coarse-grain architecture has 2-bit or 4-bit logic blocks and routing resources around the blocks. A fine-grain architecture, by contrast, has 1-bit logic blocks (lookup tables with two or sometimes three inputs, but only one output and only one stored value) with routing of lines going through the blocks (and thus making them unavailable for other purposes).

On the one hand, the larger logic block of the coarse-grain architecture is attractive, and the 4-bit block especially so, for the purpose of doing arithmetic. On the other hand, the routing of signals in the fine-grain architecture design is "local," so that portions of the chip can be identified with portions of the design. If an ultimate goal is to dynamically change part of the design on a chip, the fine-grain architecture is preferable. It avoids one of the problems of the Xilinx architecture, which is that the signals on routing resources adjacent to CLBs can come from distant parts of the design and be relatively unrelated to the computation being performed in the CLB.

We have already mentioned the issue of including memory (in quantity) with the routing and logic on an FPGA. This would allow the processor element/memory pairs of a CCM to be shrunk onto the FPGA itself (or even multiple replicated processor/memory pairs on a single FPGA).

12.3.2 Custom Processors

We have said nothing for the most part about one of the most enticing uses of FPGAs for Custom Computing Machines—the idea of a custom coprocessor or customizable processor. If one traces the development of microprocessor architecture through the 1970s and 1980s, one can find arguments both for and against the inclusion of coprocessors in modern workstations. Long ago, in the heyday of such chips as the 8086, math coprocessors also flourished to do the arithmetic functions that just would not fit on chips of that era. Now we find in most modern high-performance workstations both floating-point and integer arithmetic in the processor chip, and 64-bit arithmetic at that. One can legitimately argue that any further "special functions" that might benefit from an FPGA coprocessor are probably things that could be included in the next generation's processor as a matter of course.

On the other hand, it is probably true that among all the computations performed that need high performance, a rather broad range exists of "special functions" that would be desirable to have as processor instructions and not in software emulations. Whether any one of them would be deemed significant enough to warrant its inclusion in silicon is questionable, and the full list of such possible instructions is no doubt much longer than what would be feasible in the near future. A more interesting—and feasible—idea is that the FPGA resource could be incorporated directly onto the processor chip. If the math coprocessor can make the move, why not the customizable processor?

A further argument against coprocessors is the extent to which the low-level hardware and software of the machine must be adapted to permit the coprocessor to be used. In order for a coprocessor to be of value (implementing an instruction not found on the processor, for example, just as the 8087 implemented arithmetic not present on the 8086), the connection between processor and coprocessor must be very tight. Control of execution of the processor and coprocessor must be maintained and data passed between the two with the barest minimum of overhead. Exceptional conditions probably need to be handled in hardware. Most important, it must be possible for the compilers and the operating system to recognize when use of the coprocessor is advantageous, to arrange in advance for the coprocessor's "program" to be loaded, and to handle use of the coprocessor so that the only way a user would detect its presence would be by the decreased execution time.

If the future of coprocessors seems uncertain, the future of genuinely customizable processors seems less so. The dbC approach seems to go the old Burroughs B1700 one better than its multiple instruction set architectures. However one designs an Instruction Set Architecture, the fact will remain that much of the silicon resource on a chip is not actually in use in any given clock cycle. An advantage of the dbC approach is that, at least as far as the individual program is concerned, only those resources that are needed must be included. When the day comes that an FPGA (or its technological successor) permits dynamic reconfiguration while in execution, one could envision swapping portions of "processor hardware" in and out as needed. A more limited silicon resource would provide more capability by being reusable for multiple purposes.

The key to the above idea must come in the ability of the compiler and operating system to identify "processing units" and locality thereof, to extract and synthesize these units, and to manipulate their caching and loading with the same facility that virtual memory is handled today. And this idea will probably not be relevant to all forms of computation. There is and will no doubt continue to be a solid market for machines that do those things we now consider ordinary, and unless there is a substantial portion of a computation that is simply not done well on a traditional machine, there will be no incentive to try a reconfigurable processor—custom silicon will always be faster, and mass-market commodity machines will always be cheaper. But the quicker time-to-market of programmable hardware is an advantage, and if a selected set of niche markets were to be determined and were then targeted by commercial operations capable of carrying out successful business plans, then we feel that such reconfigurable processor machines, whose underlying processor architecture was defined only at compile-time or runtime, could become almost commonplace.

12.3.3 Languages

Without doubt, the deepest and most fascinating question regarding the evolution of CCMs is that of their programming models and languages. This is the thorny issue that has bedeviled those responsible for language software for parallel computers for nearly two decades. How much detail of the machine should the programmer see? What is the penalty in performance for a high-level view? Users of high performance computer systems have usually been willing to endure in the name of speed some agony not suffered by those for whom speed is not so vital, but it is also true that there is a limit to the patience of even these stalwarts. Should the cost of programming surpass an ill-defined and yet very real threshold, the cost is not merely an incremental loss in the number of users and applications but a rejection of the entire system.

We can look to several different experiences for insight in this issue. Most significant is our own experience with VHDL and Splash 2. After that, of course, we can make comparisons with dbC on Splash 2. Finally, there is the work of others, such as the C extension done at DEC Paris and the VHDL work done by Box at Lockheed Sanders for CHAMP [1]. All of these can also be viewed merely as the first steps taken, in part because one could capitalize on existing knowledge and tools. A necessary further step is to contemplate in the abstract what would be most desirable if one were free of the need to consider present cost, personnel, past history, and backward compatibility.

A great many of the Splash 2 applications were done not as procedural programs but as a series of processes pipelined together, through which data flowed synchronously. These resemble nothing quite so much as programs in discrete event system simulation, and a language like VHDL seems highly suitable for this kind of programming. The SIGNAL data type provides for explicitly concurrent events and allows the programmer to express in a natural way the parallelism inherent in a computation. The fact that SIGNALs are updated with every clock tick allows the programmer to specify very precisely what the synchronization of the concurrent processes is to be. The alternative of the VARIABLE data type, by contrast, is suitable for procedural segments of code or for code over whose execution the programmer need not take such care.

The negative side of the program control offered by the explicit parallelism of SIGNALs in VHDL is that the programmer *must* in fact synchronize the updates and that "off by one" errors in choreographing this process can be common. We feel that this does not argue against VHDL so much as it argues in favor of spreadsheet-like tools that facilitate such programming. The expressiveness of a genuine parallel language (which VHDL most certainly is) seems to be necessary to achieve the needed performance. Rather than abandoning the parallelism because it can make programming difficult, one must work to compensate for the difficulty, with better tools.

If many of the Splash 2 applications resemble discrete event system simulation programs, they are also like systolic programs or data flow programs. They differ from the former in that the processes can vary widely in type and size and the programs are not nearly so well-structured as are systolic programs. And they differ from data flow programs in that they have *more* structure—the expected performance advantage comes in part from the tight pipelining and synchronization of the processes, as mentioned above.

We contemplated at several points in the Splash 2 project an investigation of one or more of the various languages available for programming in which the control of execution comes not from an instruction sequencer but from the synchronous flow of the data. We have no doubt that for many applications this might be a much more natural model of computation than presently exists. That we have done no such investigation is due entirely to the fact that we had to stay focused on the main goals and could not allow ourselves to be too distracted by curiosity from those ends which had to be accomplished. In the eventual fullness of time, however, we expect that such a study would be of great value.

One major drawback to the use of a data-driven language and model of computation must be raised. Programming of Splash 2 in VHDL has already proved to be a bit of a hard sell because VHDL "just isn't C." VHDL is nonetheless a DoD standard, taught to students across the world, used in industry, and supported by very sophisticated software tools. With all this in its favor, and working against it only the religious objections and the concerned hand-wringing of middle managers whose performance appraisals depend on quantity of present output, how much harder would it be to gain acceptance of another language, which no doubt would be viewed as even more exotic?

It was to a great extent in response to the above concerns that we discussed augmenting the standard VHDL framework with features that would make programming Splash 2 much more C-like (a VHDL++, as it were), or in the other direction removing from the available VHDL language tools those aspects not needed for Splash 2 programming and potentially confusing or threatening to applications programmers (to produce VHDL−−?). Some of each would seem desirable.

We remark finally that with two different applications the price paid both in FPGA resources used and in speed of execution was about a factor of three or less between handcrafted XACT designs and synthesized VHDL code in the normal Splash 2 programming model. We feel that both are acceptable. The resource estimate was with an earlier version of the synthesis tools than is presently available, and may already have improved. The speed differential is not much different from that between high-level language and assembly code, and thus is not likely to be the deciding factor, except for those few applications that are even with XACT implementations running on the margins of acceptable speed.

If the questions surrounding Splash 2 and its normal VHDL programming model are not of capability but of acceptability, then almost the opposite is true of dbC. The language here clearly *is* C, or as close to C as one can expect to get and still be running on a SIMD machine. There are two basic questions: Can the performance be great enough to be adequate? Is the range of SIMD applications broad enough to justify the use of a different language for them?

We have remarked on the factor-of-three performance difference between XACT and VHDL. It has been further noticed that roughly the same difference exists between dbC programs and their "directly VHDL" counterparts. This comes to a factor of nearly an order of magnitude, which is probably not tolerable. (The genome sequence comparisons mentioned in Chapters 8 and 9, in contrast, show a factor of 150 superiority for the VHDL version.) There will no doubt always be some penalty for generating the code automatically through dbC; it remains to be seen whether the minimized value of this penalty is small enough.

We are much more sanguine about the breadth of SIMD applications. There are several computational problems—including much of image processing, one natural area for CCMs—that can be done very effectively as SIMD computations. An additional argument in favor of a programming model like that of dbC is that SIMD programs have the same sort of carefully sequenced flow of control that the Splash 2 VHDL programs do. Thus, although the applications are limited and there is a danger that one might need a VHDL-like programming model as well to handle non-SIMD aspects of even a largely SIMD computation, we expect that continued work on dbC is reasonable and will find use in real applications.

We comment finally on a matter that is not just a matter of language but of the entire programming process for CCMs, and that is the question of upward compatibility. It has been crucial in many computing environments for established users to be able to upgrade hardware without substantially changing programs that represent their investment of time in the process of solving their problems. It seems unlikely in this early stage of marketing of CCM that users will be able to avoid some level of discomfort at the changes in the hardware, programming, and logic synthesis tools underneath their applications. Clearly, then, to be successful, the benefits in improved performance will need to be able to overcome this drawback.

12.4 THE "KILLER" APPLICATIONS

It seems a staple of the computing industry's folklore that novel products like CCMs need to have at least one "killer" application for which the new product is so well suited that it is clearly the preferred choice. Once the product has gained a foothold in the commercial marketplace and can be viewed to "exist" in a serious sense, broader usage is then to be expected. This is part of the very real spinoff and serendipity side of technology advancement.

What, then, might be those killer applications? Three broad categories seem clear: a) image processing; b) real-time data handling and control, in which one finds large volumes of data with computations that are limited in complexity but relatively unusual if done on standard microprocessors; and c) rapid prototyping and architecture emulation, in which reconfigurability of a platform is essential to allow exploration of alternatives, but for which some sort of hardware solution is required to provide answers in a reasonably timely manner.

The two chapters on video processing and fingerprint matching are illustrative of the first of these three categories. The number of basic operations to be performed in unit time is very high. The operations themselves are not "standard," often because arithmetic using relatively few bits is possible. There is a high degree of parallelism and/or pipelining in the modest collection of algorithms that need to be implemented. These argue in favor of a hardware solution. And, arguing against ASIC development, the computations or data formats are not so totally standard and structured that today's full-custom hardware can be expected to provide a longer-term solution. Arguing further in favor of a CCM is that while hardware can be built to handle data or image compression, convolutional filtering, signal encoding or decoding, and so forth, with the use of reconfigurable hardware one can use the same hardware, or at least replicated versions of the same hardware running different programs, rather than requiring multiple distinct parts. The obvious advantages then apply with respect to building and maintaining the hardware and the application programmer/designer being able to implement and maintain programs on the final system.

Perhaps the best present example of real-time data handling or control using a CCM is the use by Moll et al. [2] of the DEC PeRLe-1 system in handling data from experiments to be run on the Large Hadron Collider soon to be built at CERN (the European Organization for Nuclear Research, Geneva, Switzerland). The plan is to use PeRLe in the second of three levels of data filtering before the data is saved off for further study. Here, there is a need for a flexible or reconfigurable processor and for high-performance processing in which substantial parallelism exists, and the data flow rate is high. A link from the PeRLe host TURBOchannel to HiPPI will provide the high data rate (a similar HiPPI-to-Splash 2 interface went through early design at SRC but was never completed for lack of a good target application or system that would use it). The flexibility of a CCM is an asset here in part because this is an experimental framework—unlike the day-to-day handling of large volumes of data that might take place in a commercial environment, one can expect the requirements at CERN to change over time with different experiments and different variations of the same experiment.

Very little has been said in this book about rapid prototyping using a CCM. This is due to our concentration with Splash 2 not on its use as an engineering tool but as a machine to be used for computing. But the use of FPGAs for prototyping is already well developed, as is evidenced by the health of companies such as Quickturn. The Quickturn hardware is geared, however, toward circuit design rather than system design. Emerging from several ongoing university projects, however, is the ability to test component-level issues rather than chip-level issues—processor interactions with memory, various memory and caching schemes, bus strategies, and such. Splash 2, for example, is presently being used to study a proposed parallel computer architecture. We suspect that, as good as hardware such as that from Quickturn is for many of the design uses to which it is put, it may not work well on higher-level architectural emulation, and that what will be needed is a system of the nature of Splash 2 with its built-in data path, explicit connections to memory, and so forth. The basic boxes of a computer architecture's block diagram are already present in Splash 2; they're just somewhat more amorphous than in a "real" computer.

Although the emulation on Splash 2 of a proposed architecture would be slower that the hardware itself, the parallelism of the machine can make it much faster than software simulation. Importantly, although one could not expect a proposed architecture to map directly to Splash 2, the partial structure of Splash 2's data and memory paths and its processor interconnections would allow many architectural features that did not fit directly to be time-multiplexed in a measurable way that would permit accurate extrapolations.

12.5 FINAL WORDS

We close this book with the not-very-bold statement that we doubt that these will be the last words spoken about Custom Computing Machines. We hope that what we have produced is more than just a project report and that a study of our system, taken as a whole, can provide insight to others planning related work. We believe we have influenced the course of research in CCMs by what we have already done, and we hope that somewhere in these pages will have been found a satisfactory explanation of the paths we took and the choices we made.

REFERENCES

[1]   B. Box, "Field Programmable Gate Array Based Reconfigurable Preprocessor," *Proc. IEEE Workshop FPGAs for Custom Computing Machines*, CS Press, Los Alamitos, Calif., 1994, pp. 40–49.

[2]   L. Moll, J. Vuillemin, and P. Boucard, "High-Energy Physics on DEC PeRLe-1 Programmable Active Memory," *Proc. FPGA95*, ACM, ACM Press, New York, 1995, pp. 47–52.

[3]   M. Shand, P. Bertin, and J. Vuillemin, "Hardware Speedups for Long Integer Multiplication," *Proc. ACM Symp. Parallel Algorithms and Architectures*, ACM, ACM Press, New York, 1990, pp. 138–145.

Splash 2 Development—The Project Manager's Summary

Duncan A. Buell

I fully admit now that when Fred More first approached me in the summer of 1991 with the idea of my supervising the general development of a second version of the Splash processor, I had no idea what I was getting into. I certainly didn't expect this to turn into a virtually full-time job for two and a half years, or else I might well have said no to the idea. In hindsight, it is clear that my ignorance was a good thing, for I think that Splash 2 was a solid success as well as the most exciting piece of work in which I've had the chance to be involved.

After some serious thinking about the issues, I told Fred I'd do it. I had been very interested in the first Splash machine, but had been unable, due to other pressures, to do direct work on it. My line management position had left me with very little time to work directly on research projects, and in every instance in which I had found time, I hadn't found enough time. I had wanted in one instance to write a program that was essentially a double loop with a table lookup in the body of the inner loop. After an entire afternoon spent trying—and failing—to construct the counter for the outer loop, I gave up. Although there were a number of people who had programmed Splash with great success, I was unlikely to become one among them.

The task that Fred More originally offered me was to rectify the problem that led to my frustrating admission of failure. The hardware of Splash was a solid success; it ran as expected and had few, if any, failures. Similarly, the software was as good as one could hope for, given the time and context. Maya Gokhale's LDG had been a tremendous advance for the intended purposes over the still-developing Xilinx tools. But the problem remained that it was an FPGA-based machine on which one could design circuitry to perform applications, but not a machine on which one could *program* applications. Fred's charge to me was to drive the development from the applications perspective and from the point of view of an applications programmer. The goal was to be able to say that programmers without a background in hardware design could write applications and achieve moderately high performance.

In accepting Fred's offer, I had one condition—I was perfectly happy to mount a search for applications that could perform well on this machine and to deal with the problem of getting the sense of "programming" into Splash 2, but I insisted that I have someone working with me who would feel responsible for the actual hardware development and someone else who would do the same for the systems software. The hardware person was to have been Andy Kopser, until he announced in late summer that he would be leaving SRC in mid-September. Elaine Davis took over the hardware, to be succeeded by Wally Kleinfelder when Elaine left for a new job the following February. The software position remained unfilled until late October, when Jeff Arnold agreed to take on the job.

From the very beginning, it was assumed that building a small system and programming kernels as benchmarks would be insufficient justification for claims of success. It would be necessary to have a system large enough to do, if not real problems, at least problems of a size comparable to real ones.

In terms of the scope and nature of the applications programming process, my agreement with SRC management was the following: We would make an honest attempt at perhaps a dozen problems. Three to six of these would be genuinely unsuccessful, either because the problems would fairly quickly be found to have a show-stopping component for Splash 2 or because the projected payoff would appear too low to warrant a complete experiment. Of the six remaining, half would prove to be successful "experiments" with nonpositive results. That is, the experiments would be complete enough that hard performance numbers could be obtained and an objective analysis of results made, but the results themselves would not show that Splash 2 was a big win or a win big enough to warrant for "production computation" the use of unusual extra hardware and the attendant problems of programming, interfacing, and maintenance. Finally, it was assumed that perhaps three of the original dozen applications would prove to be major successes, and that this would be sufficient to declare victory for Splash 2.

In order to obtain the dozen attempts at Splash 2 applications, I asked for and received from management at SRC "12 applications" worth of people, figuring the unsuccessful six applications at one to three months' effort and the successful six at three to six months' effort. Looking back, I believe that little or no revision is necessary to assert that this was, in fact, the way things went.

Funding for Splash 2 came from a special DoD "dual-use" appropriation. On October 16, 1991, an SRC presentation was one of about 35 made to various civilian government agency representatives. The requirement to obtain funding was not only that the project be technically worthy of funding; it was also necessary that some civilian agency sign on to be a recipient of the technology transfer. In our case, the recipient was the Department of Mathematical Biology of the National Cancer Institute (NCI). From the very beginning, we had contracted for delivery of a Splash 2 system and working code for the sequence comparison problem as part of a Memorandum of Understanding with NCI. Although final funding approval did not come until the spring, we had the go-ahead, rather shortly after the October 16 presentation, to continue with Splash 2.

Architectural design proceeded through the fall of 1991. The actual engineering and construction of Splash 2 were to have been done under a contract with a private company that was handling both Splash 2 and another novel machine—TERASYS—being built by SRC. TERASYS had started about four months earlier than Splash 2, and the first change in the general project plan came in February of 1992. Due to cost overruns, it was clear that TERASYS and Splash 2 could not both be completed under the outside contract. Since TERASYS was nearer completion, a decision was made to pull back into SRC the design and construction of Splash 2.

This was to be the first of several headaches. An ongoing problem was that of obtaining cabinets in which to house the Splash 2 system. The early choice of the Futurebus+ backplane by the contractor proved to be ill-advised. We went through no fewer than three complete bid procedures to obtain cabinets and backplanes— vendor A supplied one model A cabinet, then got out of the Futurebus+ business; vendor B then did the same thing, by the end of which time vendor A was back in the Futurebus+ business and supplied still a third version. Fortunately, all models actually did work, but the lack of uniformity and the effort spent in procurement was a great annoyance.

A more critical problem was the discovery, in the spring of 1992, that the TI switch chips planned for use in the crossbar were no longer in production. By this time, we had committed to a planned 10 Splash 2 systems, some 40 array boards, needing a total of 360 switch chips (plus spares). We quickly cornered the market on the switch chips known to exist, although we were naturally forced to pay a premium price for them. From then on, the number of available switch chips was the limiting factor in the number of Splash 2 systems that could be built. Later, when technology transfer was being discussed with commercial enterprises, this was the single greatest sticking point, which more than once almost brought things grinding to a halt.

Had we been able to change switch chips, even at that relatively late date, we might well have done so, but there was not then and there still does not exist a genuine substitute for the TI chips we had chosen. We felt we needed on the array card the ability to get across the crossbar in one tick and the ability to change, on a tick-by-tick basis, the configuration of the crossbar. The former capability allows a programmer to treat crossbar or linear FPGA-to-FPGA data transfers as identical, so that algorithms and programming do not require explicit pipelines or hierarchy. The latter allows flexibility in an algorithm and reduces the impact of a scarcity of resources.

Later revisionist thoughts on how the crossbar should or could have been done included using FPGAs or multiple Aptix chips. The TI chips permitted as many as eight configurations, but no applications that were implemented actually used more than four. The longer time for reconfiguration required by either alternative could have been taken care of by having as many as four devices on a board and the choice of configuration made with a multiplexor selection of one of the four "static" options.

Although progress on the Splash 2 hardware seemed at times to go in fits and starts, progress on the software was rapid through 1992. By the end of February, a working version of a simulator for the Splash 2 hardware existed, and a brief workshop was held at the end of the month to train the first guinea-pig group of programmers. Although one of the initial group was so disillusioned as to vow never to get near Splash 2 again, the general response was guardedly positive. We were indeed in uncharted waters, using for programming a language (VHDL) not intended for programming, and using VHDL tools from Synopsys and Model Technologies for purposes other than those for which they had been intended, by users much more naive (with regard to circuit design) than was ever the plan of these vendors. Also, the simulator was imperfect and incomplete at first.

All in all, programming the Splash 2 simulator in the spring and early summer of 1992 was not an entirely pleasant task. But we had begun the project with only a hazy understanding of what we needed and wanted, and it was crucial to the development of the software environment that genuine efforts be made to use the tools. We could not have laid out the specifications *a priori*; what evolved was a compromise between what was needed by the programmers and what was possible given the tools.

The patience and cooperation of the "programmers" in this period was matched only by the skill of those who were continually rewriting and upgrading the simulator and tools, notably Jeff Arnold. In a world of modern windows-based software tools, we were necessarily conducting a human-factors experiment on our own people on the level of frustration acceptable to goal-oriented application programmers working with changing tools. Remarkably, with the one exception, all the commitments were carried through to completion, and the systems software personnel for their part survived the onslaught of users clamoring for bug fixes and the instant implementation of the planned features currently holding up their progress.

Beginning with discussions with Synopsys management in June of 1992, we attempted to influence the development of VHDL simulation and synthesis tools aimed at "programming" applications on (to begin with, Xilinx) FPGAs. This led to a contract with Synopsys for a product later to become their FPGA Compiler. For several months Jeff Arnold went back and forth with Synopsys on a list of needs and wants that would make their tool look to a programmer more like a "regular compiler" for a language like C or Fortran.

Crucial to eventual success was the discovery during this period that the underlying Xilinx hardware and software was a significant improvement over what had gone before. Two problems with the XC3090 chips and their attendant `apr` software for placement and routing were that the chips themselves were a little too small to accommodate a natural "unit of computation" for many applications and that `apr`, as it existed in about 1990, had major drawbacks. It often either took too long to run or failed to route an entire design, especially if left to work "automatically," that is, without human intervention to guide the placement and routing. We intended to use the XC4010 `ppr` software as "automatic" software without any help from a user assumed to be uninterested or unable to help the design process. It was a great relief, then, to find that it was possible to write VHDL code for realistic applications that used a significant fraction (75 percent or more) of the XC4010 chips and to have the Synopsys and Xilinx tools synthesize, place, and route the program/design into a Xilinx bitfile that would allegedly execute at 10–25 MHz. One reason for this improved performance of the placement and routing software clearly seemed to be that the XC4000 series chips have a much better balance between logic resources and routing resources. In one very special instance of the DNA sequence comparison program, which has an extremely regular structure, it was possible to utilize all of the CLBs on a chip and still have the VHDL-to-bitfile translation take place without human intervention.

The summer of 1992 was a vigorous and rowdy period in the life of the Splash 2 project, in part due to the presence of five summer students working on various aspects of hardware, software, and applications programs. It was in this period that the explosive growth toward a usable programming environment took place—a large number of both small and large applications were tried, fixes or work-arounds for problems or bugs were found and shared, and tools to assist program development were written. (As always, the work of programming benefits from the deep and abiding sloth of students who insist on writing tools because they are too lazy to do things "the hard way.")

From the beginning of the project, and continuing through until about March of 1993, we had been conducting a vigorous search for good test applications. Over the course of the project we spoke at more than 20 universities, 15 companies, 10 government agencies, and 9 conferences. From the very beginning, of course, we had the sequence comparison problem from NCI as a "must do" application, and work began early in 1992 on a solution to this problem, leading to the paper presented as a later chapter of this book. But this by itself would clearly not be enough.

A potential problem from the National Center for Biotechnology Information involving clustering of bibliographic records was a moderately good match for Splash 2, but a single complete run would take two years (compared with 10 months on a Thinking Machines CM-2 supercomputer); this was dropped. Discussions with a NASA contractor on the use of Splash 2 as a platform on which to do rapid proto-typing were positive. An engineer from the company spent several weeks at SRC and came away with very positive thoughts, but the lack of extant hardware to borrow or buy was probably the show stopper in that deadline-driven world of government contracting—we were a little too far ahead of the curve for them to use Splash 2 to advantage.

I had visited VPI, however, on an early speaking trip through North Carolina and Virginia in September of 1991, and our discussions with members of the Electrical Engineering Department had continued. Peter Athanas had recently finished his Ph.D. at Brown University working on the PRISM FPGA project, and had then joined the faculty at VPI. Lynn Abbott had interesting problems in image processing and a desire to explore the use of FPGAs in hardware to accelerate the computations. The presence of Jim Armstrong suggested strong support for and solid expertise in VHDL among the students. All this was helped by the fact that John McHenry, who had spent two summers at SRC working first on Splash 1 and then on Splash 2, was finishing his Ph.D. in the department and knew the program well. When IDA Headquarters made money available for a university contract for Splash 2 applications and research, VPI was a natural choice. The ongoing relationship has been close and profitable, and a summary of their work on Splash 2 appears earlier in this book.

The variation of image processing necessary to do fingerprint matching had been discussed as a possible Splash 2 application at the October 16, 1991, presentation to government agencies. We had, at times, talked with the FBI and with potential government contractors about machines to match fingerprints, but had failed to land upon a definable experiment that could be performed. The second IDA contract thus went to Anil Jain and Diane Rover at Michigan State University after a trip I made there in January of 1993, and their work is also reported here.

Not everything was proceeding smoothly, however. What with having to pull the design back from the contractor and the switch chip and cabinet/backplane delays, a planned "hardware working" date for fall of 1992 slipped, then slipped again, then slipped still further as some of the Splash 2 engineers were time-sliced with the ongoing TERASYS project. Such delays might have killed Splash 2 in an organization that required a marketable product or needed to keep tighter control on employee time invested. At SRC, however, although we were always subject to the possibility that key players would feel compelled to drop everything to take advantage of a window of opportunity elsewhere, we were allowed to make our steady but sometimes slow progress. One could even argue (if one had to) that the hardware delays worked to the benefit of the system results by allowing more time to be spent on debugging and streamlining the process of developing applications code.

Finally, on Thursday afternoon, February 18, 1993, the first Splash 2 hardware system worked. Jeff Arnold downloaded an edge-detection program to an array board, streamed the pixels of a digitized image through the board, and received as output the edges of the image.

From then on, replication of the hardware components was rapid. Although we had stretched our resources to the limit in committing to build 10 Splash 2 systems, demand soon exceeded the supply. In addition to the systems committed to VPI, MSU, NCI, and to SRC for its own purposes, university researchers and outside companies were beginning to call to ask how copies of Splash 2 could be bought or borrowed. Even without the obvious problem presented by the switch chip, SRC was faced with a very difficult dilemma. Further Splash 2 clones were impossible without either redesigning the array board (and modifying the systems software accordingly) or designing a new, functionally equivalent and pin-compatible chip to fit into the existing board design. Neither option seemed attractive. Further, it was clear that SRC could not afford the real dollar and personnel cost of becoming the manufacturing and maintenance organization for Splash 2. Success, in this case, could come with a heavy price tag.

After some months of deliberation and at least one false start, SRC's government sponsors undertook in the first part of 1994 the technology transfer and commercialization of Splash 2. Outside private companies were to be granted, for $100, a complete data dump of schematics, diagnostics, manuals, and code, together with some guidance from SRC about things done right, things done wrong, and things that should simply be done in a different way. An initial group of potential licensees was brought to SRC for a presentation in March of 1994. The first license was issued soon after that; within six months 10 companies had obtained licenses, and by the end of calendar year 1994 the first commercial Splash 2 derivatives had become available.

Not all of the many licensees have the intention of producing anything like a commercial version of Splash 2. There are several other processors, board, and systems available or nearly available from other companies; some of the licensees have more of an interest in the software we developed for programming an FPGA-based machine or the general systems approach we took than in the specific details of Splash 2. A small consortium of licensees has formed to target an image processing market; the companies involved have divided the hardware, software, and applications into areas where each can contribute from its strength and benefit from cooperation with the others.

From the earliest days of the Splash 2 project, I had insisted that we could declare victory if any one of these criteria were met:

1. Splash 2 would be used to get real work done and not just provide demonstrations of capability.
2. Someone who did not get an SRC paycheck would use Splash 2 in his/her work and not walk away vowing "Never again!"
3. Some commercial machine would appear and have a clear and traceable ancestry to Splash 2.

It is perhaps too soon, and we are perhaps too close to the matter, to judge exactly why we succeeded; I leave such analysis to others. Having a brilliant and dedicated technical team was a major factor. Not having a particular target application helped— we were free to search for reasonable applications that would be successes. Not having marketability and "productizing" constraints helped. Not having a deadline that forced us to abandon "the right thing to do" in order to meet the deadline helped. But as it has turned out, not just one but all three of my criteria have been met. Further, we have effected something often talked about but seemingly rarely ever done—we have been able to convert proof-of-concept technology, developed at government expense as an engineering research project, into products available for sale from private-sector companies whose personnel rosters do not intersect the list of principals from the research project.

APPENDIX B

An Example Application

Jeffrey M. Arnold[1]

In this appendix we illustrate the Splash 2 programming style through an example application written in VHDL. This example, a simple digital filter, is much smaller than most Splash 2 applications, but does touch many of the issues facing the programmer. Equation 1 shows the general form of a finite impulse response (FIR) filter:

$$Q_i = \frac{\sum_j I_{i-j} F_j}{C} \tag{1}$$

where I is the input data stream, F is the set of filter coefficients, C is a constant scale factor, and Q is the output data stream.

In this example the input data is a stream of 12-bit signed integer samples, the output is a stream of 16-bit signed integers, and the filter is a five-tap low-pass filter with constant coefficients. The filter can be viewed as a weighted sum computed on a sliding window of the input data followed by the application of a constant scale factor. A block diagram of this interpretation of the filter is shown in Figure B.1.

This application is simple enough to be mapped entirely onto a single Processing Element, obviating the need to partition across multiple FPGAs. The input data arrives on the left port of the PE at the rate of one 12-bit sample per clock cycle conditioned by a valid data tag. The output data is produced at the same rate on the right port. For the sake of simplicity we assume the filter coefficients are powers of two, $F = \{1, 4, 8, 4, 1\}$, eliminating the need for combinational multipliers. The five-input add operator is implemented as a pipelined tree of two input adders. Finally, the division by the constant scale factor C is implemented by table lookup in the

---

[1]A version of this chapter appeared as Arnold and Buell [1] and is used with permission.

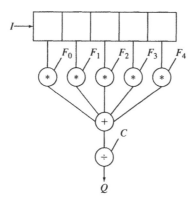

FIGURE B.1 Block Diagram of
Five-Tap FIR Filter

external RAM. The output of the add operator is used to index into the table and the contents of the addressed location is returned as the output of the filter.

Figure B.2 shows the annotated VHDL FIR program. The Processing Element entity declaration is shown in Figure 6.1 and is not reproduced here. The 12-bit input stream enters the PE on the left port (XP_Left), a weighted sum over a five-element window of the stream is computed, the sum is scaled by table lookup in the external memory, and a 16-bit result stream is sent to the right port (XP_Right). The first four lines of the architecture specify data type and parametric information that would be placed more appropriately in a separate package, but are included here for brevity. Line 2 defines the type of the input stream samples to be 12-bit signed integers. Line 3 declares the data type to be used for vectors of Samples. The number of filter taps (the data "window") is defined to be a constant 5 in line 4. Line 5 defines the set of coefficients by which each element of the window is to be multiplied. Note that for the sake of efficiency the coefficients are chosen to be powers of two, obviating the need to synthesize combinational multipliers. In general, though, the coefficient vector could be any set of constant integers; the compilation tools will synthesize the appropriate logic.

The next five lines (6–10) are declarations of internal signal objects, the storage elements of the program. Line_Buffer contains the sliding window of data samples to be filtered. sum1, sum2, and sum3 are temporary registers that hold intermediate values. The remaining signals constitute the interfaces to the external memory and to the neighboring PEs.

The body of the architecture contains two synchronous processes and one concurrent procedure call. The synchronous processes respectively compute the weighted sum and interface to the external memory. The Filter process declares an internal variable, Sum, which is used as an identifier for an intermediate value. By choosing to make Sum a variable rather than a signal, no register will be inferred. Within the body of the process, the call to the procedure Pad_Input performs type conversion from the port type RBit3 to the intrinsic Bit_Vector type. By placing the procedure call within the body of the clocked process, a pipeline register is implicitly added. This is a standard practice used on most input and output ports, designed to improve performance by allowing the IOB flip-flops in the Xilinx XC4010 FPGA to be used to stage data onto and off of the PE.

The FOR loop in lines 17–19 shifts the data window by one sample each clock cycle. Because signal assignments take effect *after* the execution of the process, all

```
1   ARCHITECTURE FIR OF Processing_Element IS
2     SUBTYPE Sample IS Integer range -(2**11) to (2**11 - 1);
3     TYPE Sample_Vector IS Array (Integer range <>) of Sample;
4     CONSTANT NTaps          : Integer := 5;
5     CONSTANT Coeff          : Sample_Vector(0 to NTaps-1) := (1,4,8,4,1);
6     SIGNAL Line_Buffer      : Sample_Vector(0 to NTaps-1);
7     SIGNAL sum1, sum2, sum3 : Integer range -(2**14) to (2**14 - 1);
8     SIGNAL madr             : Bit_Vector(MAR_RANGE-1 downto 0);
9     SIGNAL mdata_in         : Bit_Vector(MEM_WIDTH-1 downto 0);
10    SIGNAL Left, Right      : Bit_Vector(Datapath_Width-1 downto 0);
11  BEGIN  --  FIR
12    Filter : PROCESS
13       VARIABLE Sum : Integer;
14    BEGIN
15      WAIT UNTIL XP_Clk'Event and XP_Clk = '1';
16      Pad_Input(XP_Left, Left);
17      FOR i IN 1 to NTaps-1 LOOP
18        Line_Buffer(i) <= Line_Buffer(i-1);
19      END LOOP;
20      IF (Left(35) = '1') THEN
21        Line_Buffer(0) <= Conv_Integer(Left(11 downto 0));
22      ELSE
23        Line_Buffer(0) <= 0;
24      END IF;
25      sum1 <= (Line_Buffer(0) * Coeff(0)) + (Line_Buffer(1) * Coeff(1));
26      sum2 <= (Line_Buffer(2) * Coeff(2)) + (Line_Buffer(3) * Coeff(3));
27      sum3 <= Line_Buffer(4) * Coeff(4);
28      sum  := sum1 + sum2 + sum3;
29      madr <= CONV_Unsigned(sum, MAR_Range);
30    END PROCESS Filter;
31    Mem_Access : PROCESS
32    BEGIN
33      WAIT UNTIL XP_Clk'Event and XP_Clk = '1';
34      XP_Mem_Rd_L <= '0';
35      XP_Mem_Wr_L <= '1';
36      Pad_Output (XP_Mem_A, madr);
37      Pad_Input  (XP_Mem_D, mdata_in);
38      Right(15 downto 0) <= mdata_in;
39    END PROCESS Mem_Access;
40    Pad_Output(XP_Right, Right);
41  END FIR;
```

FIGURE B.2 Body of Finite Impulse Response Program

assignments occur in parallel, so the direction of iteration is not significant. Lines 20 through 25 control the loading of the window buffer: if bit 35 of the input stream is a '1' the low-order 12 bits are converted to integer and shifted into Line_Buffer; otherwise a constant zero is shifted in. The weighted sum is computed in two pipeline stages by lines 25–29. In the first stage each window element is "multiplied" by its coefficient (in zero time and area, as the coefficients are powers of two), and three partial sums are computed and stored in registers (sum1, sum2, and sum3). In

```
28a    sum4 <= sum1 + sum2;
28b    sum5 <= sum3;
28c    sum  := sum4 + sum4;    FIGURE B.3  Optimized Final Addition
```

the second stage a three-input sum is computed, the type is converted to unsigned bit vector and zero extended to the length of MAR_Range (the size of the memory address), and stored in the memory address register, madr, in preparation for the table lookup.

The second synchronous process latches the address (the weighted sum computed by Filter) to the external memory, and the scaled result returned from the memory. These pipeline stages are necessary to ensure that the memory address, data, and control signals are registered in the IOBs of the FPGA. The memory control signals, XP_Mem_Rd_L, and XP_Mem_Wr_L, are held constant by lines 34–35, forcing the memory to always read. Line 38 is an additional pipeline register on the return data prior to transmission to the next PE. By registering the data here, the assignment to the XP_Right port may be performed outside of the process by the concurrent procedure call in line 40.

There are six total pipeline stages in this program:

- the assignment of the input data to the Left signal (line 16)
- the computation of the partial sums sum1, sum2, and sum3 (lines 25–27)
- the calculation of the final sum, madr (lines 28–29)
- the assignment to the memory address register, XP_Mem_A (line 36)
- the return data from the memory, mdata_in (line 37)
- the assignment into the output data register, Right (line 38)

When this program is compiled it occupies 61 of the 400 CLBs, or 15 percent of the available real estate. The critical path delay is 106 ns, limiting the maximum clock frequency to 9.3 MHz. The static timing analyzer shows the critical path is through the three-input adder in line 28. If we needed to optimize the performance of this design further, an extra pipeline stage could be added as shown in Figure B.3.

REFERENCES

[1] J.M. Arnold and D.A. Buell, "VHDL programming on Splash 2," in W. Moore and W. Luk, eds., *More FPGAs*, Abingdon EE & CS Books, Abingdon, England, UK, 1994, pp. 182–191.

Bibliography

"Application Briefs: Computer Graphics in the Detective Business," *IEEE Computer Graphics and Applications*, Vol. 5, Apr. 1985, pp. 14–17.

A.L. Abbott et al., "Finding Lines and Building Pyramids with Splash-2," *Proc. IEEE Workshop FPGAs for Custom Computing*, CS Press, Los Alamitos, Calif., 1994, pp. 155–163.

A.L. Abbott, R.M. Haralick, and X. Zhuang, "Pipeline Architectures for Morphologic Image Analysis," *Machine Vision and Applications*, Vol. 1, No. 1, 1988, pp. 23–40.

L. Agarwal, M. Wazlowski, and S. Ghosh, "An Asynchronous Approach to Efficient Execution of Programs on Adaptive Architectures Utilizing FPGAs," *Proc. IEEE Workshop FPGAs for Custom Computing*, CS Press, Los Alamitos, Calif., 1994, pp. 101–110.

Algotronix Ltd., *The Configurable Logic Data Book*, Algotronix Ltd., Edinburgh, Scotland, UK, 1990.

R. Amerson et al., "Teramac—Configurable Custom Computing," *Proc. IEEE Symp. FPGAs for Custom Computing Machines*, CS Press, Los Alamitos, Calif., 1995, pp. 32–38.

A.A. Apostolico et al., "Efficient Parallel Algorithms for String Editing and Related Problems," *SIAM J. on Computing*, Vol. 19, 1990, pp. 968–988.

J.M. Arnold, "The Splash 2 Software Environment," *Proc. IEEE Workshop FPGAs for Custom Computing Machines*, CS Press, Los Alamitos, Calif., 1993, pp. 88–94.

J.M. Arnold, "The Splash 2 Software Environment," *J. of Supercomputing*, Vol. 9, 1995, pp. 277–290.

J.M. Arnold and D.A. Buell, "VHDL Programming on Splash 2," in W. Moore and W. Luk, eds., *More FPGAs*, Abingdon EE & CS Books, Abingdon, England, UK, 1994, pp. 182–191.

J.M. Arnold, D.A. Buell, and E.G. Davis, "Splash 2," *ACM Symp. Parallel Algorithms and Architectures*, ACM Press, New York, 1992, pp. 316–322.

J.M. Arnold et al., "The Splash 2 Processor and Applications," *Proc. Int'l Conf. Computer Design*, CS Press, Los Alamitos, Calif., 1993, pp. 482–485.

J.M. Arnold and M.A. McGarry, "Splash 2 Programmer's Manual," Tech. Report SRC-TR-93-107, SRC, Bowie, Md., 1993.

P.M. Athanas, "Functional Reconfigurable Architecture and Compiler for Adaptive Computing," *Proc. 1993 Int'l Phoenix Computer and Comm. Conf.*, CS Press, Los Alamitos, Calif., 1993, pp. 49–55.

P.M. Athanas and A.L. Abbott, "Processing Images in Real Time on a Custom Computing Platform," in R.W. Hartenstein and M.Z. Servít, eds., *Field-Programmable Logic: Architectures, Synthesis, and Applications*, Springer-Verlag, Berlin, 1994, pp. 156–167.

P.M. Athanas and K.L. Pocek, eds., *Proc. IEEE Symp. FPGAs for Custom Computing Machines*, CS Press, Los Alamitos, Calif., 1995.

P.M. Athanas and H.F. Silverman, "An Adaptive Hardware Machine Architecture for Dynamic Processor Reconfiguration," *Proc. Int'l Conf. Computer Design*, CS Press, Los Alamitos, Calif., 1991, pp. 397–400.

P.M. Athanas and H.F. Silverman, "Processor Reconfiguration through Instruction Set Metamorphosis: Architecture and Compiler," *Computer*, Vol. 26, No. 3, Mar. 1993, pp. 11–18.

J. Babb, R. Tessier, and A. Agarwal, "Virtual Wires: Overcoming Pin Limitations in FPGA-Based Logic Emulators," *Proc. IEEE Workshop FPGAs for Custom Computing Machines*, CS Press, Los Alamitos, Calif., 1993, pp. 142–151.

S.L. Bade and B.L. Hutchings, "FPGA-Based Stochastic Neural Networks—Implementation," *Proc. IEEE Workshop FPGAs for Custom Computing Machines*, CS Press, Los Alamitos, Calif., 1994, pp. 189–199.

J.P. Banâtre, D. Lavenier, and M. Vieillot, "From High Level Programming Model to FPGA Machines," *Proc. IEEE Workshop FPGAs for Custom Computing Machines*, CS Press, Los Alamitos, Calif., 1994, pp. 119–125.

R.A. Bergamaschi, "High-Level Synthesis in a Production Environment: Methodology and Algorithms," in J.P. Mermet, ed., *Fundamentals and Standards in Hardware Description Languages*, Kluwer Academic Publishers, Boston, 1993, pp. 195–230.

N.W. Bergmann and J.C. Mudge, "Comparing the Performance of FPGA-Based Custom Computers with General-Purpose Computers for DSP Applications," *Proc. IEEE Workshop FPGAs for Custom Computing Machines*, CS Press, Los Alamitos, Calif., 1994, pp. 164–172.

P. Bertin, *Mémoires Actives Programmables: Conception, Réalisation et Programmation*, PhD thesis, Université Paris 7, 1993.

P. Bertin, D. Roncin, and J. Vuillemin, "Programmable Active Memories: A Performance Assessment," in G. Borriello and C. Ebeling, eds., *Research on Integrated Systems: Proceedings of the '93 Symposium*, MIT Press, Cambridge, Mass., 1993, pp. 88-102.

P. Bertin and H. Touati, "PAM Programming Environments: Practice and Experience," *Proc. IEEE Workshop FPGAs for Custom Computing Machines*, CS Press, Los Alamitos, Calif., 1994, pp. 133–139.

B. Box, "Field Programmable Gate Array Based Reconfigurable Preprocessor," *Proc. IEEE Workshop FPGAs for Custom Computing Machines*, CS Press, Los Alamitos, Calif., 1994, pp. 40–49.

B. Box and J. Nieznanski, "Common Processor Element Packaging," *Proc. IEEE Symp. FPGAs for Custom Computing Machines*, CS Press, Los Alamitos, Calif., 1995, pp. 39–46.

F. Brooks, *The Mythical Man-Month*, Addison-Wesley, Reading, Mass., 1975. (The notion of "second-system effect" seems to come from Brooks, although this precise definition comes from *The Hacker's Dictionary*, by Guy L. Steele, Jr.)

S.D. Brown et al., *Field-Programmable Gate Arrays*, Kluwer Academic Publishers, Boston, 1992.

D.A. Buell and K.L. Pocek, eds., *Proc. IEEE Workshop FPGAs for Custom Computing Machines*, CS Press, Los Alamitos, Calif., 1993.

D.A. Buell and K.L. Pocek, eds., *Proc. IEEE Workshop FPGAs for Custom Computing Machines*, CS Press, Los Alamitos, Calif., 1994.

D.A. Buell and K.L. Pocek, "Custom Computing Machines: An Introduction," *J. of Supercomputing*, Vol. 9, 1995, pp. 219–230.

D.A. Buell and N. Shirazi, "A Splash 2 Tutorial," Tech. Report SRC-TR-92-087 (revised), SRC, Bowie, Md., 1993.

P.J. Burt and E.H. Adelson, "The Laplacian Pyramid as a Compact Image Code," *IEEE Trans. Comm.*, Vol. COM-31, No. 4, Apr. 1983, pp. 532–540.

R. Camposano et al., "The IBM High-Level Synthesis System," R. Camposano and Wayne Wolf, eds., *High Level Synthesis*, Kluwer Academic Publishers, Boston, 1991, pp. 79–104.

J.M. Carrera et al., "Architecture of a FPGA-Based Coprocessor: The PAR-1," *Proc. IEEE Symp. FPGAs for Custom Computing Machines*, CS Press, Los Alamitos, Calif., 1995, pp. 20–29.

S. Casselman, "Virtual Computing and the Virtual Computer," *Proc. IEEE Workshop FPGAs for Custom Computing Machines*, CS Press, Los Alamitos, Calif., 1993, pp. 43–49.

P.K. Chan and M.D.F. Schlag, "Architectural Tradeoffs in Field-Programmable-Device-Based Computing Systems," *Proc. IEEE Workshop FPGAs for Custom Computing Machines*, CS Press, Los Alamitos, Calif., 1993, pp. 152–162.

L. Chen, "Fast Generation of Gaussian and Laplacian Image Pyramids Using an FPGA-based Custom Computing Platform," master's thesis, Virginia Polytechnic Inst., Blacksburg, Va., 1994.

H.A. Chow, H. Alnuweiri, and S. Casselman, "FPGA-Based Transformable Computers for Fast Digital Signal Processing," *Proc. IEEE Symp. FPGAs for Custom Computing Machines*, CS Press, Los Alamitos, Calif., 1995, pp. 197–203.

Concurrent Logic Inc., *Cli6000 Series Field-Programmable Gate Arrays*, Concurrent Logic Inc., Sunnyvale, Calif., 1992.

N.G. Core et al., "Supercomputers and Biological Sequence Comparison Algorithms," *Computers and Biomedical Research*, Vol. 22, No. 6, 1989, pp. 497–515.

C.P. Cowen and S. Monaghan, "A Reconfigurable Monte-Carlo Clustering Processor (MCCP)," *Proc. IEEE Workshop FPGAs for Custom Computing Machines*, CS Press, Los Alamitos, Calif., 1994, pp. 59–66.

C.E. Cox and W. Ekkehard Blanz, "Ganglion—a Fast Hardware Implementation of a Connectionist Classifier," IBM Research Report RJ8290, *Proc. 1991 IEEE Custom Integrated Circuits Conf.*, IEEE Press, Piscataway, N.J., 1991, pp. 6.5.1–6.5.4.

S.A. Cuccaro and C.F. Reese, "The CM-2X: A Hybrid CM-2/Xilinx Prototype," *Proc. IEEE Workshop FPGAs for Custom Computing Machines*, CS Press, Los Alamitos, Calif., 1993, pp. 121–131.

M. Dahl et al., "Emulation of the Sparcle Microprocessor with the MIT Virtual Wires Emulation System," *Proc. IEEE Workshop FPGAs for Custom Computing Machines*, CS Press, Los Alamitos, Calif., 1994, pp. 14–23.

M. Dao et al., "Acceleration of Template Based Ray Casting for Volume Visualization Using FPGAs," *Proc. IEEE Symp. FPGAs for Custom Computing Machines*, CS Press, Los Alamitos, Calif., 1995, pp. 116–124.

J. Darnauer et al., "A Field Programmable Multi-Chip Module (FPMCM)," *Proc. IEEE Workshop FPGAs for Custom Computing Machines*, CS Press, Los Alamitos, Calif., 1994, pp. 1–11.

Datacube, Inc., *The MaxVideo 200 Reference Manual*, Datacube, Inc., Danvers, Mass., 1994.

A. DeHon, "DPGA-Coupled Microprocessors: Commodity ICs for the Early 21st Century," *Proc. IEEE Workshop FPGAs for Custom Computing Machines*, CS Press, Los Alamitos, Calif., 1994, pp. 31–40.

A.S. Deshpande, D.S. Richards, and W.R. Pearson, "A Platform for Biological Sequence Comparison on Parallel Computers," *CABIOS*, Vol. 7, No. 2, April 1991, p. 237.

P.M. Dew, R.A. Earnshaw, and T.R. Heywood, eds., *Parallel Processing for Computer Vision and Display*, Addison-Wesley, Reading, Mass., 1989.

P. Dhaussy et al., "Global Control Synthesis for an MIMD/FPGA Machine," *Proc. IEEE Workshop FPGAs for Custom Computing Machines*, CS Press, Los Alamitos, Calif., 1994, pp. 72–82.

T. Drayer et al., "MORRPH: A MOdular and Reprogrammable Real-Time Processing Hardware," *Proc. IEEE Symp. FPGAs for Custom Computing Machines*, CS Press, Los Alamitos, Calif., 1995, pp. 11–19.

R.O. Duda and P.E. Hart, "Use of the Hough Transform to Detect Lines and Curves in Pictures," *Comm. of the ACM*, Vol. 15, 1972, pp. 11–15.

J.G. Eldredge and B.L. Hutchings, "Density Enhancement of a Neural Network Using FPGAs and Run-Time Reconfiguration," *Proc. IEEE Workshop FPGAs for Custom Computing Machines*, CS Press, Los Alamitos, Calif., 1994, pp. 180–189.

R. Elliott, "Hardware Implementation of a Straight Line Detector for Image Processing," master's thesis, Virginia Polytechnic Inst., Blacksburg,Va., 1993.

Federal Bureau of Investigation, *The Science of Fingerprints: Classification and Uses*, U.S. Govt. Printing Office, Washington, D.C., 1984.

P.W. Foulk, "Data Folding in SRAM Configurable FPGAs," *Proc. IEEE Workshop FPGAs for Custom Computing Machines*, CS Press, Los Alamitos, Calif., 1993, pp. 163–172.

P.C. French and R.W. Taylor, "A Self-Reconfiguring Processor," *Proc. IEEE Workshop FPGAs for Custom Computing Machines*, CS Press, Los Alamitos, Calif., 1993, pp. 50–60.

K.A. Frenkel, "The Human Genome Project and Informatics," *Comm. of the ACM*, Vol. 34, No. 11, 1991, pp. 41–51.

D. Gajski, ed., *Silicon Compilation*, Addison-Wesley, Reading, Mass., 1988.

D. Galloway, "The Transmogrifier C Hardware Description Language and Compiler for FPGAs," *Proc. IEEE Symp. FPGAs for Custom Computing Machines*, CS Press, Los Alamitos, Calif., 1995, pp. 136–144.

G.J. Gent, S.R. Smith, and R.L. Haviland, "An FPGA-Based Custom Coprocessor for Automatic Image Segmentation Applications," *Proc. IEEE Workshop FPGAs for Custom Computing Machines*, CS Press, Los Alamitos, Calif., 1994, pp. 172–180.

M. Gokhale, W. Holmes, and K. Iobst, "Processing in Memory: The Terasys Massively Parallel Processor Array," *Computer*, Vol. 28, No. 4, Apr. 1995, pp. 23–31.

M. Gokhale et al., "Building and Using a Highly Parallel Programmable Logic Array," *Computer*, Vol. 24, No. 1, Jan. 1991, pp. 81–89.

M. Gokhale et al., "The Logic Description Generator," Tech. Report SRC-TR-90-011, SRC, Bowie, Md., 1990.

M. Gokhale and R. Minnich, "FPGA Programming in a Data Parallel C," *Proc. IEEE Workshop FPGAs for Custom Computing Machines*, CS Press, Los Alamitos, Calif., 1993, pp. 94–102.

M. Gokhale and B. Schott, "Data Parallel C on a Reconfigurable Logic Array," *J. of Supercomputing*, Vol. 9, 1995, pp. 291–314.

J.P. Gray and T.A. Kean, "Configurable Hardware: A New Paradigm for Computation," C.L. Seitz, ed., *Advanced Research in VLSI*, MIT Press, Cambridge, Mass., 1989, pp. 279–295.

H. Grünbacher and R.W. Hartenstein, eds., *Field Programmable Gate Arrays: Architectures and Tools for Rapid Prototyping*, Springer-Verlag, Berlin, 1993. (Lecture Notes in Computer Science #705).

S.A. Guccione and M.J. Gonzalez, "A Data-Parallel Programming Model for Reconfigurable Architectures," *Proc. IEEE Workshop FPGAs for Custom Computing Machines*, CS Press, Los Alamitos, Calif., 1993, pp. 79–88.

R.K. Gupta and C.N. Coelho Jr., "Program Implementation Schemes for Hardware-Software Systems," *Computer*, Vol. 27, No. 1, Jan. 1994, pp. 48–55.

J. Hadley and B. Hutchings, "Design Methodologies for Partially Reconfigured Systems," *Proc. IEEE Symp. FPGAs for Custom Computing Machines*, CS Press, Los Alamitos, Calif., 1995, pp. 78–84.

R.W. Hartenstein, R. Kress, and H. Reinig, "A Reconfigurable Data-Driven ALU for Xputers," *Proc. IEEE Workshop FPGAs for Custom Computing Machines*, CS Press, Los Alamitos, Calif., 1994, pp. 139–147.

S. Hauck and G. Borriello, "Pin Assignment for Multi-FPGA Systems," *Proc. IEEE Workshop FPGAs for Custom Computing Machines*, CS Press, Los Alamitos, Calif., 1993, pp. 11–14.

K. Hayashi et al., "Reconfigurable Real-Time Signal Transport System Using Custom FPGAs," *Proc. IEEE Symp. FPGAs for Custom Computing Machines*, CS Press, Los Alamitos, Calif., 1995, pp. 68–75.

B.U. Heeb, *Debora: A System for the Development of Field-Programmable Hardware, and Its Application to a Reconfigurable Computer*, PhD thesis, VDF, Informatik Dissertationen 45, ETH Zürich, Zürich, Switzerland, 1993.

B.U. Heeb and C. Pfister, "Chameleon, a Workstation of a Different Color," in H. Grünbacher and R.W. Hartenstein, eds., *Field Programmable Gate Arrays: Architectures and Tools for Rapid Prototyping*, Springer-Verlag, Berlin, 1993, pp. 152–161.

J.H. Hennessy and D.A. Patterson, *Computer Architecture: A Quantitative Approach*, Morgan Kauffmann Publishers, San Mateo, Calif., 1990.

H.-J. Herpel et al., "A Reconfigurable Computer for Embedded Control Applications," *Proc. IEEE Workshop FPGAs for Custom Computing Machines*, CS Press, Los Alamitos, Calif., 1993, pp. 111–121.

Sir W.J. Herschel, *The Origin of Fingerprinting*, AMS Press, New York, 1974.

W.D. Hillis, *The Connection Machine*, MIT Press, Cambridge, Mass., 1986.

D.T. Hoang, "A Systolic Array for the Sequence Alignment Problem," Tech. Report CS-92-22, Brown Univ., Providence, R.I., 1992.

D.T. Hoang, "Searching Genetic Databases on Splash 2," *Proc. IEEE Workshop FPGAs for Custom Computing Machines*, CS Press, Los Alamitos, Calif., 1993, pp. 185–192.

D.T. Hoang and D.P. Lopresti, "FPGA Implementation of Systolic Sequence Alignment," in H. Grünbacher and R.W. Hartenstein, eds., *Field Programmable Gate Arrays: Architectures and Tools for Rapid Prototyping*, Springer-Verlag, Berlin, 1993, pp. 183–191.

H. Högl et al., "Enable++: A Second Generation FPGA Processor," *Proc. IEEE Symp. FPGAs for Custom Computing Machines*, CS Press, Los Alamitos, Calif., 1995, pp. 45–53.

P.V.C. Hough, "A Method and Means for Recognizing Complex Patterns," U.S. Patent No. 3,069,654, 1962.

R.P. Hughey, *Programmable Systolic Arrays*, PhD thesis CS-91-34, Brown Univ., Providence, R.I., 1991.

IEEE Standard VHDL Language Reference Manual, Std 1076-1987, IEEE Press, New York, 1988.

IEEE Standard VHDL Language Reference Manual, Std 1076-1992, IEEE Press, New York, 1992.

C. Iseli and E. Sanchez, "Spyder: A Reconfigurable VLIW Processor Using FPGAs," *Proc. IEEE Workshop FPGAs for Custom Computing Machines*, CS Press, Los Alamitos, Calif., 1993, pp. 17–25.

C. Iseli and E. Sanchez, "A C++ Compiler for FPGA Custom Execution Units Synthesis," *Proc. IEEE Symp. FPGAs for Custom Computing Machines*, CS Press, Los Alamitos, Calif., 1995, pp. 173–179.

C. Iseli and E. Sanchez, "Spyder: A SURE, SUperscalar and REconfigurable, Processor," *J. of Supercomputing*, Vol. 9, 1995, pp. 231–252.

B. Jahne, *Digital Image Processing*, Springer-Verlag, New York, 1991.

A.K. Jain, "Advances in Statistical Pattern Recognition," in *Pattern Recognition Theory and Applications*, P.A. Devijer and J. Kittler, eds., Springer-Verlag, New York, 1987, pp. 1–19.

A. Jantsch et al., "A Case Study on Hardware/Software Partitioning," *Proc. IEEE Workshop FPGAs for Custom Computing Machines*, CS Press, Los Alamitos, Calif., 1994, pp. 111–119.

C. Jones et al., "Issues in Wireless Video Coding Using Run-Time-Reconfiguration FPGAs," *Proc. IEEE Symp. FPGAs for Custom Computing Machines*, CS Press, Los Alamitos, Calif., 1995, pp. 85–89.

R. Jones, "Protein Sequence and Structure Comparison on Massively Parallel Computers, *Int'l J. of Supercomputer Applications*, Vol. 6, No. 2, 1992, pp. 138–146.

T.A. Kean, *Configurable Logic: A Dynamically Programmable Cellular Architecture and Its VLSI Implementation*, PhD thesis, Univ. of Edinburgh Dept. of Computer Science, Edinburgh, Scotland, UK, 1988.

T.A. Kean and C. Carruthers, "Bipolar CAL Chip Doubles the Speed of FPGAs," in W. Moore and W. Luk, eds., *FPGAs*, Abingdon EE & CS Books, Abingdon, England, UK, 1991, pp. 46–53.

T.A. Kean and J.P. Gray, "Configurable Hardware: Two Case Studies of Micrograin Computation," *J. of VLSI Signal Processing*, Vol. 2, 1990, pp. 9–16.

A. Kopser, "Splash 2: Architectural Motivation," tech. report, SRC, Bowie, Md., 1991.

H.T. Kung, "Why Systolic Architectures?" *Computer*, Vol. 15, 1982, pp. 37–46.

H.T. Kung and C.E. Leiserson, "Systolic Arrays for VLSI," in C.A. Mead and L.C. Conway, eds., *Introduction to VLSI Systems*, Addison-Wesley, Reading, Mass., 1980, pp. 271–292.

E.S. Lander, R. Langridge, and D.M. Saccocio, "Computing in Molecular Biology: Mapping and Interpreting Biological Information," *Computer*, Vol. 24, No. 11, Nov. 1991, pp. 6–13.

E.S. Lander, R. Langridge, and D.M. Saccocio, "Mapping and Interpreting Biological Information," *Comm. of the ACM*, Vol. 34, 1991, pp. 32–39.

H.C. Lee and R.E. Gaensslen, *Advances in Fingerprint Technology*, Elsevier, New York, 1991.

E. Lemoine and D. Merceron, "Run Time Reconfiguration of FPGA for Scanning Genomic Databases," *Proc. IEEE Symp. FPGAs for Custom Computing Machines*, CS Press, Los Alamitos, Calif., 1995, pp. 90–98.

A. Lew and R. Halverson, "A FCCM for Dataflow (Spreadsheet) Programs," *Proc. IEEE Symp. FPGAs for Custom Computing Machines*, CS Press, Los Alamitos, Calif., 1995, pp. 2–10.

D.M. Lewis, M.H. van Ierssel, and D.H. Wong, "A Field Programmable Accelerator for Compiled-Code Applications," *Proc. IEEE Workshop FPGAs for Custom Computing Machines*, CS Press, Los Alamitos, Calif., 1993, pp. 60–68.

J. Li and C.K. Cheng, "Routability Improvement Using Dynamic Interconnect Architecture," *Proc. IEEE Symp. FPGAs for Custom Computing Machines*, CS Press, Los Alamitos, Calif., 1995, pp. 61–67.

X.-P. Ling and H. Amano, "WASMII: A Data Driven Computer on a Virtual Hardware," *Proc. IEEE Workshop FPGAs for Custom Computing Machines*, CS Press, Los Alamitos, Calif., 1993, pp. 33–43.

X.-P. Ling and H. Amano, "WASMII: A MPLD with Data Driven Control on a Virtual Hardware," *J. of Supercomputing*, Vol. 9, 1995, pp. 253–276.

R.J. Lipton and D.P. Lopresti, "A Systolic Array for Rapid String Comparison," *Proc. 1985 Chapel Hill Conf. VLSI*, Computer Science Press, Rockville, Md., 1985, pp. 363–376.

D.P. Lopresti, *Discounts for Dynamic Programming with Applications in VLSI Processor Arrays*, PhD thesis, Princeton Univ., Princeton, N.J., 1987.

D.P. Lopresti, "Fast Dictionary Searching on Splash," tech. report, SRC, Bowie, Md., 1991.

D.P. Lopresti, "Rapid Implementation of a Genetic Sequence Comparator Using Field Programmable Logic Arrays," in C.H. Séquin, ed., *Advanced Research in VLSI*, MIT Press, Cambridge, Mass., 1991, pp. 138–152.

D.P. Lopresti and R.J. Lipton, "Comparing Long Strings on a Short Systolic Array," Tech. Report CS-TR-026-86, Princeton Univ., Princeton, N.J., 1986.

M.E. Louie and M.D. Ercegovac, "A Digit-Recurrence Square Root Implementation for Field Programmable Gate Arrays," *Proc. IEEE Workshop FPGAs for Custom Computing Machines*, CS Press, Los Alamitos, Calif., 1993, pp. 178–184.

M.E. Louie and M.D. Ercegovac, "A Variable Precision Square Root Implementation for Field Programmable Gate Arrays," *J. of Supercomputing*, Vol. 9, 1995, pp. 315–336.

W. Luk, "Pipelining and Transposing Heterogeneous Array Designs," *J. of VLSI Signal Processing*, Vol. 5, 1993, pp. 7–20.

W. Luk, "A Declarative Approach to Incremental Custom Computing," *Proc. IEEE Symp. FPGAs for Custom Computing Machines*, CS Press, Los Alamitos, Calif., 1995, pp. 164–172.

W. Luk, V. Lok, and I. Page, "Hardware Acceleration of Divide-and-Conquer Paradigms: A Case Study," *Proc. IEEE Workshop FPGAs for Custom Computing Machines*, CS Press, Los Alamitos, Calif., 1993, pp. 192–202.

W. Luk, T. Wu, and I. Page, "Hardware-Software Codesign of Multidimensional Programs," *Proc. IEEE Workshop FPGAs for Custom Computing Machines*, CS Press, Los Alamitos, Calif., 1994, pp. 82–91.

P. Marchal and E. Sanchez, "CAFCA (Compact Accelerator for Cellular Automata): The Metamorphosable Machine," *Proc. IEEE Workshop FPGAs for Custom Computing Machines*, CS Press, Los Alamitos, Calif., 1994, pp. 66–72.

W.J. Masek and M.S. Paterson, "How to Compute String-Edit Distances Quickly," in *Time Warps, String Edits, and Macromolecules: The Theory and Practice of Sequence Comparison*, D. Sankoff and J. Kruskal, eds., Addison-Wesley, Reading, Mass., 1983.

MasPar, Inc., *MasPar Application Language Reference Manual*, MasPar, Inc., Sunnyvale, Calif., 1990.

J.T. McHenry, "Dictionary Search Application on Splash," tech. report, SRC, Bowie, Md., 1991.

J.T. McHenry and A. Kopser, "Keyword Searching on Splash," tech. report, SRC, Bowie, Md., 1991.

Mead Data Central, *LEXIS Quick Reference*, Mead Data Central, New York, 1976.

R. Meier, "Rapid Prototyping of a RISC Architecture for Implementation in FPGAs," *Proc. IEEE Symp. FPGAs for Custom Computing Machines*, CS Press, Los Alamitos, Calif., 1995, pp. 190–196.

P.J. Menchini, "An Introduction to VHDL," in J.P. Mermet, ed., *Fundamentals and Standards in Hardware Description Languages*, Kluwer Academic Publishers, Boston, 1993, pp. 359–384.

B. Miller, "Vital Signs of Identity," *IEEE Spectrum*, Vol. 31, No. 2, Feb. 1994, pp. 22–30.

G. Milne et al., "Realizing Massively Concurrent Systems on the SPACE Machine," *Proc. IEEE Workshop FPGAs for Custom Computing Machines*, CS Press, Los Alamitos, Calif., 1993, pp. 26–33.

L. Moll, J. Vuillemin, and P. Boucard, "High-Energy Physics on DEC PeRLe-1 Programmable Active Memory," *Proc. FPGA95*, ACM, ACM Press, New York, 1995, pp. 47–52.

S. Monaghan and C.P. Cowen, "Reconfigurable Multi-Bit Processor for DSP Applications in Statistical Physics," *Proc. IEEE Workshop FPGAs for Custom Computing Machines*, CS Press, Los Alamitos, Calif., 1993, pp. 103–111.

W. Moore and W. Luk, eds., *FPGAs*, Abingdon EE & CS Books, Abingdon, England, UK, 1992. (Proc., Oxford 1991 Int'l Workshop on Field Programmable Logic and Applications.)

W. Moore and W. Luk, eds., *J. of VLSI Signal Processing*, 1993, (Special Issue on Field-Programmable Gate Arrays.)

W. Moore and W. Luk, eds., *More FPGAs*, Abingdon EE & CS Books, Abingdon, England, UK, 1994. (Proc., Oxford 1993 Int'l Workshop on Field Programmable Logic and Applications.)

Q. Motiwala, "Optimizations for Acyclic Dataflow Graphs for Hardware-Software Codesign," master's thesis, Virginia Polytechnic Inst., Blacksburg, Va., 1994.

Nat'l Library of Medicine, *MEDLARS, The Computerized Literature Retrieval Services of the Nat'l Library of Medicine*, Publication NIH 79-1286, U.S. Dept. of Health, Education and Welfare, Washington, D.C., 1979.

M. Newman, W. Luk, and I. Page, "Constraint-Based Hierarchical Hardware Compilation of Parallel Programs," in R.W. Hartenstein and M.Z. Servít, eds., *Field-Programmable Logic: Architectures, Synthesis, and Applications.* Springer-Verlag, Berlin, 1994, pp. 220–229.

R.J. Offen, *VLSI Image Processing*, McGraw-Hill, New York, 1985.

J.K. Ousterhout, *Tcl and the Tk Toolkit*, Addison-Wesley, Reading, Mass., 1994.

I. Page and W. Luk, "Compiling Occam in FPGAs," in W. Moore and W. Luk, eds., *FPGAs*, Abingdon EE & CS Books, Abingdon, England, UK, 1991, pp. 271–283.

D.L. Perry, *VHDL*, McGraw-Hill, New York, 1991.

D.L. Perry, *VHDL*, McGraw-Hill, New York, 2nd ed., 1994.

W.K. Pratt, *Digital Image Processing*, Wiley, New York, 1978.

D.V. Pryor, M.R. Thistle, and N. Shirazi, "Text Searching on Splash 2," *Proc. IEEE Workshop FPGAs for Custom Computing Machines*, CS Press, Los Alamitos, Calif., 1993, 172–178.

G. Purcell and D. Mar, "SCOUT: Information Retrieval from Full-Text Medical Literature," Knowledge Systems Lab. Report KSL-92-35, Stanford Univ., Palo Alto, Calif., 1992.

G.M. Quénot et al., "A Reconfigurable Compute Engine for Real-Time Vision Automata Prototyping," *Proc. IEEE Workshop FPGAs for Custom Computing Machines*, CS Press, Los Alamitos, Calif., 1994, pp. 91–101.

R. Rachakonda, "Region Detection and Labeling in Real-time Using a Custom Computing Platform," master's thesis, Virginia Polytechnic Inst., Blacksburg, Va., 1994.

F. Raimbault et al., "Fine Grain Parallelism on a MIMD Machine Using FPGAs," *Proc. IEEE Workshop FPGAs for Custom Computing Machines*, CS Press, Los Alamitos, Calif., 1993, pp. 2–9.

N.K. Ratha, A.K. Jain, and D.T. Rover, "Fingerprint Matching on Splash 2," tech. report, Dept. of Computer Science, Michigan State Univ., East Lansing, Mich., Mar. 1994.

N.K. Ratha, A.K. Jain, and D.T. Rover, "Convolution on Splash 2," *Proc. IEEE Symp. FPGAs for Custom Computing Machines*, CS Press, Los Alamitos, Calif., 1995, pp. 204–213.

A. Rosenfeld and A. Kak, *Digital Picture Processing*, 2nd ed., Academic Press, New York, 1982.

G. Salton, *Automatic Text Processing*, Addison-Wesley, Reading, Mass., 1989.

G. Salton and M.J. McGill, *Introduction to Modern Information Retrieval*, McGraw-Hill, New York, 1983.

D. Sankoff and J. Kruskal, eds., *Time Warps, String Edits, and Macromolecules: The Theory and Practice of Sequence Comparison*, Addison-Wesley, Reading, Mass., 1983.

J. Schlesinger and M. Gokhale, dBC Reference Manual. Tech. Report SRC-TR-92-068, Revision 2, SRC, Bowie, Md., 1993.

H. Schmit et al., "Behavioral Synthesis for FPGA-Based Computing," *Proc. IEEE Workshop FPGAs for Custom Computing Machines*, CS Press, Los Alamitos, Calif., 1994, pp. 125–133.

H. Schmit and D. Thomas, "Implementing Hidden Markov Modelling and Fuzzy Controllers in FPGAs," *Proc. IEEE Symp. FPGAs for Custom Computing Machines*, CS Press, Los Alamitos, Calif., 1995, pp. 214–221.

J. Serra, *Image Analysis and Mathematical Morphology*, Academic Press, London, 1982.

M. Shand, "Flexible Image Acquisition Using Reconfigurable Hardware," *Proc. IEEE Symp. FPGAs for Custom Computing Machines*, CS Press, Los Alamitos, Calif., 1995, pp. 125–134.

M. Shand, P. Bertin, and J. Vuillemin, "Hardware Speedups for Long Integer Multiplication," *ACM Symp. Parallel Algorithms and Architectures*, ACM, ACM Press, New York, 1990, pp. 138–145.

N. Shirazi, "Implementation of a 2-D Fast Fourier Transform on an FPGA-based Computing Platform," master's thesis, Virginia Polytechnic Inst., 1995.

N. Shirazi, A. Walters, and P. Athanas, "Quantitative Analysis of Floating-Point Arithmetic on FPGA-based Custom Computing Machines," *Proc. IEEE Symp. FPGAs for Custom Computing*, CS Press, Los Alamitos, Calif., Apr. 1995, pp. 155–162.

S. Singh, "Architectural Description for FPGA Circuits," *Proc. IEEE Symp. FPGAs for Custom Computing Machines*, CS Press, Los Alamitos, Calif., 1995, pp. 145–154.

S. Singh and P. Bellec, "Virtual Hardware for Graphics Applications Using FPGAs," *Proc. IEEE Workshop FPGAs for Custom Computing Machines*, CS Press, Los Alamitos, Calif., 1994, pp. 49–59.

N. Sitkoff et al., "Implementing a Genetic Algorithm on a Parallel Custom Computing Machine," *Proc. IEEE Symp. FPGAs for Custom Computing Machines*, CS Press, Los Alamitos, Calif., 1995, pp. 180–187.

C. Stanfill and B. Kahle, "Parallel Free-Text Search on the Connection Machine System," *Comm. of the ACM*, Vol. 29, No. 12, 1986, pp. 1229–1239.

J. Stigliani, *Writing SBus Device Drivers*, Sun Microsystems, Inc., Mountain View, Calif., 1990.

Synopsys, Inc., *Design Compiler Reference Manual*, Synopsys, Inc., Mountain View, Calif., 1991.

Synopsys, Inc., *VHDL Compiler Reference Manual*, Synopsys, Inc., Mountain View, Calif., 1991.

Synopsys, Inc., *FPGA Compiler Reference Manual*, Synopsys, Inc., Mountain View, Calif., 1994.

A. Tarmaster, "Median and Morphological Filtering of Images in Real Time Using an FPGA-based Custom Computing Platform," master's thesis, Virginia Polytechnic Inst., Blacksburg, Va., 1994.

Texas Instruments Inc., *The SN74ACT8800 Family Data Manual (SCSS006A)*, Texas Instruments Inc., Dallas, 1988.

Thinking Machines, Inc., *C* Programming Guide*, Thinking Machines, Inc., Cambridge, Mass., 1993.

D.E. Thomas and P.R. Moorby, *The Verilog Hardware Description Language*, Kluwer Academic Publishers, Boston, 1991.

S.M. Trimberger, ed., *Field Programmable Gate Array Technology*, Kluwer Academic Publishers, Boston, 1994.

Reference Manual for the Ada Programming Language, ANSI/MIL-STD-1815A-1983, U.S. Department of Defense, Washington, D.C., Feb. 1983.

L. Uhr, ed., *Parallel Computer Vision*, Academic Press, New York, 1987.

M. van Daalen, P. Jeavons, and J. Shawe-Taylor, "A Stochastic Neural Architecture That Exploits Dynamically Reconfigurable FPGAs," *Proc. IEEE Workshop FPGAs for Custom Computing Machines*, CS Press, Los Alamitos, Calif., 1993, pp. 202–212.

D.E. Van den Bout, "The Anyboard: Programming and Enhancements," *Proc. IEEE Workshop FPGAs for Custom Computing Machines*, CS Press, Los Alamitos, Calif., 1993, pp. 68–78.

G. VanDerWal and P. Burt, "A VLSI Pyramid Chip for Multiresolution Image Analysis," *Int'l J. of Computer Vision*, Vol. 8, No. 3, 1992, pp. 177–189.

R. Vogt, *Automatic Generation of Morphological Set Recognition Algorithms*, Springer-Verlag, New York, 1989.

J. Vuillemin et al., "Programmable Active Memories: Reconfigurable Systems Come of Age," *IEEE Trans. VLSI Systems*, to be published in Mar. 1996.

M. Wazlowski et al., "PRISM II: Compiler and Architecture," *Proc. IEEE Workshop FPGAs for Custom Computing Machines*, CS Press, Los Alamitos, Calif., 1993, pp. 9–17.

J.H. Wegstein, *An Automated Fingerprint Identification System*, Special Publication 500–89, Nat'l Bureau of Standards, Washington, D.C., 1982.

R. Wieler, Z. Zhang, and R. McLeod, "Emulating Static Faults Using a Xilinx Based Emulator," *Proc. IEEE Symp. FPGAs for Custom Computing Machines*, CS Press, Los Alamitos, California, 1995, pp. 110–115.

M. Wirthlin and B. Hutchings, "A Dynamic Instruction Set Computer," *Proc. IEEE Symp. FPGAs for Custom Computing Machines*, CS Press, Los Alamitos, Calif., 1995, pp. 99–107.

M.J. Wirthlin, B.L. Hutchings, and K.L. Gilson, "The Nano Processor: A Low Resource Reconfigurable Processor," *Proc. IEEE Workshop FPGAs for Custom Computing Machines*, CS Press, Los Alamitos, Calif., 1994, pp. 23–31.

D. Wo and K. Forward, "Compiling to the Gate Level for a Reconfigurable Co-Processor," *Proc. IEEE Workshop FPGAs for Custom Computing Machines*, CS Press, Los Alamitos, Calif., 1994, pp. 147–155.

L.F. Wood, "High Performance Analysis and Control of Complex Systems Using Dynamically Reconfigurable Silicon and Optical Fiber Memory," *Proc. IEEE Workshop FPGAs for Custom Computing Machines*, CS Press, Los Alamitos, Calif., 1993, pp. 132–142.

Xilinx, Inc., *The Programmable Gate Array Data Book*, Xilinx, Inc., San Jose, Calif., 1993.

Xilinx, Inc., *The XC4000 Data Book*, Xilinx, Inc., San Jose, Calif. 1994.

C.-C. Yeh, C.-H. Wu, and J.-Y. Juang, "Design and Implementation of a Multicomputer Interconnection Using FPGAs," *Proc. IEEE Symp. FPGAs for Custom Computing Machines*, CS Press, Los Alamitos, Calif., 1995, pp. 56–60.

Index

Contributors

A. Lynn Abbott, Bradley Department of Electrical Engineering, Virginia Polytechnic Institute and State University, Blacksburg, Virginia 24061. 703-231-4472

Jeffrey M. Arnold, Center for Computing Sciences, 17100 Science Drive, Bowie, Maryland 20715. 301-805-7479

Peter Athanas, Bradley Department of Electrical Engineering, Virginia Polytechnic Institute and State University, Blacksburg, Virginia 24061. 703-231-7010

Duncan A. Buell, Center for Computing Sciences, 17100 Science Drive, Bowie, Maryland 20715. 301-805-7372

Maya Gokhale, David Sarnoff Research Center, CN 5300, Princeton, New Jersey 08543. 609-734-3119

Dzung T. Hoang, Department of Computer Science, Duke University, Durham, North Carolina 27706. 919-660-6598

Anil Jain, Department of Computer Science, Michigan State University, East Lansing, Michigan 48824. 517-353-5150

Walter J. Kleinfelder, Center for Computing Sciences, 17100 Science Drive, Bowie, Maryland 20715. 301-805-7355

Daniel V. Pryor, Center for Computing Sciences, 17100 Science Drive, Bowie, Maryland 20715. 301-805-7407

Nalini Ratha, Department of Computer Science, Michigan State University, East Lansing, Michigan 48824. c/o A. Jain 517-353-5150

Diane Rover, Department of Electrical Engineering, Michigan State University, East Lansing, Michigan 48824. 517-353-7735

Nabeel Shirazi, Bradley Department of Electrical Engineering, Virginia Polytechnic Institute and State University, Blacksburg, Virginia 24061. c/o P. Athanas 703-231-7010

Mark R. Thistle, Center for Computing Sciences, 17100 Science Drive, Bowie, Maryland 20715. 301-805-7413

Additional Advances Board Titles

A Probabilistic Analysis of Test-Response Compaction
    Slawomir Pilarski and Tiko Kameda

The Cache Coherence Problem in Shared-Memory Multiprocessors: Software Solutions
    Igor Tartalja and Veljko Milutinović

The Cache Coherence Problem in Shared-Memory Multiprocessors: Hardware Solutions
    Igor Tartalja and Veljko Milutinović

Advanced Multimicroprocessor Bus Architectures
    Janusz Zalewski

IEEE Computer Society Press Publications

The world-renowned Computer Society Press publishes, promotes, and distributes a wide variety of authoritative computer science and engineering texts. These books are available in two formats: 100 percent original material by authors preeminent in their field who focus on relevant topics and cutting-edge research, and reprint collections consisting of carefully selected groups of previously published papers with accompanying original introductory and explanatory text.

Submission of proposals: For guidelines and information on CS Press books, send e-mail to csbooks@computer.org or write to the Acquisitions Editor, IEEE Computer Society Press, P.O. Box 3014, 10662 Los Vaqueros Circle, Los Alamitos, CA 90720-1314. Telephone +1 714-821-8380. FAX +1 714-761-1784.

IEEE Computer Society Press Proceedings

The Computer Society Press also produces and actively promotes the proceedings of more than 130 acclaimed international conferences each year in multimedia formats that include hard and softcover books, CD-ROMs, videos, and on-line publications.

For information on CS Press proceedings, send e-mail to csbooks@computer.org or write to Proceedings, IEEE Computer Society Press, P.O. Box 3014, 10662 Los Vaqueros Circle, Los Alamitos, CA 90720-1314. Telephone +1 714-821-8380. FAX +1 714-761-1784.

Additional information regarding the Computer Society, conferences and proceedings, CD-ROMs, videos, and books can also be accessed from our web site at www.computer.org.

Printed and bound by CPI Group (UK) Ltd, Croydon, CR0 4YY

27/10/2024

14580344-0002